GRAMMAR TO GO

How It Works and How to Use It

5e

GRAMMAR TO GO

How It Works and How to Use It

5e

BARBARA GOLDSTEIN
Hillsborough Community College

JACK WAUGH
Hillsborough Community College

KAREN LINSKY
Hillsborough Community College

CENGAGE
Learning®

Australia • Brazil • Mexico • Singapore • United Kingdom • United States

CENGAGE
Learning®

Grammar to Go: How It Works and How to Use It, 5e
Barbara Goldstein, Jack Waugh, and Karen Linsky

Product Director: Liz Covello

Sr. Product Manager: Andrew Rawson

Content Developer: Maggie Barbieri

Associate Content Developer: Elizabeth Rice and Kathryn Jorawsky

Product Assistant: Jacob Schott

Media Developer: Elizabeth Neustaetter

Sr. Marketing Brand Manager: Necco McKinley

IP Analyst: Ann Hoffman

IP Project Manager: Amber Hosea

Manufacturing Planner: Betsy Donaghey

Art and Design Direction, Production Management, and Composition: Cenveo® Publisher Services

Cover Image © Rich Legg/E+/Getty Images

For product information and technology assistance, contact us at
Cengage Learning Customer & Sales Support, 1-800-354-9706

For permission to use material from this text or product, submit all requests online at **www.cengage.com/permissions**. Further permissions questions can be emailed to **permissionrequest@cengage.com**.

Library of Congress Control Number: 2014946045

Student Edition:
ISBN: 978-1-305-10376-4

Cengage Learning
20 Channel Center Street
Boston, MA
USA

Cengage Learning is a leading provider of customized learning solutions with office locations around the globe, including Singapore, the United Kingdom, Australia, Mexico, Brazil, and Japan. Locate your local office at **international.cengage.com/region**.

Cengage Learning products are represented in Canada by Nelson Education, Ltd.

For your course and learning solutions, visit **www.cengage.com**.

Purchase any of our products at your local college store or at our preferred online store **www.cengagebrain.com**.

Instructors: Please visit **login.cengage.com** and log in to access instructor-specific resources.

Printed in the United States of America
Print Number: 01   Print Year: 2014

Contents

Preface

When we began work on the first edition more than a decade ago, it was out of frustration. We thought it would be easy to find a college-level text that simplified the study of English grammar, which would begin at the basic foundations and add more sophisticated concepts in easy-to-understand, short increments, but, alas, we were mistaken. We had to create our own, and we are proud that so many instructors have become believers in our pedagogy. It has been such an honor to create the fifth edition of *Grammar to Go*.

The best part about creating a new edition is that we are able to make the text even better, and the fifth edition is no exception. This new edition continues to present a clear, systematic, and thorough approach to teaching English grammar to beginning college students, starting with the parts of speech and basic sentence patterns. New concepts build upon those already mastered, so by the time students reach the end of Part 1, verbals and clauses are no longer mysteries but logical extensions of what they already know.

We have continued to include Word Watchers, a popular addition since the second edition, and we have considerably strengthened some of the features added to the later editions. The fifth edition includes many more integrated exercises on interesting and varied topics, from the Greek gods to baseball legend Bill Maseroski, from the oldest city in the United States to little-known tidbits about our presidents. In addition, GrammarSpeak, a popular feature we introduced in the fourth edition, has now been incorporated throughout the text, helping to correct some of the common misspoken words and phrases that students hear in everyday life. These exercises will help students establish new patterns and build better oral language habits.

However, we are most excited about the extended and improved Write Now feature. This feature now includes specific writing assignments for students, enabling them to practice the new grammar skills they have learned while constructing paragraphs on assigned topics. Instructors who wish can require students to extend these paragraphs into full essays as well. You will find Write Now assignments in every chapter.

Then there's the diagramming. Some of our users love it while others skip over it. For those who do not include the diagramming instruction in their courses, the diagramming exercises have been modified to include practice without the diagram, so it is not necessary to omit any of the practice sets. For those who love diagramming, we have included more instruction on our ancillary website. Those who want to take their students further than diagramming sentences with prepositional phrases have a step-by-step guide to help them teach the more complex diagramming of verbals and clauses. There is also a quick diagramming guide inside the front cover of the text for easy reference.

Our old friends will also notice a big change in Chapter 16. Once a review chapter, the final chapter of the text now offers parts of speech concepts for further study. These include, for example, a more in-depth look at verbs than you will find earlier in the text, including tenses, moods, voice, and irregular forms. In addition, it provides more instruction on adjectives and adverbs, discussing base forms, comparatives, and superlatives more in depth.

Finally, while we are still philosophically opposed to providing answers in the back of the text, we have continued to include the "Test Yourself" feature in each chapter, with answers provided, to enable students to check their understanding of the material. We have also continued to include the answer key to the "Word Watchers" practice sets.

NEW *GRAMMAR TO GO* FEATURES AT A GLANCE

This new edition of *Grammar to Go* features the following:

- more integrated exercises on interesting and varied topics.
- GrammarSpeak exercises incorporated throughout the text.
- extended and improved Write Now features with specific writing assignments for students.
- diagramming instruction that has been modified, so practices can be completed with or without diagramming, at the discretion of the instructor.
- a revised Chapter 16 that enhances parts of speech study and provides more advanced instruction in verb tense and form and adjectives and adverbs, including comparatives and superlatives.

APPROACH

Grammar to Go gives students the opportunity to learn through a step-by-step, interactive approach that minimizes memorizing rules out of context. Instead, the text incorporates pertinent information when students need it to understand the material they are studying. The book uses small, incremental steps to move from simple concepts to more complex ones. For example, Part 1 teaches how the English language works, providing a foundation for the conventions of usage explained in Part 2. Seeing the complete picture gives students the tools to analyze their own writing from a grammatical perspective. With every step in this process, *Grammar to Go* provides reinforcement and encouragement.

CONTENT AND ORGANIZATION

Chapter 1 supplies students with the basic terminology—the parts of speech and the parts of the sentence—that they need to navigate the remainder of the text. Chapter 2 presents the five basic sentence patterns as the building blocks of the English language, moving from the simplest subject/verb pattern to the more complex patterns containing complements. Chapter 3 adds single-word modifiers to the basic sentence patterns. Chapters 4 and 5 add phrases to the patterns, starting with simple prepositional phrases and moving to the more complex verbals and verbal phrases. Chapter 6 reinforces the patterns, showing that they remain the same even when word order changes. Chapters 1 through 6 prepare students to understand the complex concepts of clauses presented in Chapters 7 and 8. Part 1 ends with "Types of Sentences," reinforcing all of the concepts mastered in the first portion of the book.

Part 2 addresses specific writing issues, putting them into the grammatical framework learned in Part 1. Students apply these concepts to their own writing because they now understand how the language works. Chapter 9 begins with sentence fragments and run-on sentences, thus directly building on the compound and complex sentences found in Chapters 7 and 8. Chapter 10, covering comma placement, and Chapter 11, reviewing other punctuation, also present concepts that require an understanding of phrases, clauses, and sentence types.

The remaining chapters on pronouns, agreement, modifiers, and sentence coherence are now approachable; they simply build on the lessons of the previous chapters. Part 2 ends with a section of "further study" of parts of speech. Parts 1 and 2 progress in small steps, providing encouragement at every stage of the learning process. Unlike many traditional texts that offer exercises only at the end of large sections and chapters, *Grammar to Go* includes level-appropriate exercises at every step, checking student mastery and providing feedback.

FEATURES

The chapters in *Grammar to Go* offer the following features:

Practice Sets: These exercises, which follow every concept presented, give students the opportunity to check their mastery of the lesson.

Quick Tips: These easily identifiable boxes offer students mnemonic devices, shortcuts, and other hints to simplify various grammatical concepts.

Test Yourself: In each chapter, these practice tests allow students to check their understanding of the material presented. Answers are provided in the back of the text.

Word Watchers: The mini-lessons at the end of each chapter focus on confusing pairs, frequently misspelled words, and language and tone. Each includes a practice set, with answers provided in the back of the text.

GrammarSpeak: GrammarSpeak exercises help correct some of the common misspoken words and phrases that students hear in everyday life. These exercises will help students establish new patterns and build better oral language habits.

Write Now: Chapters 2 through 15 conclude with the "Write Now" feature, which provides a specific writing assignment based on the lessons just covered. These assignments can also be extended to become full essays.

Grammar to Go uses a new approach to a traditional way to understand grammar. Reed and Kellogg diagramming, a system developed in the late 1800s, was a staple of teaching English grammar for three-quarters of a century. The new millennium is seeing a resurgence in this century-old system of understanding how sentences work. Diagramming is learning by doing, allowing a hands-on examination of the connections involved in constructing a sentence. Students visualize the relationship among sentence parts as the diagrams break down complicated sentences into simple, easy-to-see segments. It does not replace the study of grammar; it enhances it.

Grammar to Go introduces diagramming in three early chapters—"Sentence Patterns," "Adjectives and Adverbs," and "Phrases"—as a way to help students visualize basic sentence patterns. These chapters include practice sets that can be completed with or without the use of diagramming, making them appropriate for all instruction.

ANCILLARY MATERIAL

Instructor's Resource Manual. The instructor's manual continues to contain learning objectives, key terms, teaching suggestions, and additional chapter review exercises. It provides an answer key to the exercises found in the text, as well as an answer key for the additional chapter review exercises specific to the manual. A new section called "Making the Connection" is now included for each chapter in Part 1 of *Grammar to Go*. This section will help students connect the skills they are learning to the rules for writing clear sentences.

Many users have told us how much the diagramming in the first four chapters has added to the learning process for their students and how they wished they were able to continue the diagramming lessons through clauses. The instructor's manual includes a step-by-step explanation of the diagramming process for verbals, word order variations, clauses, and types of sentences. We've added diagramming exercises for instructors who wish to carry the process beyond the instruction provided in the main text.

ACKNOWLEDGMENTS

Many thanks to our students, especially the hundreds of students in various English classes at Hillsborough Community College, Dale Mabry Campus, Tampa, Florida, who used this text in its many incarnations. Their suggestions and encouragement have been invaluable.

Thanks also to those who reviewed our manuscript for all of their suggestions and ideas.

Finally, thanks to our spouses, Bruce, Lynda, and Michael, for their support and optimism, and to other family members and our many friends, whose names appear in exercises throughout the book, especially the world's greatest grandchildren: Gavin, Asher, Davis, Laya, Jax, Morgan, Sydney, Samantha, Wilson, Jackson, Carson, Meredith, Mali, Owen, Ellie W., Claire, Ellie S., Jake, and Slade.

Learning Grammar Basics

PART 1

Getting Started

*G*rammar to Go is a book that will help you learn English grammar in a fast and logical way. You will process information in small, simple steps that will help you understand some of the concepts that you may have found difficult to learn in the past.

To master English grammar, start by learning some basic terms and some simple rules. These elements will help you understand the way language works. In this "Getting Started" chapter, you will become familiar with the eight parts of speech, learn about and practice finding the subject and verb in a sentence, and see how the parts of speech function in a sentence. In the chapters that follow, you will revisit these basics, adding to what you have already learned.

Consider this situation: A new football coach stands in front of his seventy-five potential players for the first time. Before he can field this team, he must learn some important lessons about them. He knows that there are several different kinds of players: tackle, end, receiver, or quarterback. He also knows that each player has a specific job to do on the field. The coach must learn who does what before he can put a single play together.

Think of grammar as the game of football. You are the coach. Your "players" are the eight parts of speech. Each one has a specific name and function. In football, there are times when some players can play different positions. For example, a tackle may become a receiver when there is a turnover. Likewise, the same word may serve different functions in a sentence. For example, the word *play* can act as a noun or a verb, depending on how it is used in a sentence. As you work through this book, you will see how using grammar compares with fielding a football team. First, meet your "players," the parts of speech.

PARTS OF SPEECH BASICS

Verb Basics

Verbs are words that show action or state of being. They also indicate the time the action or state of being occurs: present, past, or future.

Look at the verbs that show action in the following sentences:

Action in the present: The spider *weaves* a web.

Action in the past: The spider *wove* a web during the night.

Action in the future: The spider *will weave* a new web after the storm.

Verbs like *am, is, are, was, were, seem, feel,* and *become* usually express a state of being. These verbs are called **linking verbs**.

Look at the linking verbs that show state of being in the following sentences:

State of being in the present: I *am* tired.

State of being in the past: After my workout, I *became* very weak.

State of being in the future: I *will be* strong tomorrow.

Practice Set 1–1

Directions: In the following sentences, underline all the verbs twice. Write "A" for action or "L" for linking over each underlined verb. On the blank indicate whether the verb shows present, past, or future time.

            L

Example: Gary seemed moody.   past ____________

1. The ozone layer protects the earth from the sun's harmful rays.   ____________

2. Some people are always late.   ____________

3. Glass littered the street after the accident.   ____________

4. Eventually coal will become diamonds.   ____________

5. The carton contains orange juice.   ____________

Noun Basics

Nouns are words that name persons, places, things, or ideas. Notice the six nouns in the following sentences:

Julia played *tennis.*

Safety became a *concern.*

Mr. Todd lives in *London.*

Julia, Mr. Todd, and *London* are called **proper nouns**. Proper nouns name specific persons, places, things, or ideas. They start with capital letters.

Common nouns, like *tennis, safety,* and *concern,* do not begin with capital letters unless they begin a sentence.

The words *a*, *an*, and *the* are **articles**, and they always signal that a noun will follow.

noun

I ate *a* pickle.

noun

They had *an* argument.

noun

The information seems important.

Other words may come between *a*, *an*, or *the* and the noun.

I ate *a sour pickle*.

They had *a terrible argument*.

The new information seems important.

Many nouns appear without *a*, *an*, or *the*.

I ate *dinner*.

They had *problems*.

Information comes from many sources.

Practice Set 1–2

Directions: Underline the nouns in the following sentences.

   Example: Sundari finally found her way to the station.

1. Grammar is the study of the main elements of a language.

2. Words and phrases must make sense in a sentence.

3. Certain grammar rules help make the meaning of sentences clear.

4. Most people who speak a common language agree on correct usage.

5. Students studying a language learn which forms are acceptable.

Pronoun Basics

A **pronoun** is a word that takes the place of a noun. Notice how pronouns replace some of the nouns in the following sentences:

Julia plays tennis.   *She* plays tennis.

Safety became a concern.   *It* became a concern.

Mr. Todd lives in London.   *He* lives in London.

These words that substitute for specific persons, places, or things are **personal pronouns**. They are the most common pronouns. Other personal pronouns include *I, me, we, us, you, him, her, they,* and *them*.

Indefinite pronouns, on the other hand, do not refer to specific persons, places, or things. They include words like *each, everyone, everybody, anyone, somebody, both, some, all,* and *most.* Look at these sentences that contain indefinite pronouns:

Everyone bought a ticket.

The storm caught *all* of the workers by surprise.

Anybody can learn English grammar.

Practice Set 1–3

Directions: Underline all the pronouns in the following sentences. Over each one write "P" for personal pronoun or "I" for indefinite pronoun.

              I   P

Example: Anyone may take him to soccer practice.

1. She gave both the dogs a bath.

2. It really does not affect someone like me.

3. He is a better actor than anyone on the stage.

4. They surprised everyone by choosing Jake instead of her.

5. You have completed all of the assignments.

Adjective Basics

Adjectives are words that describe nouns or pronouns. Adjectives usually come right before the words that they describe; however, sometimes they come after linking verbs. The articles *a, an,* and *the* are always adjectives.

Look at the following sentences that contain adjectives:

Adjectives before nouns: *High* waves make *happy* surfers.

Adjectives after linking verbs: The waves are *high.* The surfers are *happy.*

Practice Set 1–4

Directions: Underline all the adjectives in the following sentences.

Example: Several people made low scores on the exam.

1. An unusual thing happened on a recent fishing trip.

2. Several passengers saw a gray fin in the choppy water near the boat.

3. They seemed nervous and afraid.

4. The alert captain steered the small vessel into the shallow water.

5. A dangerous situation ended in welcome relief.

> ## WRITE NOW
>
> The sentences in Practice Set 1–4 tell a little story about a fishing trip that became dangerous. Write a paragraph of 5–8 sentences about a dangerous situation that you have experienced. Use as many descriptive adjectives as you can. Then underline all the adjectives in your story.

Adverb Basics

Adverbs are words that describe verbs, adjectives, or other adverbs. When trying to find adverbs, look for words that tell *how*, *when*, or *where*. Remember that many adverbs—but not all—end in *-ly*.

Look at the following sentences that contain adverbs:

Adverb telling how:	Marcus walked *carefully* along the narrow ledge.
Adverbs telling when:	He *always* takes risks. He walks the ledge *daily*.
Adverb telling where:	I will not walk *there*.

Practice Set 1–5

Directions: Underline all the adverbs in the following sentences. On the blanks, write whether the adverbs tell how, when, or where.

Example: The phone rang loudly.   how _____ _____

1. Yesterday Rocky failed his math test.   _____ _____

2. The instructor immediately asked him to stay late to retake the test.   _____ _____

3. He soon realized that he had unfortunately made other plans.   _____ _____

4. He quickly asked his teacher to give him the test tomorrow.   _____ _____

5. Then he came to school early, hurriedly took the test, and scored well.   _____ _____

Preposition Basics

Prepositions are words that connect a noun or a pronoun to the rest of the sentence. Prepositions include words like *around, during, in, of, on, to, under, with*. A **prepositional phrase** starts with a preposition and ends with a noun or a pronoun.

Look at the following sentences that contain prepositional phrases:

A vase *of flowers* fell *on the floor*.

During my break, I went *to the snack bar*.

A car *with a flat tire* came *around the corner*.

Directions: Place parentheses ( ) around all the prepositional phrases in the following sentences. Underline the prepositions.

Example: I stood (with the graduates) (for two hours).

1. The dog with muddy paws is sleeping on the couch.

2. After dinner, we will go to the mall.

3. The letter with my signature is in the mail.

4. Several of his creations are on display.

5. Behind that bush is a nest of wasps.

Conjunction Basics

Conjunctions are words that join two or more words, groups of words, or sentences. Conjunctions that join equal sentences or equal parts of sentences are **coordinating conjunctions**. They are *and, but, or, nor, for, so, yet*.

Look at the following sentences that contain coordinating conjunctions:

Coordinating conjunction joining two words: Salt *and* pepper are popular seasonings.

Coordinating conjunction joining two groups of words: Look in the garage *or* on the workbench.

Coordinating conjunction joining two sentences: Simon will come early, *but* Miriam will be late.

Subordinating conjunctions join parts of sentences that are not equal. These include words like *after, although, because, before, if, since, until,* and *where*.

Look at the following sentences that contain subordinating conjunctions:

If I get a new job, I will be able to pay my bills.

Sandra chose the used car *because* it came with a service contract.

The boys like to travel *where* they can snowboard.

Practice Set 1–7

Directions: Underline the conjunctions in the following sentences. On the blank write whether they are coordinating or subordinating.

Example: I will stop on the way home, <u>or</u> I will run out of gas.
coordinating _____

1. If you are going to be late, call me on my cell phone.
_____

2. Have you seen my car keys and my wallet?
_____

3. The storm is severe, but it will miss our city.
_____

4. The car stalled because it ran out of gas.
_____

5. The scary part is over, so you can open your eyes.
_____

Interjection Basics

Interjections show strong feeling or emotion and are usually set off from the rest of the sentence with an exclamation point. Mild interjections—words like *oh*, *well*, *yes*, *no*—are set off by commas. Interjections are not grammatically related to the rest of the sentence.

Look at the following sentences that contain interjections:

Well, I think it's time to leave.   *No*, I don't have a ride.

Wow! You got the job!   *Ouch*! That really hurt.

PARTS OF SENTENCES BASICS

Subject and Verb Basics

We are now ready to see how parts of speech function in sentences. Nouns serve as the main parts of the sentence, but when they do, we refer to them by their function: subject, direct object, indirect object, subject complement, object complement, or object of the preposition. For example, we don't say "the noun" of the sentence; we say the *subject* of the sentence. However, verbs are always referred to by their part of speech name: the *verb*. The first step to understanding how any sentence is constructed is to determine its subject and verb. Since the verb is the heart of the sentence, it is a good idea to identify it first.

The verb can show action: The car *jumped* the curb.

The verb can show a state of being: The new cruise ship *is* huge.

The verb may be more than one word—a main verb with its **helping verbs**. Helping verbs combine with main verbs to show the time of the action.

The hurricane *is coming* ashore.   My answer *should have been* correct.

HELPING VERBS	
Forms of *to be*:	am, is, are, was, were, be, being, been
Forms of *to have*:	has, have, had
Forms of *to do*:	do, does, did
Modals:	can, could, may, might, must, shall, should, will, would

Practice Set 1–8

Directions: In the following sentences, underline the verbs twice.

Example: Judith finished her wedding dress.

Example: Lydia may have found the missing pieces.

Example: The news was good.

1. Sherman's interview lasted three hours.

2. Swimming is good exercise.

3. My neighbor has offered her help.

4. I carefully printed the fliers for the trip.

5. Damien usually arrives early.

6. The computer has been making a funny sound.

7. Carla felt disappointed after the concert.

8. The situation seems dangerous.

9. The parade floats crowded the narrow street.

10. The motorcycles roared through the quiet park.

Subjects

Subjects are nouns or pronouns that cause the action or state of being to happen. They answer the questions *who* or *what* before the verb. In the following examples, the subjects are italicized and the verbs are underlined twice. Look at the subjects in the following sentences:

Common noun as subject:	The *waitress* served ten tables.
Proper noun as subject:	*Marty Brink* served ten tables.
Personal pronoun as subject:	*She* served ten tables.
Indefinite pronoun as subject:	*Somebody* served ten tables.

Notice that all the subjects tell *who* served.

Practice Set 1–9

Directions: Underline the subjects in the following sentences. On the blank, write whether the subject is a noun or pronoun.

Example: <u>Each</u> came to the seminar with creative ideas.   pronoun

1. The circus comes to the fairgrounds next week.   _____

2. Everyone enjoys the clowns.   _____

3. One performer walks a high tightrope without a safety net.   _____

4. She trained on a low wire for twenty years.   _____

5. The audience loves her dangerous act.   _____

You have now learned the basics of the parts of speech and how subjects and verbs form the main parts of sentences. You have also learned how these words work together to form sentences. The chapters that follow will build upon these basics, revisiting many of the same concepts, adding more detail to what you already know.

TEST YOURSELF

Directions: Underline the verb twice and the subject once. Then label all parts of speech in the sentences below.

              Noun   verb adj adj   noun
Example: <u>Marco Polo</u> <u>was</u> a famous explorer.

1. Marco Polo planned a trip to the East.

2. He started his journey from Venice, Italy and ended in China.

3. Wow! That was an incredible journey!

4. Polo entered the Mongol diplomatic service in China.

5. His travels led him through Asia for fifteen years.

6. The Genoese eventually captured him.

7. He wrote a book about his adventures.

8. Many people read his book and thought about this courageous explorer.

9. Everybody was excited about China.

10. His adventures revealed the riches of the East.

WRITE NOW

The sentences in Practice Set 1–9 tell a story about the circus coming to town. Write a paragraph of 5–8 sentences about a theatrical performance or concert that you have seen or read about. Underline all subjects and verbs in your sentences.

Sentence Patterns

Think about the different types of possibilities involved in a football play. When the center hikes the ball to the quarterback, the quarterback passes it to a receiver, hands it off, or perhaps keeps the ball himself and runs with it. Those who really understand football, however, know that only a limited number of patterns are possible in the game. Similarly, English sentences use a limited number of patterns. In this chapter, you will learn the five basic English sentence patterns. The first type is the Subject/Verb pattern.

SENTENCE PATTERN 1: SUBJECT/VERB

The basic Subject/Verb sentence pattern consists of a subject and a verb. The following sentence is in this pattern:

Fido barks.

First find the verb. The part of the sentence that includes the verb is called the **predicate**. To find the verb, ask yourself, "What happens?" Find the word that shows action or being. In the sentence above, the action is *barks*, so *barks* is the verb. The **simple subject** is the word that acts or causes the action. The **complete subject** includes any modifiers or other words that go with the simple subject. To find the simple subject, ask yourself, "Who barks?" Fido does, so *Fido* is the subject. The simple subject is always a noun or a pronoun.

Here are some more examples in the Subject/Verb pattern:

    S   V
Anthony left early.

                S   V
The ancient *plumbing leaked* badly.

           S   V
The noisy *frog* in the pond *croaked* throughout the night.

Practice Set 2–1

Directions: In the following sentences, underline the verbs twice and the simple subjects once.

Example: Florence sat on the couch.

1. The roof collapsed.

2. The skaters wait for their turn.

3. The airplanes circled above the airport.

4. He travels by car.

5. The meeting began on time.

Diagramming Subject/Verb Sentence Patterns

Visualizing sentences is helpful in understanding the structure of English. Linguists have devised a system of diagrams to illustrate the pattern of a sentence. **Diagramming** a sentence involves placing words on lines that connect to form a frame that shows how all of the words are related.

The diagram for a Subject/Verb pattern looks like this:

subject	verb

In the sentence *Fido barks*, you already know that *barks* is the verb. To determine the simple subject, ask, "Who or what barks?" The answer is Fido, so *Fido* goes in the subject part of the diagram. Note that all capitalized words in the sentence are also capitalized on the diagram frame.

Fido	barks

Practice Set 2–2

Directions: In the sentences that follow, underline the verbs twice and the simple subjects once.

Optional diagramming: Place the simple subject and verb in their appropriate places on the diagram frames. Draw the diagrams on a separate sheet of paper.

Example: Lindsay left before the finale.

Lindsay	left

1. Hector sneezed.

2. The fire blazed.

3. The old swimming hole freezes in the winter.

4. They celebrated after the game.

5. In the middle of the sixth inning, the pitcher balked.

Directions: On a separate sheet of paper, write five sentences in the Subject/Verb pattern. Underline the verbs twice and the simple subjects once.

Optional diagramming: Place the subjects and verbs in their appropriate positions on the diagram frame.

SENTENCE PATTERN 2: SUBJECT/VERB/DIRECT OBJECT

Some verbs take a **direct object**, which is a noun or pronoun that receives the action of the verb. Examine this sentence:

John drove the car.

Begin by finding the verb. What happened? Somebody *drove*. To find the subject, ask who or what did the action. Who drove? John did, so *John* is the subject. To find a direct object, ask *whom or what* after the verb. What did John drive? He drove the car, so *car* is the direct object. Thus, the subject does the action, and the direct object receives the action.

Here are more examples in the Subject/Verb/Direct Object pattern:

        S   V   DO
The *New York Giants won* the *game*.

      S   V   DO
The *chef cooked* a great *dinner*.

Remember, pronouns can also serve as subjects or direct objects. Consider the following example:

  S   V   DO
She asked him to the movies.

  S   V DO
They flew us on their private airplane.

Directions: In the sentences that follow, underline the verb twice and the simple subject once. Write DO above the direct object.

                     DO
Example: Rafael found his jacket.

                  DO
Example: She kissed me on the forehead.

1. The technician took the test.

2. This garage has many entrances.

3. They sent him away.

4. Jax lost his phone.

5. The students received new computers.

6. Greed often ruins relationships.

7. The Forest Hills Falcons played their last game.

8. Mariah found the answer quickly.

9. Everything upsets him.

10. We excused them early.

DIRECT OBJECTS: WHOM OR WHAT

Not all verbs take a direct object. Direct objects answer the question *whom* or *what*—not *how* or *when*—after the verb.

I ate the sandwich.

I ate what? I ate the sandwich. In this sentence, *sandwich* tells *what* about the verb, so it is a direct object.

I ate quickly.

Does *quickly* tell whom or what? No, it tells how. In this sentence, *quickly* is not a direct object; it is an adverb.

Practice Set 2–5

Directions: In the sentences that follow, underline the verb twice and the simple subject once. Write DO above the direct object. Not all sentences have a direct object.

Example: The engineer planned the project carefully.

The engineer planned ahead.

1. We ate spaghetti for dinner.

2. We ate in the kitchen.

3. Marti called her for help.

4. Marti called for help.

5. The hiker climbed to the top of the mountain

6. The hiker climbed the mountain easily.

7. The babysitter left early

8. The babysitter left her purse on the bench.

9. The company pays bonuses for creativity.

10. The company pays well.

Diagramming Subject/Verb/Direct Object Sentence Patterns

The Subject/Verb/Direct Object pattern diagram looks like this:

subject	verb	direct object

Place a short vertical line after the verb and then add the direct object. Notice that the line dividing the subject and the verb crosses through the horizontal base line to separate the words belonging to the subject from the rest of the sentence. The line separating the verb from the direct object stops at the horizontal line rather than crossing through it. Look at the following diagram for placement:

subject	verb	direct object
John	**drove**	**car**

Practice Set 2–6

Directions: In the following sentences, underline the verb twice and the simple subject once. Write DO above the direct object.

Optional diagramming: Place the subjects, verbs, and direct objects in their appropriate positions on the diagram frame. Draw the diagrams on a separate sheet of paper.

Example: George ate too much candy.

George	ate	candy

1. Sydney called Morgan.

2. The jury made the correct decision.

3. Liam congratulated me for winning.

4. Sophie completed the difficult assignment.

5. Everyone needs a friend.

6. Nobody won the lottery in March.

7. He married her during halftime.

8. The company gave bonuses for Christmas.

Challenge question: Honesty provides its own rewards.

WRITING YOUR OWN SENTENCES

Directions: In the blanks provided, use the cues to help you write your own sentences in the Subject/Verb/Direct Object pattern. You may add *a*, *an*, or *the*, if needed.

_____   _____   _____
     noun or pronoun   verb   noun or pronoun that
                                                                completes the thought

Try another one:

_____   _____   _____
     noun or pronoun   verb   noun or pronoun that
                                                                completes the thought

Now try one on your own:

_____

Practice Set 2–7

Directions: On a separate sheet of paper, write five sentences in the Subject/Verb/Direct Object pattern. Underline the verb twice and the simple subject once. Write DO above the direct object.

Optional diagramming: Place the subjects, verbs, and direct objects in their appropriate positions on the diagram frame.

SENTENCE PATTERN 3: SUBJECT/VERB/INDIRECT OBJECT/DIRECT OBJECT

This third pattern is similar to the Subject/Verb/Direct Object pattern but with an addition. In the Subject/Verb/Indirect Object/Direct Object pattern, you go one step beyond asking *whom or what* after the verb. The **indirect object** answers the question *to whom or what* or *for whom or what*. The indirect object always appears between the verb and the direct object.

Here is a sentence in the Subject/Verb/Indirect Object/Direct Object pattern:

I sent John a gift.

In this sentence, *sent* is the verb. To find the subject, ask, "Who sent?" The answer is I sent, so *I* is the subject. To find the direct object, ask, "What did I send?" I sent a gift, so *gift* is the direct object. To find the indirect object, ask, "To whom did I send the gift?" I sent the gift to John, so *John* is the indirect object.

To find the indirect object, ask the following questions about the verb:

To whom?   I offered Lizzie a sandwich. =
                 I offered (to) Lizzie a sandwich.

To what?   I mailed the electric company my check. =
                 I mailed (to) the electric company my check.

For whom?   I baked Zachary some brownies. =
I baked (for) Zachary some brownies.

For what?   The chef prepared the guests a special dessert. =
The chef prepared (for) the guests a special dessert.

Here are some other examples in the Subject/Verb/Indirect Object/Direct Object pattern:

  S   V   IO   DO
Travis offered Melanie an *explanation.*

        S   V   IO   DO
The *actors gave* the *audience* a *hand.*

    S   V   IO   DO
Marisol sent her *friend* a long *email.*

Like subjects and direct objects, indirect objects are nouns or pronouns

    N   N   N
Winston taught Denny a song.

Certain verbs, such as *ask, bring, buy, give, send, show, teach,* and *tell,* often have indirect objects.

Be careful not to confuse sentences that look alike because they contain nouns that appear to occupy the same positions. Consider these two sentences:

 S V   IO   DO
I sent Marcy some flowers.

In this sentence, *flowers* is the direct object, telling what I sent. *Marcy* is the indirect object: I sent (to) *Marcy* some flowers.

 S V   DO
I sent Marcy to the store.

In this second sentence, *Marcy* is the direct object. *To the store* is a prepositional phrase telling where I sent her. The direct object tells *whom* or *what,* not *where.* This sentence does not contain an indirect object.

Try another example.

Glenna painted her teacher a picture.

Painted is the verb. Glenna painted, so *Glenna* is the subject. Remember to ask the correct questions to distinguish the direct object from the indirect object. For the direct object, ask, "*What* did Glenna paint?" Glenna painted the picture, so *picture* is the direct object. For the indirect object, ask "*For whom* did Glenna paint?" Glenna painted for her teacher, so *teacher* is the indirect object.

A sentence cannot have an indirect object without a direct object. For example, look at the sentence *Glenna painted her teacher a picture.* If the direct object (*a picture*) is deleted, the sentence says, *Glenna painted her teacher.*

QUICK TIP

In a sentence containing an indirect object, the words *to* or *for* do not actually appear before the indirect object.

    I sent John a gift contains an indirect object.

    I sent a gift to John does not contain an indirect object. *To John* is a prepositional phrase.

Practice Set 2–8

Directions: In the following sentences, underline the verbs twice and the simple subjects once. Then write IO above the indirect object and DO above the direct object. Not all sentences contain direct objects or indirect objects.

                     IO   DO

  Example: Asher gave his brother a book.

1. Jackson told me the truth.
2. Michelle taught her cousin a lesson about manners.
3. Kyle gave Madison the wrong directions to his house.
4. They smuggled cans of soda into the stadium.
5. Carson showed his friends his new apartment.
6. Dora sat calmly by the window during the thunderstorm.
7. Ellie kept the stray puppy in her garage.
8. Rob went to dinner with his girlfriend.
9. Lauren teaches dolphins sign language.
10. Nicki sent the company her resume.

Challenge question: I give anyone in social work much respect.

Challenge question: I sold my electric guitar to Emilio.

Diagramming Subject/Verb/Indirect Object/Direct Object Sentence Patterns

To diagram Subject/Verb/Indirect Object/Direct Object sentence patterns, begin with the parts you already know. For example, in the sentence *Glenna painted her teacher a picture*, you have already determined that *Glenna* is the subject, *painted* is the verb, and *picture* is the direct object:

                      Glenna | **painted** | **picture**

Under the verb, place the indirect object on a horizontal line (_____) attached to a backslash diagonal, which extends slightly below the horizontal line.

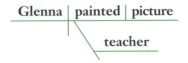

Practice Set 2–9

Directions: In the following sentences, underline the verbs twice and the simple subject once. Then write IO above the indirect object and DO above the direct object. Not all sentences contain direct objects or indirect objects.

Optional Diagramming: Place the subjects, verbs, indirect objects, and direct objects in their appropriate positions on the diagram frame. Draw the diagrams on a separate sheet of paper.

Example: The teacher gave the entire class a lecture.

1. The supervisor asked Meredith some difficult questions.

2. The man sold Carolyn some land in North Carolina.

3. Terri fed her iguanas a beautiful salad.

4. Dr. Totten sent the laboratory a detailed report.

5. Madonna sang the audience another encore.

6. She brought him a pineapple pizza for lunch.

7. Valerie presented him an ultimatum.

8. The job offered her a chance for advancement.

WRITING YOUR OWN SENTENCES

Directions: Fill in the blanks below, using the cues to help you write your own sentences in the Subject/Verb/Indirect Object/Direct Object pattern. You may add *a*, *an*, or *the*, if needed.

_____	_____	_____	_____
noun or pronoun	**choose one of the following verbs:** *ask, bring, buy, give*	**noun or pronoun**	**noun or pronoun that completes the thought**

Try another one:

_____   _____   _____   _____
noun or pronoun   **choose one of the following verbs:**   **noun or pronoun**   **noun or pronoun that completes the thought**
    send, show, teach, tell

Now try one on your own:

_____

Practice Set 2–10

Directions: On a separate sheet of paper, construct five of your own sentences in the Subject/Verb/Indirect Object/Direct Object pattern. Underline the verbs twice and the simple subjects once. Write IO above the indirect objects and DO above the direct objects.

Optional diagramming: Place the subjects, verbs, direct objects, and indirect objects in the appropriate positions on the diagram frame.

SENTENCE PATTERN 4: SUBJECT/VERB/DIRECT OBJECT/OBJECT COMPLEMENT

This pattern contains the subject, verb, and direct object, but it adds another word, the object complement. An **object complement** always follows the direct object and either renames or describes the direct object. Object complements can be nouns, pronouns, or adjectives. Consider this sentence:

She named the baby Bruce.

The verb is *named*. To find the subject, ask, "Who named?" She named, so *she* is the subject. Now ask, "Whom did she name?" She named the baby, so *baby* is the direct object. Any word following the direct object that renames or describes the direct object is an object complement. She named the baby Bruce, so *Bruce* is the object complement.

Here is another sentence in the Subject/Verb/Direct Object/Object Complement pattern. To find the direct object, remember to ask *whom or what* about the verb. To find the object complement, remember to ask *what* about the direct object.

      S   V   DO OC
The *dye turned* the *shirt red*.

Turned is the verb; *dye* is the subject. The dye turned *what*? It turned the shirt, so *shirt* is the direct object. Now ask *what* about shirt. The dye turned the shirt *what*? The dye turned the shirt red, so *red* is the object complement.

Look at some more examples in this pattern:

      S   V   DO   OC (noun)
The *panel selected Dong Li Miss Universe*.

      S   V   DO   OC (adjective)
The *doctor considered* the patient's *feelings important*.

        S   V   DO   OC (adjective)

The *party* at the amusement park *made* the little girl's *friends happy*.

Be careful not to confuse sentences that look alike. Consider these two sentences:

He called the man a liar.

In this sentence *called* is the verb, and *he* is the subject. *Man* is the direct object. So now let's ask *what* about him. *Liar* renames the man; he called the man *what*? He called the man a liar, so *liar* is the object complement.

He called the man yesterday.

Like the first sentence, in this sentence *called* is the verb, and *he* is the subject. *Man* is the direct object. The adverb *yesterday* tells when, not what, so it cannot be an object complement.

When an adjective functions as the object complement, it describes the direct object that comes before it, rather than renaming it:

I painted my nails *green*.

Painted is the verb. Who painted? I did, so *I* is the subject. What did I paint? I painted my nails, so *nails* is the direct object. What did I paint them? I painted them green, so *green* is the object complement describing nails.

Certain verbs, such as *appoint, believe, call, choose, consider, elect, keep, leave, make, name, paint, prove, select, think, turn,* and *vote,* commonly appear in patterns with object complements.

Practice Set 2–11

Directions: In the following sentences, underline the verbs twice and the simple subjects once. Then label the direct objects DO and object complements OC.

                         DO   OC

Example: We named our boat *Hog Heaven*.

1. He called his brother a genius.

2. The dye turned my hair purple.

3. I proved him wrong today.

4. The comedian left the audience hungry for more.

5. I kept Nicky busy during the boring speech.

6. The committee appointed me the leader.

7. Carlie made me sorry about my behavior.

8. I consider you my friend.

Diagramming Subject/Verb/Direct Object/Object Complement Sentence Patterns

To diagram a sentence in the Subject/Verb/Direct Object/Object Complement pattern, begin with the parts you already know.

$$\text{subject} \mid \text{verb} \mid \text{direct object}$$

The object complement follows a backslash placed next to the direct object. Notice how the line points back to the direct object, the word the object complement renames or describes.

$$\text{subject} \mid \text{verb} \mid \text{direct object} \setminus \text{object complement}$$

$$\text{I} \mid \text{painted} \mid \text{nails} \setminus \text{green}$$

Practice Set 2–12

Directions: In the following sentences, underline the verbs twice and the simple subjects once. Label the direct objects DO and object complements OC.

Optional diagramming: On a separate sheet of paper, place the subjects, verbs, direct objects, and object complements in their appropriate positions on the diagram frame.

Example: We elected Jack secretary

$$\text{We} \mid \text{elected} \mid \text{Jack} \setminus \text{secretary}$$

1. The remark made Carmen happy.

2. Aisha's friends considered her song a hit.

3. A rescue team found the climbers alive.

4. The students elected Manny president of the council.

5. Jim Martin thought the whole plan unnecessary.

6. My sister painted her room red.

7. The generous donation from the foundation kept our dream alive.

8. She considered her mother her best friend.

9. I called my neighbor's barking dog a pest.

10. The café made the coffee too strong.

WRITING YOUR OWN SENTENCES

Directions: Fill in the blanks provided, using the cues to help you write your own sentences in the Subject/Verb/Direct Object/Object Complement pattern. You may add *a*, *an*, or *the*, if needed.

noun or pronoun	one of the following verbs: *appoint, believe, call, choose, consider, elect, keep*	noun or pronoun	noun, pronoun, or adjective that renames or describes the noun or pronoun just before it

Try another one:

noun or pronoun	one of the following verbs: *leave, make, name, paint, prove, select, think, turn, vote*	noun or pronoun	noun, pronoun, or adjective that renames or describes the noun or pronoun just before it

Now try one on your own:

_____

Directions: On a separate sheet of paper, construct five of your own sentences in the Subject/Verb/ Direct Object/Object Complement pattern. Underline the verbs twice and the simple subjects once. Label the direct objects DO and object complements OC.

Optional diagramming: Place the subjects, verbs, direct objects, and object complements in the appropriate positions on the diagram frame.

SENTENCE PATTERN 5: SUBJECT/LINKING VERB/ SUBJECT COMPLEMENT

The verbs examined so far have been action verbs. You have learned that action verbs do not always take a direct object. Remember Fido? Fido *barks*. At other times, action verbs do take a direct object. Remember John and his car? John drove the car, so *car* is the direct object.

Not all verbs show action, however. **Linking verbs** have a special purpose—to link the subject to a word in the predicate in order to explain or enhance the subject's meaning. The word that renames or describes the subject is called the subject complement. Here is a sentence in the subject/linking verb/subject complement pattern:

Lindsay seems lucky.

In this sentence, *lucky* tells something about the subject, *Lindsay*. The verb *seems* links the word *Lindsay* to *lucky*. Verbs such as *seem, appear,* and *become* are usually linking verbs. Other verbs can also be linking verbs, such as those involving the senses, including *feel, look, sound, smell,* and *taste.* These verbs are linking verbs only when they connect the subject to a word that renames or describes it. Be careful not to consider them linking verbs when they show action. Examine these two sentences:

> Hilda tastes the chocolate.

> The chocolate tastes bitter.

In the first sentence, Hilda is doing something. She tastes the chocolate. Here *tastes* shows action. In the next sentence, *tastes* connects (or links) the subject *chocolate* to the word that describes it, *bitter.* In this sentence, *tastes* is a linking verb.

QUICK TIP

A good trick to determine if a verb is a linking verb is to substitute the word *seems* for the verb. If the sentence still makes sense, the verb is a linking verb.

> The food *looked* spoiled.

> The food *seemed* spoiled.

Seemed works, so *looked* is a linking verb in the sentence above.

> I *looked* at the dark clouds.

> I *seemed* at the dark clouds.

Seemed doesn't work, so *looked* is not a linking verb in the preceding sentence.

Practice Set 2–14

Directions: In the following sentences, underline the verbs twice and then determine whether the verbs are linking verbs or action verbs.

Examples:

He looked at the instructions carefully.	action
He looked confused.	linking

1. Jason suddenly appeared in the window. _____

2. The track star's running shoes smelled terrible. _____

3. I felt the rough surface of the tabletop. _____

4. She sounded the bell at midnight. _____

5. The Tin Man appeared rusty. _____

6. I really feel sorry for you. _____

7. The campers smelled the skunk in the woods. _____

8. His excuse sounds insincere to me. _____

9. The climber became weary near the summit. _____

10. He became a member of the team. _____

The "to be" verb

The most common linking verb is the verb *to be*.

> Albert *is* an actor.

> Jessica *was* fortunate.

Any form of the verb *to be* can be a linking verb: *am, is, are, was, were. Be, been,* and *being* can also be linking verbs when they appear with helping verbs (*will be, has been, are being*).

Like the verbs of the senses, forms of *to be* are not always linking verbs. Sometimes they are **helping verbs,** that is, verbs that combine with other verbs to form a verb phrase:

> **verb phrase**
> I *am running*

> **verb phrase**
> You *were snoring*.

Practice Set 2–15

Directions: In the sentences below, underline the linking verbs twice and the simple subjects once.

Example: He was hungry all week.

1. They are sailors in the United States Navy.

2. Martine is sorry about her mistake.

3. I am certain that Darcy left.

4. My sister was happy when I called her.

5. The twins are ushers at that movie theater.

6. You are silly.

7. Michael and Thomas were friends in kindergarten.

8. I am careful about what I say.

You can now recognize three types of linking verbs:

> Verbs such as *appear, become,* and *seem*

> Verbs dealing with the senses, such as *feel, look, smell, sound,* and *taste*

> Forms of *to be,* such as *am, is, are, was, were, be, been, being*

When a sentence has a linking verb, the word that it links to the subject is called the subject complement. A **subject complement** is a word that follows a linking verb and renames or describes the subject. Subject complements can be nouns, pronouns, or adjectives:

     S   LV SC (noun)
Shelly is a *student* of history.

     S   LV   SC (noun)
Jack became a tour *director* in Europe.

         S   LV SC (pronoun)
The person in charge is *she*.

   S   LV   SC (adjective)
She was *alone* for three years.

        S   LV   SC (adjective)
The sky appeared *black* before the storm.

      S   LV   SC (adjective)
Marianne looked *healthy*.

        S   LV   SC (noun)
Mr. Martinelli is a large *man*.

> **QUICK TIP**
>
> Don't confuse subject complements with direct objects. Direct objects follow action verbs; subject complements follow linking verbs. Consider the following sentence:
>
>   Amelia Earhart was a pilot.
>
> Here, *pilot* is a subject complement, not a direct object, because it follows the linking verb was. Pilot does not receive the action of the verb but instead renames the subject, *Amelia Earhart*.

Diagramming Subject/Linking Verb/Subject Complement Sentence Patterns

The Subject/Verb/Subject Complement diagram frame is similar to the Subject/Verb/Direct Object diagram frame. The only difference is that the line between the verb and the subject complement slants to the left, pointing back to the subject renamed or described.

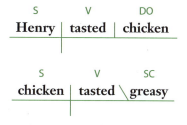

Directions: In the following sentences, underline the linking verb twice and the subject once. Label the subject complement (SC).

Optional diagramming: Place the subjects, verbs, and subject complements in their appropriate positions on the diagram frame. Draw the diagrams on a separate sheet of paper.

                                     SC
Example: The windows <u><u>were</u></u> foggy.

        windows | were \ foggy

1. The trophy was enormous.

2. Wynton Marsalis is a trumpeter.

3. The tacos looked spicy.

4. The winner was he.

5. My answer sounded stupid.

6. The cold seemed unbearable.

7. My uncles were fishermen.

8. Austin is the capital of Texas.

WRITING YOUR OWN SENTENCES

Directions: Fill in the blanks provided, using the cues to help you write your own sentences in the Subject/Linking Verb/Subject Complement pattern.

_____	_____	_____
noun or pronoun	**linking verb, like *be, seem, become, appear***	**noun, pronoun, or adjective linking to the subject**

Try another one:

_____	_____	_____
noun or pronoun	**linking verb of the senses**	**noun, pronoun, or adjective linking to the subject**

Now try one on your own:

_____

Directions: On a separate sheet of paper, construct five of your own sentences in the Subject/Linking Verb/ Subject Complement pattern. Underline the linking verbs twice and the simple subjects once. Label the subject complements (SC).

Optional diagramming: Place the subjects, linking verbs, indirect objects, and subject complements in the appropriate positions on the diagram frame.

Practice Set 2–18

Directions: In the following sentences, label the main sentence parts (subject, verb, DO, IO, OC, SC). Then write the sentence patterns on the lines provided.

        S   V   DO

Example: Kevin asked a silly question.   S/V/DO

1. Arthur sold Ricky his old car.   _____

2. Bert is a very smart guy.   _____

3. Katherine won first prize at the fair.   _____

4. Elena considered her son brilliant.   _____

5. Mashid left his keys in his locked car.   _____

6. Our hot water heater broke over the weekend.   _____

7. Mazie colored the tree orange.   _____

8. The speaker told the crowd the story of his life.   _____

9. They were all good dancers.   _____

10. The final exam was very easy.   _____

TEST YOURSELF

Directions: Label the sentence patterns in the following paragraph. We've done the first one for you.

               S/LV/SC

    Bill Mazeroski was one of the greatest second basemen ever in Major League Baseball. He played for the Pittsburgh Pirates from 1956 to 1972. This fine athlete entered the Baseball Hall of Fame in 2001. He holds the Major League record for double plays by a second baseman. This accomplishment earned him the nickname "The Glove." However, his bat made him even more famous. He was the last batter in the ninth inning of the 1960 World Series. He hit the only home run ever to win a World Series in game seven. The Pirates won with a score of 10 to 9. Bill Mazeroski taught sports fans an important lesson: a master outfielder can hit the most dramatic home run in the history of baseball.

WRITE NOW

Directions: Write one sentence in each of the five sentence patterns. Include at least one of the words from the Word Watchers exercise in each sentence (*accept, except, affect, effect, between, among, capital, capitol, choose, chose*).

GrammarSpeak: ⟶

Here is another exercise to help you establish better oral language habits. The following exercise contains some commonly mispronounced words containing silent letters. Practice saying the correct pronunciations aloud, keeping the silent letters silent.

	Instead of:	Say:
Herbs	HERBS	ERBS
Gourmet	GourMET	gour MAY
Sword	SWORD	SORD
Subtle	SUBtle	SUTTLE
Thyme	THYME	Time

WORD WATCHERS

The words in the pairs below are frequently misused. Be sure to use the words that you mean.

accept/except　*Accept* is a verb meaning *to receive:* I accept your apology.

Except is a preposition meaning *but:* Everyone was invited except Tim.

affect/effect　Both can mean *influence. Affect* is always a verb: How does the weather affect your mood?

Effect is usually a noun: The weather has no effect on my mood.

It can also mean consequence or result: The effect of the tornado was total devastation.

Effect can also be a verb meaning *to bring about:* I want to effect a change in policy.

between/among　Use *between* for two; use *among* for more than two: I divided the chores between the twins but among the triplets.

capital/capitol　The *capital* is a city; the *capitol* is a building: The capital of Florida is Tallahassee. Many state capitols have copper domes.

choose/chose　*Choose*, rhyming with *fuse*, is present tense and means *select*: Please choose your partner.

Its past tense is *chose,* rhyming with *hose:* He chose the same partner last week.

Word Watchers Practice Set

Directions: Circle the correct word in the parentheses.

1. How does this grade (affect/effect) my overall average?
2. Mr. Callahan spread the workload (between/among) all of the students in the class.
3. The (capital/capitol) of Vermont is Montpelier.
4. Tie a ribbon on every chair (accept/except) that one.
5. Lilly (choose/chose) the low-calorie dessert.
6. The senator gave his speech on the steps of the (capital/capitol) building.
7. You must (accept/except) responsibility for your actions.
8. The accident at the nuclear reactor had a devastating (affect/effect) on the village.
9. You can (choose/chose) the path you wish to take in life.
10. Please place your luggage (between/among) the two posts.

Adjectives and Adverbs

ADJECTIVES

Although there are many kinds of adjectives, the following two rules apply to all of them:

1. Adjectives **modify** (describe) **nouns** and **pronouns**.

   Adjective modifying a noun: The *pretty dress* had a hole in it.

   Adjective modifying a pronoun: *Almost everybody* brought a gift.

2. Adjectives tell **which one, what kind,** and **how many**.

   Adjective telling which one: The **purple** jacket is on sale.

   Adjective telling what kind: A **kind** word can change the world.

   Adjective telling how many: Four geese escaped from the pen.

   An adjective usually appears before the noun or pronoun it modifies.

   I love my *new* car.

   What word does *new* describe? It describes the noun *car*. Thus, you know that *new* is an adjective because it describes a noun. It tells *which* car or *what kind of* car—my *new* car.

   Nearly everyone likes pizza.

   Everyone is a pronoun. It may be harder to see what *nearly* tells us about everyone, but since it describes a pronoun, it is an adjective.

Articles

English has two indefinite articles, *a* and *an*, and one definite article, *the*. Since articles modify nouns and pronouns, they are adjectives. Articles are like signposts on a highway. They show that a noun is coming, though the noun may not be the very next word. For this reason, they are **noun indicators**. The article may come just before the noun, or there may be some modifiers between the article and the noun.

   She found *an* apple in *the* refrigerator.

   A rusty hinge broke.

Possessives

A **possessive** shows ownership. Possessive words are adjectives when they modify nouns and pronouns.

I love *Angie's* dress.

What word does *Angie's* describe? It describes the *dress*. Because *dress* is a noun, the word *Angie's* must be an adjective. The adjective *Angie's* tells which dress. Possessives also imply indirect ownership: *today's* news, *society's* values.

Like possessive nouns, some possessive pronouns (*my*, *your*, *his*, *her*, *its*, *our*, and *their*) modify nouns and function as adjectives.

My leg is broken.   They offered *their* apology.

Predicate Adjectives

Adjectives don't always appear next to the word they modify.

My problem was *serious*.

Serious describes the noun *problem*. It tells what kind of problem—a *serious* problem. This sentence follows the Subject/Linking Verb/Subject Complement sentence pattern. Subject complements can be only three parts of speech—nouns, pronouns, or adjectives.

When adjectives serve as subject complements, they always appear in the predicate of the sentence. For this reason, they are called predicate adjectives. **Predicate adjectives** follow linking verbs and modify the subject; thus, *serious* is a predicate adjective.

Adjectives that modify pronouns often appear as subject complements:

She is *happy*.

Directions: Circle the adjectives and draw an arrow to the words they modify.

Example: Almost nobody completed the difficult assignment.

Example: They are happy about the new rules.

Example: My grandmother is really old.

1. The antique mirror cost a small fortune.

2. Lily told practically everybody about the big sale.

3. His next decision is very important.

4. Their former skating teacher made the Olympic team.

5. Melissa's partner was not sorry about the mistake.

6. His biography is the untold story of a heroic farm boy.

7. She became nervous when her car's engine light began blinking.

8. The corporation's new policy affects practically everybody.

9. Your Internet provider may offer new subscribers a generous discount.

10. The second person in line offered my friend his ticket.

There are many types of adjectives, but they all have two things in common. They all show which one, what kind, or how many, and they all modify nouns and pronouns.

Proper Adjectives

Proper adjectives are derived from proper nouns, and like proper nouns, they begin with a capital letter. They refer to specific people, places, languages, or groups.

This *Renaissance* painting is very valuable.

Demonstrative Adjectives

When *this*, *that*, *these*, and *those* modify nouns, they are demonstrative adjectives. *This* and *that* modify singular nouns; *these* and *those* modify plural nouns.

This meat is raw.   *That* answer is wrong.

These people are waiting.   *Those* pickles are sour.

Indefinite Adjectives

When *each, every, either, neither, another, all, some, many, most,* and *both* modify nouns, they are indefinite adjectives.

Every child deserves a good home.

Interrogative Adjectives

When *what, which,* and *whose* modify nouns within a question, they are interrogative adjectives.

Which answer is correct?

Relative Adjectives

When *what, whatever, which, whichever,* and *whose* modify nouns, they are relative adjectives.

Whatever answer I choose will be correct.

Numerical Adjectives

When cardinal numbers (the whole numbers, like *one, two, three*) or ordinal numbers (the numbers that show position, like *first, second, third*) modify nouns, they are numerical adjectives.

Two people offered to help me.   My *first* reason is simple.

Practice Set 3–2

Directions: Circle the adjectives and draw an arrow to the words they modify.

Example: Three graduates filled these positions.

1. Early telephones carried audible messages from place to place.

2. What instrument could actually record these messages?

3. Thomas Edison invented the first phonograph to record the human voice and other sounds.

4. American listeners could have whatever music they liked in their homes.

5. The original machine had a foil drum with a small needle.

6. Could any invention be better than this one?

7. The next improvement was the famous gramophone invented by Emile Berliner.

8. This machine recorded on a large flat disc made of shellac.

9. These inventors paved the way for portable devices like cell phones.

10. Today, a small phone can also store a thousand songs.

Adding Adjectives to the Diagram

Adjectives have two positions on the diagram frame. Predicate adjectives, the adjectives that follow linking verbs and serve as subject complements, appear on the main line, following the linking verb and a backslash diagonal line:

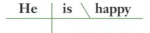

All other adjectives go on a backslash diagonal line beneath the word they modify. If more than one adjective modifies the same word, each has its own diagonal. Do not place an adjective directly under a verb since adjectives never modify verbs.

The strong, healthy athlete exercised.

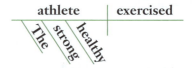

The poor, lonesome beggar gave the wealthy man his last dime.

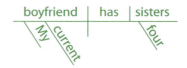

Practice Set 3–3

Directions: In the following sentences, underline the verb twice and the simple subject once; then label all the adjectives.

Optional diagramming: Diagram the sentences on a separate sheet of paper.

Example: My current boyfriend has four sisters.

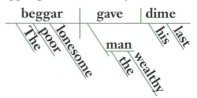

1. I met an old Russian woman.

2. Several English courses are available.

3. Three strange sea creatures occupied the aquarium.

4. Karen's math teacher gave the confused student some additional notes.

5. That requirement seems unnecessary.

6. Mrs. Spear sold the expensive house.

7. The contest judges gave each contestant a cheap plastic medal.

8. Which sandwich tastes fresh?

9. Dr. Patel is an American citizen.

10. The handsome prince sent the beautiful princess a fragrant rose.

ADVERBS

Two rules apply to all adverbs:

1. Adverbs modify **verbs, adjectives,** and other **adverbs**.

An adverb modifying a verb:	She **sang** *beautifully*. (describes how she **sang**)
An adverb modifying an adjective:	He is *very* **sorry**. (describes how **sorry** he is)
An adverb modifying another adverb:	He walked *quite* **slowly**. (describes how **slowly he walked**)

2. Adverbs tell **where, when, how, why,** and **to what degree**.

An adverb telling where:	She placed the paper *there*.
An adverb telling when:	He *never* lies to me.
An adverb telling how:	She spoke *angrily*.
An adverb telling to what degree:	He is *not* happy.

Adverbs that tell why usually appear as phrases or clauses:

An adverb clause telling why:	I am angry *because she is late*.

Adverbs Ending in -*ly*

Adverbs often end in -*ly*. When modifiers have two forms, one with the -*ly* ending and one without, distinguishing the adverb from the adjective is easy. For example, *real* is an adjective, and *really* is an adverb. However, some words that are not adverbs end in -*ly*. Consider this example:

She is a lovely girl.

Although *lovely* ends in -*ly*, it modifies a noun, *girl*. Thus, it is an adjective, not an adverb. Rather than simply noting the -*ly* ending, ask yourself what part of speech the word modifies.

Interrogative Adverbs

The interrogative words *how, when, why,* and *where* are adverbs. We use these adverbs to ask questions.

Why did you do that?   *Where* is my hat?

Practice Set 3–4

Directions: Label the adjectives (adj.) and adverbs (adv.) and draw an arrow to the words they modify.

       adj.   adj.   adj.   adv.

Example: The bright moonlight lit the yard brilliantly.

1. The math instructor reluctantly changed the grade.

2. Today the price is very reasonable.

3. The new music is simply wonderful!

4. James sold the very old cabinet rather quickly.

5. Clemencio posted a very long blog.

6. Claudia gave the audience a long, boring lecture.

7. I finally painted the rusty, old shed drab green.

8. Marlesia always gives older people special attention.

9. They appeared very gracious tonight.

10. Rosa surely wants some recognition quickly.

Adding Adverbs to the Diagram

Use a backslash diagonal to place the adverb beneath the word it modifies. If the adverb modifies another word (an adjective or another adverb) that is already written on a backslash diagonal, add a short connecting line to the first backslash before creating a new one.

Practice Set 3–5

Directions: In the following sentences, underline the verb twice and the simple subject once; then label all adjectives and adverbs.

Optional diagramming: Diagram the sentences on a separate sheet of paper.

         adv.   adj. adv.   adj.   adv.

Example: Iris nearly lost her very pretty ring yesterday.

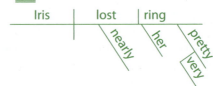

1. The lazy dog slept.

2. Daniel laughed hysterically.

3. The president's staff was very helpful.

4. Each father proudly gave his son a merit badge.

5. Robert's wife is a lawyer.

6. Those incredibly ancient ruins attract many tourists yearly.

7. He is never late.

8. I always call my mother "Mama."

9. The finicky eater gave the angry server a new order.

10. That very sensitive information became public yesterday.

11. Your lame excuse is definitely not acceptable.

12. He quickly emailed his new boss a long apologetic memo.

TEST YOURSELF

Directions: Label all the adjectives and adverbs in the following sentences and draw arrows to the words they modify.

Example: Some people think Jamestown was the first city in the United States.

but St. Augustine is really older.

1. When we talk about the oldest city, we really mean the oldest European settlements.

2. Numerous ancient Native American settlements were established much earlier than any of the great cities we now call our "oldest" ones.

3. St. Augustine is located in the northeastern part of Florida and is now a popular destination for many tourists.

4. In the sixteenth century, the Spanish government desperately wanted to establish a secure base to protect their New World settlements from the English and the French, who were also anxious to explore the region.

5. Admiral Pedro Menendez de Aviles, a somewhat famous conquistador, claimed the contested land for Spain in 1565, and St. Augustine served as the capital of Spanish Florida for two centuries.

6. Following a bloody century of skirmishes with the native population and some English privateers, the industrious Spanish built a secure fort, The Castillo de San Marcos.

7. The sturdy fort still stands today, the oldest masonry fort in the continental United States, and it is certainly the most popular tourist attraction in the old city.

8. Henry Flagler, a wealthy oil tycoon, helped transform the ancient city to a popular tourist resort for very wealthy people during the late nineteenth and early twentieth century.

9. He built several hotels there, including the magnificent Ponce de Leon, a luxurious retreat for extremely rich and famous people.

10. Since 1968 the lovely hotel has served as Flagler College, a private, four-year college.

WRITE NOW

Directions: Write a paragraph about the city where you were raised; remember to include many colorful adjectives and adverbs to make your ideas specific. Label all adjectives and adverbs. The paragraph should be at least five sentences in length.

GrammarSpeak ▬▬▶

Be careful not to use adjectives when your sentence requires adverbs or adverbs when your sentence requires adjectives. Practice using the proper part of speech by repeating these corrected sentences aloud:

Instead of:	**Say:**
I did **good** on my test.	I did **well** on my test.
He is **real** sorry about his mistake.	He is **really** sorry about his mistake.
I feel **badly** about your loss.	I feel **bad** about your loss.
He is **near** finished.	He is **nearly** finished.
They drive very **slow**.	They drive very **slowly**.

WORD WATCHERS

Some words sound alike but have very different meanings. Be sure to use the words that you mean.

cite/site/sight

Cite refers to giving reference: You must cite each article you read for this research paper.

Site refers to a place: This corner is the site of the accident.

Sight refers to vision: John Milton lost his sight before he wrote *Paradise Lost*.

complement/compliment	Remember the vowels to keep these straight.
	Complement means *to complete* and the spelling is similar: Your purse really complements your outfit.
	To *compliment*—with an *i*—means to say something nice about someone: I like to get a compliment. Thanks for paying me that compliment!
continuous/continual	When something is *continuous*, it goes without a break: The dog's continuous barking disturbed the entire neighborhood.
	Something that is *continual* happens regularly and frequently, but not necessarily continuously: His continual interruptions angered the instructor.
emigrate/immigrate	Remember the vowels. People emigrate FROM a country and immigrate TO a new country. Remember the vowels: **e**migrate = exit; **i**mmigrate = into: The O'Rourkes emigrated from Ireland in 1988. Thousands of people immigrate to the United States each year.
farther/further	*Farther* refers to distance: They live farther away than they used to.
	Further refers to quantity or degree: I do not wish to discuss this topic any further.

Word Watchers Practice Set

Directions: Choose the correct word in the parentheses.

1. The (continuous/continual) dripping of the faucet kept everyone awake.
2. If you escalate this argument any (farther/further), you will lose my support.
3. We chose an unusual (cite/site) for the annual picnic.
4. The red wine (complemented/complimented) the filet mignon perfectly.
5. Before she (emigrated/immigrated) to the United States, Luisa completed her college education in Bolivia.
6. Nebraska Avenue is (farther/further) from the expressway than Kennedy Boulevard.
7. Their (continuous/continual) arguing is going to wreck their marriage.
8. The professor (cited/sited/sighted) Albert Einstein in his lecture.
9. May I (complement/compliment) you on your good manners?
10. Anatoly brought his violin with him when he (emigrated/immigrated) from Russia.

Phrases

A phrase is a group of related words that functions as a single part of speech—a noun, a verb, an adjective, or an adverb. It does not contain both a subject and a verb. Several types of phrases exist in English. One of the most common types of phrases begins with words called prepositions.

PREPOSITIONAL PHRASES

A **preposition** is a word that connects a noun or pronoun to other words in a sentence. A preposition is usually one word, but sometimes a group of words can act as a preposition. Below is a list of common prepositions:

about	beside	in spite of	through
above	between	inside	throughout
according to	beyond	instead of	to
across	but (meaning "except")	into	together with
after	by	like	toward
against	by way of	near	under
along	concerning	of	underneath
along with	despite	off	until
among	down	on	up
around	during	onto	up to
as	except	out	upon
as well as	for	out of	with
at	from	outside	with reference to
because of	in	over	with regard to
before	in addition to	past	with the exception of
behind	in back of	regarding	within
below	in case of	since	without
beneath	in front of	than	

A **prepositional phrase** always begins with a preposition and ends with a noun or a pronoun, which is called the **object of the preposition**. Between the preposition and the object, some modifiers may appear. When we are examining the parts of a sentence, we traditionally put parentheses around prepositional phrases to make them stand out.

prep. obj.
The meaning (*of life*) is a mystery.

prep.   obj.
I found my ring (*among* the old *newspapers*).

Practice Set 4–1

Directions: Place parentheses around all prepositional phrases. Circle the prepositions and underline the objects of the prepositions.

Example: The winner (of the game) advances (to the finals).

1. Because of the poor weather conditions, there were several serious accidents in town.

2. We have not received your payment for January.

3. According to the CEO, a person like him is always an asset to this firm.

4. He proposed to her during the football game.

5. Everyone except Felicia knows about the meeting on Friday.

6. I parked in front of the building in case of an emergency.

7. I bought these shoes in spite of her objections about the cost.

8. She lied about the burglary that had taken place during their trip to Canada in March.

9. At night, my ferret sleeps among the boxes under my bed.

10. Rolando found the missing map inside the rusty watering can that we had thrown in front of the storage shed.

Prepositional Phrases–Never the Subject

Prepositional phrases—and any words within them—can never be the subject of the sentence. Prepositional phrases always act as adjectives or adverbs, but the subject of the sentence must be a noun or pronoun. It's easy to be tricked into thinking that the object of the preposition is the subject of the sentence since both are nouns. When you are trying to find the subject, it's a good idea to put parentheses around prepositional phrases and then cross them out, so they won't confuse you. Then the subject is easier to see:

The reason (for his mistakes) is not clear.

Practice Set 4–2

Directions: Put parentheses around the prepositional phrases and then cross them out. Underline the verb twice and the simple subject once.

Example: The purpose (of these demonstrations) is to teach you how to cook.

1. The photograph of her children is ready for editing.

2. The recipe for the dessert calls for unusual ingredients.

3. The newspapers on the porch are wet from the rain.

4. My friends from my old job take a vacation in June.

5. The ribbons in her hair blew gently in the wind.

6. Unplanned trips to the mall cost me a lot of money.

7. The socks behind the dryer have so much lint on them.

8. After the snowstorm, the roads were nearly impassable.

9. Opportunities like that one come once in a lifetime.

10. The paramedics at the scene first treat the victims with the worst injuries.

PREPOSITIONAL PHRASES AS ADJECTIVES AND ADVERBS

Prepositional phrases always act as adjectives or adverbs.

Adjective Phrases

When prepositional phrases function as adjectives, they describe **which one** or **what kind** about a **noun** or a **pronoun**, just as single-word adjectives do.

The snake *in that cage* is poisonous.

(The prepositional phrase *in that cage* tells **which** snake.)

You should not submit a résumé *with a typographical error*.

(The prepositional phrase *with a typographical error* tells **what kind** of résumé.)

Practice Set 4–3

Directions: Place each prepositional phrase in parentheses and write it in the blank. In the second blank, write the word that the phrase modifies.

Example: I thought the program (about the election) was very interesting.

Prepositional phrase: _about the election_____

Word it modifies: _program_____

1. The members of our club hope you will join soon.

   Prepositional phrase: _____

   Word it modifies: _____

2. Shanita told a funny story about her nosy uncle.

   Prepositional phrase: _____

   Word it modifies: _____

3. I asked the boy in front of me to step aside.

   Prepositional phrase: _____

   Word it modifies: _____

4. The shop around the corner sells what you need.

   Prepositional phrase: _____

   Word it modifies: _____

5. I wrote him a letter concerning his recent engagement to Sophia.

   Prepositional phrase: _____

   Word it modifies: _____

   Prepositional phrase: _____

   Word it modifies: _____

Adverb Phrases

When prepositional phrases function as adverbs, they modify **verbs, adjectives,** or other **adverbs**. They tell **where, when, how, why,** and **to what degree** about the words they modify, just as single-word adverbs do.

   I put the report *in the file*.

(The prepositional phrase *in the file* tells **where** I put the report.)

   She planted the tomatoes *in the spring*.

(The prepositional phrase *in the spring* tells **when** she planted the tomatoes.)

   The baker made this cake *with a blender*.

(The prepositional phrase *with a blender* tells **how** the baker made this cake.)

I was nervous *about the upcoming test*.

(The prepositional phrase *about the upcoming test* tells **why** I was nervous.)

Practice Set 4–4

Directions: Place each prepositional phrase in parentheses and write it in the blank. In the second blank, write the word that the phrase modifies.

Example: (Throughout the production), the actors spoke (in rhyme).

Prepositional phrase: Throughout the production

Word it modifies: spoke

Prepositional phrase   in rhyme

Word it modifies   spoke

1. She stored the stolen letters behind the cabinet.

   Prepositional phrase: _____

   Word it modifies: _____

2. I took these pictures with an old box camera.

   Prepositional phrase: _____

   Word it modifies: _____

3. Our neighbors live beyond their means.

   Prepositional phrase: _____

   Word it modifies: _____

4. We can join you for lunch immediately after class.

   Prepositional phrase: _____

   Word it modifies: _____

   Prepositional phrase: _____

   Word it modifies: _____

5. At noon I left the assignment on her desk.

   Prepositional phrase: _____

   Word it modifies: _____

   Prepositional phrase: _____

   Word it modifies: _____

Practice Set 4–5

Directions: Place each prepositional phrase in parentheses and write it in the blank. Next, determine the word and the part of speech of that word that each phrase modifies. Then indicate whether the prepositional phrase acts as an adjective or an adverb.

Example: The parrot (in the cage) can talk.

Prepositional phrase: in the cage

Word it modifies: parrot

Part of speech of the word it modifies: noun

Prepositional phrase functions as this
part of speech: adjective

1. Before the Olympics, the athletes train hard.

    Prepositional phrase: _____

    Word it modifies: _____

    Part of speech of the word it modifies: _____

    Prepositional phrase functions as this
    part of speech: _____

2. The point of his argument is clear.

    Prepositional phrase: _____

    Word it modifies: _____

    Part of speech of the word it modifies: _____

    Prepositional phrase functions as this
    part of speech: _____

3. I put the money in a safe place.

    Prepositional phrase: _____

    Word it modifies: _____

    Part of speech of the word it modifies: _____

    Prepositional phrase functions as this
    part of speech: _____

4. The waves crashed against the sea wall.

    Prepositional phrase: _____

    Word it modifies: _____

    Part of speech of the word it modifies: _____

    Prepositional phrase functions as this
    part of speech: _____

5. The picture above the cabinet fell on the floor.

Prepositional phrase: _____

Word it modifies: _____

Part of speech of the word it modifies: _____

Prepositional phrase functions as this
part of speech: _____

Prepositional phrase: _____

Word it modifies: _____

Part of speech of the word it modifies: _____

Prepositional phrase functions as this
part of speech: _____

Adding Prepositional Phrases to the Diagram

The diagram frame for the prepositional phrase is a backslash diagonal line for the preposition, extending slightly below a horizontal line for its object. Place any modifiers on backslash diagonals beneath the object of the preposition.

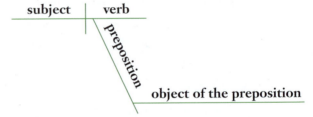

Prepositional phrases always go beneath the words they modify.

To decide where to place the prepositional phrase frame, determine whether the phrase is an adjective or an adverb. What does the phrase tell?

If the phrase tells **which one** or **what kind,** it is an **adjective phrase**.

If the phrase tells **where, when, why,** or **how,** it is an **adverb phrase**.

What part of speech does the phrase modify?

If the phrase modifies a **noun** or **pronoun**, it is an **adjective phrase**.

If the phrase modifies a **verb**, an **adjective**, or an **adverb**, it is an **adverb phrase**.

Examine this sentence:

The meaning of life is a mystery.

The diagram of the sentence looks like this:

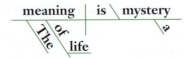

Of life tells **what kind** of meaning. Since it tells **what kind** and modifies a noun, it is an adjective phrase.

Sometimes a prepositional phrase can modify the object of a different prepositional phrase. Consider this sentence:

I put the ticket on the corner of my desk.

On the corner and *of my desk* are both prepositional phrases, but what does each modify? *On the corner* tells **where** I put the ticket. Since it tells **where** and describes a verb, it is an adverb phrase.

What does *of my desk* tell? It tells **which** corner. Since it tells **which one** and it describes a noun, it is an **adjective** phrase. It modifies the object of the preposition—*corner*. Diagram it like this:

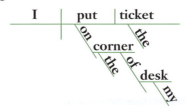

QUICK TIP

Remember the diagram position of the indirect object.

He gave Jake a gift.

The diagrams for indirect objects and prepositional phrases are very similar. Because the indirect object tells *to whom, for whom,* or *to what, for what* about the verb, this similarity is logical. *He gave the gift to Jake* is another way to say *He gave Jake a gift.* If the sentence actually contained the prepositional phrase *to Jake* instead of an indirect object, the diagram frame would look the same. The only difference would be the inclusion of the preposition on the diagonal line.

He gave gift Jake	He gave gift to Jake
Indirect Object	**Prepositional Phrase**

Practice Set 4–6

Directions: Place each prepositional phrase in parentheses and write it in the blank. On the next blank, write the word that the phrase modifies and on the final blank, write whether the phrase functions as an adjective or an adverb.

Optional diagramming: Diagram the sentences on a separate sheet of paper.

Example: The capital (of Idaho) is Boise.

Prepositional phrase: of Idaho

Word it modifies: capital

Prepositional phrase functions as: adjective

capital | is \ Boise
The \ of \ Idaho

1. On Tuesday I have three classes.

Prepositional phrase: _____

Word it modifies: _____

Prepositional phrase functions as: _____

2. They discontinued the search for the lost pilot after ten days.

Prepositional phrase: _____

Word it modifies: _____

Prepositional phrase functions as: _____

Prepositional phrase: _____

Word it modifies: _____

Prepositional phrase functions as: _____

3. My best friend from camp arrived by train.

Prepositional phrase: _____

Word it modifies: _____

Prepositional phrase functions as: _____

Prepositional phrase: _____

Word it modifies: _____

Prepositional phrase functions as: _____

4. The Rays played a double-header at Tropicana Field on Sunday afternoon.

Prepositional phrase: _____

Word it modifies: _____

Prepositional phrase functions as: _____

Prepositional phrase: _____

Word it modifies: _____

Prepositional phrase functions as: _____

5. The hamster slept soundly on a towel in the closet.

Prepositional phrase: _____

Word it modifies: _____

Prepositional phrase functions as: _____

Prepositional phrase: _____

Word it modifies: _____

Prepositional phrase functions as: _____

Practice Set 4-7

Directions: Draw an arrow from each bolded prepositional phrase to the word it modifies. Then, label the prepositional phrase as either an adjective phrase or adverb phrase.

adv.   adj.

Example: When we travel **to new places**, we often like to take photos **of our trip**.

Lighting a Photograph

A good photo begins **with good lighting**. Photographers should check the sunlight **from all sides** because the angle **of the sun** greatly affects the outcome **of the photo**. When the sun is located **behind the subjects**, you are shooting **into the light**. Then the automatic features **of your camera** will put your camera **on the wrong settings** and underexpose the people **in your photograph**. Everything **except the people** will be properly exposed. The problem with sunlight **over your shoulder** is that the camera will be **on the proper settings** but your subjects will be squinting **at the sun** and will look funny **in the pictures**. **During the shot**, if the sunlight is **on the left or right**, the shadows **on your subjects** will ruin the picture. **In spite of these issues**, natural light works best **for most people**. The solutions **to these problems** are simple. Try to find a spot **in the shade** to give your subjects a break **from the harsh sunlight**. You can also try using a flash when the sun is **behind the subjects**. Understanding the lighting **for your photos** can have a great impact **on your results.**

WRITE NOW

Directions: Write a paragraph on something that you know how to do (e.g. bake a cake, drive a car, study for a test). Try to use a prepositional phrase in each sentence. Underline the prepositional phrases in your paragraph and draw an arrow to the words they modify. Then label the prepositional phrases as adjective phrases (adj.) or adverb phrases (adv.).

VERB PHRASES

You may have noticed in our discussion of verbs so far that the verbs in a sentence are not always single words; sometimes they are verb phrases. A **verb phrase** consists of a main verb and its **helping verbs** (also called *auxiliary verbs*):

Forms of *to be*:	am, is, are, was, were, be, being, been
Forms of *to have*:	has, have, had
Forms of *to do*:	do, does, did
Modals:	can, could, may, might, must, shall, should, will, would

      AV   MV

He *is singing* a song.

It can also include several auxiliary verbs plus a main verb:

     AV   AV   AV   MV

She *should have been exercising* daily.

Practice Set 4–8

Directions: Underline the verb twice and the simple subject once.

  Example: Margerite should have arrived by now.

1. The doctor will return your call in the morning.
2. That mechanic can fix anything on wheels.
3. Ashley should ask someone else that question.
4. She does have a good method for budgeting her time.
5. They have had too much time on their hands.
6. You could have told me your problem sooner.
7. Raphael might have been telling the truth.
8. I am devising a new plan.
9. Kiara would have done the job herself.
10. Lindsay may have stumbled upon a real bargain.

Adverbs Within the Verb Phrase

Frequently, adverbs appear within the verb phrase, but they are not part of the verb. Consider this sentence:

He *is* always *telling* stupid jokes.

Is telling is the verb phrase, and *always* is an adverb that describes when he is telling the jokes. Be particularly careful about the word *not*.

He *has* not *been doing* his homework.

The verb phrase is *has been doing*. *Not* tells how he has been doing. Thus, it is an adverb, not part of the verb. Don't forget that *n't* is a contraction, for *not* and is not part of the verb phrase.

He *was*n't *telling* the truth.

The verb phrase is simply *was telling*.

Practice Set 4–9

Directions: Underline the verb twice and the simple subject once.

Example: Harvey should not have answered so quickly.

1. Julieta would never break her promise to you.
2. You must not tell anyone your secret.
3. I have just sold my first painting.
4. He wouldn't have given you the money.
5. They should have never been swimming in that dangerous area.
6. Everett is still waiting for his refund check.
7. This spy story can't possibly be true.
8. The twins will never have the chance to know their father.
9. The child shouldn't be sitting on the wet grass.
10. Allison is always bragging about her children.

Adjectives Vs. Verb Phrases

It is important to distinguish between adjectives that follow linking verbs (The magician is *amazing*) and verb phrases (The magician *is amazing* the audience). To determine whether the word following a form of the verb *to be* is part of the verb phrase or is a subject complement, ask yourself whether it shows action or describes the subject.

Joseph Dover and Janice Fox were married for over 30 years.

Married describes Joseph Dover; thus the verb is *were*, and *married* is a subject complement.

Joseph Dover married Janice Fox in a small private ceremony at Lake Tahoe.

Married shows action, so it is a verb. *Janice Fox* is the direct object.

Practice Set 4–10

Directions: Indicate whether the word in boldface is a subject complement or is part of the verb.

Examples:

My new pen is **missing**.   subject complement

She is obviously **missing** her mother.   verb

1. The doctor **worried** about his patient's recovery. _____

2. My mother was **worried** about my car accident. _____

3. They have **gone** to the mountains to ski. _____

4. Elvis is **gone** but not forgotten. _____

5. The mystery play is **surprising** the audience. _____

6. Your offer is quite **surprising**. _____

7. I knew at once that the game was **lost**. _____

8. She **lost** her sweater at the movies. _____

9. We have **exhausted** our water supply. _____

10. The runners are really **exhausted**. _____

Diagramming Verb Phrases

The entire verb phrase is placed in the verb position on the diagram frame. Examine this sentence:

He is doing his homework.

In this sentence, the complete verb is the verb phrase *is doing*. To diagram this sentence, you must put the entire verb phrase in the verb position on the diagram frame.

$$\text{He} \mid \text{is doing}$$

He is doing what? He is doing his homework, so *homework* is the direct object. *His* is an adjective modifying *homework*. The completed diagram looks like this:

Here is another sentence:

He may have been wrong.

To diagram this sentence, put the entire verb phrase in the verb position on the diagram frame. Since *may have been* is a form of the verb *to be*, it is a linking verb; therefore, *wrong* appears in the subject complement position.

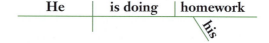

Practice Set 4–11

Directions: Underline all verb phrases twice.

Optional diagramming: Diagram the sentences on a separate sheet of paper.

Example: Martin is not running the business successfully.

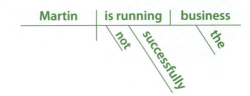

1. Keanna has never enjoyed a fancy gourmet meal.

2. Mara was happily dancing to the loud music.

3. Katie's new book has not been printed yet.

4. Estefan might have needed some help.

5. *Annie* is often revived on Broadway.

6. Nathan should have been the first one in line.

7. The parking lot has been empty today.

8. The doctor's office will never open on Friday.

9. The new rules are being discussed in that committee.

10. We don't always see the obvious solution.

APPOSITIVE PHRASES

An **appositive** renames a noun or a pronoun. It usually follows the noun and identifies, explains, or adds to the meaning of the noun. An **appositive phrase** consists of the appositive and its modifiers.

           noun   **appositive**

My dentist, Dr. Kanter, pulled my tooth.

                         noun   **appositive**

Ernest Hemingway wrote the novel *For Whom the Bell Tolls*.

The entire title acts as the appositive because it renames *novel*.
An appositive or an appositive phrase can appear next to any noun in a sentence:

                   subject   **appositive**

Appositive with subject: Dr. Rockwell, my professor, has office hours on weekends.

Appositive with object of the preposition:

               object of the preposition   **appositive**

I left the package with   Mr. Foxworth,   the doorman.

DO   appositive

Appositive with direct object: I was playing Hearts, a card game.

IO   appositive

Appositive with indirect object: I gave Alma, my girlfriend, a single rose.

SC   appositive

Appositive with subject complement: He is our leader, the man in charge.

OC   appositive

Appositive with object complement: We called her Sammy, a family nickname.

Practice Set 4–12

Directions: Circle the appositive phrase and underline the noun it renames.

> **Example:** The campus book store was selling the <u>textbook</u> (*Chemistry I*) at a discount.

1. Mrs. Dumeyer, my drama coach, is starring in a new play.

2. The award goes to Valerie Muñoz, our most valuable player.

3. The character Voldemort appears in *Harry Potter and the Deathly Hallows*.

4. Kwanzaa, an African-American cultural festival, is celebrated in December.

5. She is the winner, the fastest runner in the school.

6. I invited Davis, my best friend, to the party.

7. The movie tells the story of the *Titanic*, the doomed ship.

8. The judge gave Ted, my supervisor, a suspended sentence.

9. Judy Garland starred in the movie *The Wizard of Oz*.

10. Max's is my favorite restaurant, the best diner in town.

Diagramming Appositive Phrases

To diagram an appositive phrase, place the appositive in parentheses in the same position as the noun it renames, with its modifiers beneath it.

Stephanie, my oldest daughter, left for college yesterday.

Optional diagramming: Diagram the sentences in Practice Set 4–12.

Example: I offered Mrs. Gale, the secretary, an apology.

Directions: Add appropriate phrases to each of the following sentences.

Example: Add an appositive: I sold the necklace to Annie, *my friend from Pittsburgh*.

Example: Add a verb phrase: The tennis team *should have won* the tournament.

Example: Add a prepositional phrase: I drove my car *into a tree*.

Add appositives:

1. Cousin Wilbur, _____ , will not be coming to the reunion this year.

2. A careless shopper backed into my new car, _____ .

3. Istanbul, _____ , has the largest open-air market in the world.

4. I forwarded the memo to Sophie Moss, _____ .

Add verb phrases:

5. The Help the Children Campaign _____ $25,000 by the end of the month.

6. Ellie _____ on the phone for two hours.

7. My sister _____ a job as a firefighter.

Add prepositional phrases:

8. _____ , I prefer to eat a hearty breakfast of whole grains, fruit, and yogurt.

9. _____ , my boyfriend gave me a box of candy.

10. Sean found a diamond bracelet _____ .

Directions: In the blanks at the right, indicate whether the underlined phrase is a prepositional phrase, a verb phrase, or an appositive phrase.

Example: I <u>have been thinking</u> about summer vacation.   verb phrase

1. Many electrical cords are needed <u>for a new computer hook-up</u>.   _____

2. Monet, <u>an impressionist painter</u>, experimented with reflected light.   _____

3. After my doctor's appointment <u>on Wednesday</u>, I will go back to work.   _____

4. When we heard the siren, we knew the time <u>of real danger</u> was over.   _____

5. Smitty <u>has never seen</u> a live manatee.   _____

6. Mother <u>has been donating</u> most of her spare time to charity.   _____

7. Frances Perkins, <u>the first female in a U. S. president's cabinet</u>, was appointed by Franklin Roosevelt in 1933.   _____

8. <u>During the frog dissection demonstration</u>, Sylvia had to leave the room.   _____

9. Many chalkboards <u>have been replaced</u> by whiteboards.   _____

10. <u>For the last ten years</u>, he has hidden his money under his mattress.   _____

▼ TEST YOURSELF

Directions: In the following paragraph, identify the phrase in boldface as a prepositional phrase, a verb phrase, or an appositive phrase.

verb phrase

Example: Sometimes people who **have experienced** adversity make a great

prep. ph.

mark **in history**.

Theodore Roosevelt, (1) **the twenty-sixth President of the United States**, was born two years (2) **before the Civil War**. He suffered (3) **from asthma** and was a sickly child, but as an adult he (4) **would engage** in activities that required great physical abilities. Roosevelt, (5) **the only native of New York City to become President**, made a name for himself as the leader of the Rough Riders (6) **during the Spanish-American War**. Roosevelt's talents extended to many areas, and he (7) **would have been remembered** even if he (8) **had** never **held** office. He was an established historian and naturalist, a well-known authority (9) **on large American mammals**. His birthplace (10) **in Manhattan** is now a National Historic Site.

WRITE NOW

Directions: Write a paragraph of at least 8–10 sentences about a favorite movie or television show. Include either an appositive, a verb phrase, or a prepositional phrase in each sentence.

GrammarSpeak ⊢——————➤

The following exercise contains some commonly misspoken phrases. Practice saying the phrases aloud.

Instead of:	Say:
Take it for granite	Take it for *granted*
It's a doggy dog world	It's a *dog-eat-dog* world
For all intensive purposes	For *all intents and purposes*
Of upmost importance	Of *utmost* importance
Nip it in the butt	Nip it in the *bud*
I could care less	I could *not* care less
Statue of limitations	*Statute* of limitations
360 degree change	*180* degree change
Escape goat	*Scapegoat*
Hone in on	*Home* in on

WORD WATCHERS

Some words sound alike but have very different meanings. Be sure to use the words that you mean.

fewer/less	If you count them, use *fewer*; if you weigh or measure them, use *less:* There are fewer roses on the bush this year because I used less fertilizer.
lead/led	*Lead*, rhyming with *bead*, means *to go in front:* Martin wants to lead the parade.
	Its past tense is *led:* Yesterday, Martin led the parade.
	Lead, rhyming with *head*, is a metal: The fisherman used a lead sinker on his line.
loose/lose	*Loose* means *not tight*. It rhymes with *goose*. When you *lose* something, you can't find it: If my bracelet is too loose, it may fall off, and I will lose it.
number/amount	If you count it, use *number;* if you weigh or measure it, use *amount*. This is the same rule as *fewer/less*. A small number of students used a large amount of paint.

passed/past	*Passed* is the past tense of the verb *pass:* I passed my test with flying colors.
	Past can be a noun referring to an earlier time: In the past, women wore corsets and hoop skirts.
	Past can be an adjective describing something or someone from an earlier time: Our past president is resigning from the club.
	Past can be an adverb: We drove past.
	Past can be a preposition: They walked past the house.

Word Watchers Practice Set

Directions: Choose the correct word in parentheses.

1. Try not to (loose/lose) all of your money when you go to Las Vegas.
2. Marguerite (lead/led) the class in the Pledge of Allegiance.
3. The (number/amount) of oranges on my tree has doubled since the weather turned warm.
4. On my way to work this morning, I (passed/past) the house where I used to live.
5. You can check out in the express lane if you have ten items or (fewer/less).
6. I lost my earring because the back was (loose/lose).
7. There are (fewer/less) typos in this paragraph than in your previous one.
8. Superman cannot see through anything made of (lead/led).
9. Emma was afraid to marry him because of his troubled (passed/past).
10. I will follow wherever you (lead/led).

Verbals and Verbal Phrases

Verbals are words that are formed from verbs but do not function as verbs. Because verbals come from verbs, it is sometimes difficult to see the difference, but a word cannot be a verb and a verbal at the same time.

There are three types of verbals: participles, gerunds, and infinitives.

PARTICIPLES

Participles are verbals that function as adjectives. Present participles end in *-ing (singing)*; past participles usually end in *-ed (excited)*, *-t (built)*, *-k (drunk)*, or *-n (eaten)*. Because participles function as adjectives, they usually appear next to the noun or pronoun they modify.

participle noun
The singing waiter entertained my mother.

participle noun
The excited child opened his presents.

participle pronoun
Abandoned, he walked alone in the forest.

Sometimes it is difficult to distinguish a participle from the main verb of the sentence. Singing sounds like a verb. However, if you carefully examine the phrase *the singing waiter*, you notice that *waiter* is a noun and *singing* is an adjective that shows **what kind** of waiter. Thus, it is a verbal, not a verb. The verb in the sentence is *entertained*.

A **participial phrase** contains a participle and the words that go with it.

The player *wearing the red shirt* was obviously the fastest.

The phrase *wearing the red shirt* tells **which** player.

Arriving late, the beautiful bride slipped past the guests in the lobby.

Just as the word *beautiful* is an adjective, the participle *arriving late* also functions as an adjective describing *bride*. When we ask, "**What kind** of bride?" the answer is an *arriving late* bride. Remember that like adjectives, participles usually modify the noun that they are next to, so the phrase modifies the noun closest to it.

61

Practice Set 5–1

Directions: Circle the nouns or pronouns modified by the participles and participial phrases in boldface.

Examples: She cried when she heard the (missionary) **telling his story**.

They threw the **broken** (toys) into the box.

Offering his apology, (Jason) picked up the groceries he had knocked on the floor.

1. The plumber is going to repair the **leaking** pipes.

2. **Breaking his silence**, the witness finally related what he had seen that night.

3. We should honor our **fallen** soldiers every day, not just on Veterans Day.

4. The coyote **howling in the moonlight** frightened the campers.

5. She smiled at the **faded** photograph.

6. **Impressed with my work**, the contractor offered me the job.

7. The fire destroyed their **recently built** home.

8. The detective found the murder weapon **hidden in the fireplace**.

9. **Driven to work each day**, the movie star did not understand why people complained about the traffic.

10. They offered a replacement product to everyone **wanting a refund**.

Verb Phrases

Remember that verbs can also come in phrases. Sometimes the main verb needs "assistance" by a helping (or auxiliary) verb. The entire phrase is the verb of the sentence.

Don't confuse verb phrases with participial phrases. Ask yourself whether the phrase is showing action, indicating a verb phrase, or describing a noun, indicating a participial phrase.

verb phrase

Action: My cousin *has been helping* me with my homework.

participial phrase

Description: The girl *helping me with my homework* is really smart.

verb phrase

Action: The thief *might have been watching* our house.

participial phrase

Description: The thief *watching our house* waited until we left.

Practice Set 5–2

Directions: Identify the word in boldface as a verb or a participle.

Examples: He **crumpled** the paper and threw
it in the garbage.

verb

He found the **crumpled** map in the glove
compartment.

participle

This store might be **offering** a discount.

verb

I want to shop at the store **offering** a discount.

participle

1. The snow had been **falling** all night. _____

2. Davis left a partially **eaten** apple on my bed. _____

3. The man **asking** that question is a reporter
for Channel 10. _____

4. Asher **painted** the room bright green. _____

5. The car's price is its best **selling** point. _____

6. She caught the **falling** dish before it hit
the floor. _____

7. You have not **eaten** your lunch yet. _____

8. He was **asking** me questions about the
assignment. _____

9. I ruined my pants when I sat on the newly
painted bench. _____

10. The Girl Scouts will be **selling** their cookies
this month. _____

Practice Set 5–3

Directions: Underline all of the participles or participial phrases. Then circle the nouns or pronouns they modify. A sentence may have more than one participle or participial phrase.

Examples: The fallen (soldier) lay motionless on the battlefield.

The (boy) entering the room introduced himself to the (crowd) waiting for him.

1. Following my instructions, someone left the package on the doorstep.

2. I saw the half-eaten sandwich in the refrigerator.

3. The photograph bearing his signature is quite valuable.

4. During the raging storm, he comforted the frightened child.

5. He called to the police officer standing by the cruiser.

6. Built in 1911, this building has been condemned.

7. Lisa stopped to talk to the frustrated man selling his paintings at the art fair.

8. Worried about his grade, he made an appointment with his professor.

9. The short story written by Alice Walker won the coveted award.

10. The smiling project manager showed the boss her finished product.

GERUNDS

Gerunds are verbals that always end in *-ing*, but unlike participles, they function as nouns.

Studying is important.

The gerund *studying* is the subject of the sentence. **Gerund phrases** consist of the gerund and the words that go with it.

Studying the lesson is important.

To decide whether an *-ing* word is a gerund or a participle, try to identify its function in the sentence.

Gerunds act as nouns, so think about where you would find nouns in a sentence. Nouns can be **subjects**, **direct objects**, **indirect objects**, **subject complements**, or **objects of a preposition.** These basic sentence parts cannot usually be taken out of the sentence. Likewise, because gerunds function as these basic sentence parts, the gerund phrase cannot be left out of the sentence.

Participles, on the other hand, act as adjectives, which describe a noun or pronoun. Because adjectives are simply modifiers, participles can always be left out of the sentence.

Try the "leave-out" test with these two sentences:

Driving in the rain can be dangerous.

Driving in the rain, she became nervous.

In the first sentence, the linking verb is *can be*. The *-ing* phrase is a gerund functioning as a noun, and more specifically, the subject. If you leave it out, the sentence is incomplete: *Can be dangerous.* In the second sentence, the linking verb is *became*, and the subject is *she*. The *-ing* phrase is a participle. It acts as an adjective modifying the subject *she*. If you leave it out, the sentence, although not as detailed, is still complete: *She became nervous.*

Once you have decided that an *-ing* phrase is a gerund, look at it in relation to the main verb of the sentence. Then consider the sentence patterns and determine how the gerund functions.

Subject:	*Writing an essay* requires concentration.
Direct object:	He enjoys *cooking gourmet meals for his family*.
Indirect object:	He gave *training for the marathon* his total effort.
Subject complement:	His lifelong dream is *traveling around the world*.
Object of the preposition:	Before *setting the table* you should wash your hands.

Practice Set 5–4

Directions: Underline the gerunds and gerund phrases.

Examples: <u>Dancing</u> is good exercise.

His hobby is <u>collecting old newspapers</u>.

1. Laughing out loud got me in trouble.

2. Rashaad loves teasing his brother.

3. Before planning a party, you should decide on the menu.

4. Jake was almost fired for losing the customer's order.

5. The final straw was finding him asleep on the job.

6. I resent being interrupted during a phone conversation.

7. Creating a disturbance is a way to get attention.

8. I like going to car shows that feature muscle cars.

9. Playing on a team requires cooperation.

10. After moving to a new apartment, Maya sold her old furniture.

Practice Set 5–5

Directions: Underline the verbal phrases and identify them as participles or gerunds.

Examples:	
<u>Watching the lizard</u>, the kitten began to purr.	participle
<u>Ironing the shirt</u> took a long time.	gerund

1. Shaking frantically, the suspect blurted out his confession. _____

2. This unusual vase, crafted by hand, is very expensive. _____

3. Selling everything cheaply was important to him. _____

4. Elena does not mind lending the money. _____

5. The two spaniels sleeping peacefully by the fire did not bother the burglar. _____

6. You can make a lot of money by investing it carefully. _____

7. Developed by a team of surgeons, the new procedure saved Evan's life. _____

8. Losing ten pounds is my goal for this month. _____

9. I found my heavy winter jacket by cleaning my closet.

_____

10. The electrician was unraveling the electrical wires twisted by the storm.

_____

Practice Set 5–6

Directions: Identify the words in boldface as verbs or verbals. If the word is a verbal, label it as a participle or a gerund.

Example: She was **running** for vice president.   verb _____

These **running** shoes have holes in the soles.   verbal—participle _____

Running is great exercise.   verbal—gerund _____

1. His **speeding** ticket cost him $250.   _____

2. Angel is **working** toward earning a degree in computer programming.   _____

3. **Knowing** how an engine works is the key to auto repair.   _____

4. The **demanding** customer really irritated the sales clerk.   _____

5. **Speeding** on an icy road is dangerous.   _____

6. You will need to have your **working** papers before I can offer you a job.   _____

7. She gave me a **knowing** look as she left the room.   _____

8. He is always **demanding** to have his own way.   _____

9. I enjoy **working** in the garden when the weather is warm.   _____

10. If you are **speeding,** the officer will give you a ticket.   _____

INFINITIVES

Infinitives are verbals that begin with *to*, followed by the base form of the verb.

I love *to sing*.

Infinitive phrases include the infinitive and the words that go with it.

I want *to buy a new car*.

Infinitives and infinitive phrases function as nouns, adjectives, or adverbs.

Infinitives as Nouns

When infinitives are used as nouns, they act as either subjects, direct objects, subject complements, or objects of prepositions.

Infinitive phrase as subject: *To answer my question* took an hour.

Infinitive phrase as direct object: I like *to read in bed*.

Infinitive phrase as subject complement: My goal is *to make money*.

Infinitive phrase as object of a preposition: Except *to visit the doctor*, the old woman rarely left home.

Infinitives as Adjectives

When infinitives are used as adjectives, they modify nouns or pronouns and show **which one** and **what kind.**

Infinitive phrase modifying a noun: The rent *to be paid in April* was late.

Infinitive phrase modifying a pronoun: He was always looking for someone *to blame*.

Infinitives as Adverbs

When infinitives are used as adverbs, they modify verbs, adjectives, or other adverbs, and they answer questions like **why, how,** or **to what extent.**

Infinitive phrase modifying a verb: *To catch a butterfly*, use a net.

Infinitive phrase modifying an adjective: You are right *to complain*.

Infinitive phrase modifying an adverb: He ran too slowly *to win the race*.

QUICK TIP

All infinitives begin with the word *to*, but remember that not all phrases beginning with the word *to* are infinitives. Prepositional phrases also can begin with the word *to*.

to plus a **noun** = prepositional phrase:

We traveled *to* **China**.

to plus a **verb** = infinitive:

I like *to* **hike**.

Practice Set 5–7

Directions: Underline the infinitive phrases.

Examples: I want to buy a new phone.

To answer my question, she tried to find the answer online.

1. She wants to offer him an apology.

2. To be successful, he had to make sacrifices.

3. To meet life's challenges is our goal.

4. My fondest desire is to visit China.

5. The tire to change is in the trunk.

6. To clean the pool, I must first skim off the leaves.

7. To choose a strong topic, you must be interested in the subject.

8. The general's hope was to attack at dawn.

9. His decision to submit his application early made the difference.

10. To plant a productive garden, you must start with sturdy seedlings.

Practice Set 5–8

Directions: Identify the words in boldface as verbs or infinitives.

Example: She keeps trying **to speak** out of turn.   Infinitive

Example: I will **find** a way out of this predicament.   Verb

1. She tried to **finish** the assignment before he returned.   _____

2. To **unlock** the file, you will need three keys.   _____

3. Christopher Columbus didn't really **discover** America.   _____

4. She will **answer** you whenever she has the time.   _____

5. It is important to **dress** for success.   _____

6. My mother can never **finish** her sentences without my brother interrupting.   _____

7. I will **unlock** the door so the painters can get in.   _____

8. The only way to **discover** who you truly are is to **be** honest with yourself.   _____

9. My job is to **answer** the telephone and take messages.   _____

10. She will **dress** the mannequins for the window display.   _____

Practice Set 5–9

Directions: Identify the words in boldface as verbs or verbals. If they are verbals, indicate whether they are participles, gerunds, or infinitives.

Examples: The **laughing** toddler made every one smile.

verbal—participle

The toddler was **laughing**.

verb

1. The old man had such **wrinkled** skin. _____

2. I **wrinkled** the paper and threw it in the trash. _____

3. Horseback **riding** is a lot of fun. _____

4. The jockey was **riding** a sure winner. _____

5. This campsite has **running** water. _____

6. He is **running** a great campaign. _____

7. I love **to run** in cold weather. _____

8. **Running** in place, Shanice sprained her ankle. _____

9. **To record** a message, please wait for the tone. _____

10. Before **recording** a message, wait for the tone. _____

11. A **recorded** message is sometimes hard to understand. _____

12. He **recorded** the message carefully. _____

13. The **recording** artist won a Grammy. _____

14. **Recording** a message, Mike left the information and hung up. _____

15. I am **recording** my message for you. _____

Practice Set 5–10

Directions: Underline all the verbals and verbal phrases in the following sentences. Label each one as *P* for participle, *G* for gerund, or *I* for infinitive.

            G   P

Example: Knitting a sweater is a forgotten art.

1. Anticipating an accident, he swerved away from the approaching car.

2. My pressing dilemma is whether to sign the contract now or to wait until next year.

3. The swollen river rose two feet a day, overflowing its banks.

4. Exhausted from the drive, the college student decided to stop at a motel.

5. Mastering the game of chess takes hours of concentrated effort.

6. Her accumulated wealth increased her ability to help needy children.

7. Singing arias gave the trained tenor the practice he needed.

8. Eating healthy foods can lead to a prolonged life.

9. Avoiding tobacco and alcohol improved his condition.

10. Avoiding tobacco and alcohol, he was able to improve his condition.

 TEST YOURSELF

Directions: Label all of the underlined phrases as participles (P), gerunds (G), or infinitives (I). [The first sentence is an example.]

P

Arturo Sandoval, one of the most celebrated jazz musicians of our time, was born near Havana, Cuba, in 1949. His early training was as a classical musician, but at age twelve, upon hearing his first jazz recordings, he knew that he wanted to be a jazz trumpeter. A founding member of Irakere, a band blending traditional Latin sounds with jazz, rock, and classical music, Sandoval tried to explore new musical territory but was frequently censored by the Castro regime. Aided by jazz great Dizzy Gillespie, Sandoval defected to the United States in 1990. His wife and son joined him later. Nominated twelve times for Grammies and awarded three, Sandoval continues to excite music lovers throughout the world. Cuban-born actor Andy Garcia, fascinated by his countryman's amazing life, wanted to tell Sandoval's story to the world. He was able to do so when he starred in an HBO television movie, *For Love or Country: The Arturo Sandoval Story*. In 2013, honoring Sandoval for his many achievements, President Barack Obama awarded him the Presidential Medal of Freedom.

 WRITE NOW

Directions: Write a paragraph of 8–12 sentences on one of your favorite recording artists or movie stars. Use a participle, a gerund, or an infinitive in each sentence. These verbals may occur as single words or in phrases. Underline each verbal or verbal phrase. You may use the Internet to help you research if you wish, but be sure not to plagiarize by using any phrases or sentences that you have read in your research. If you do research, be sure to include the name and Web address of your source at the end of your paragraph.

GrammarSpeak ⊢——————▶

Here is another exercise to help you establish better oral language habits. The following exercise contains some commonly mispronounced words containing silent letters. Practice saying the correct pronunciations aloud, keeping the silent letters silent.

	Instead of:	Say:
Salmon	SAL Mon	SAM-uhn
Corps	CORPSE	CORE
Buffet	BUFF et	Buf FAY
Gyro	J+EYE ROW	YEER Oh (if you mean the Greek sandwich on pita bread)
Zoology	ZOO ology	ZOH ology

WORD WATCHERS

Some words sound alike but have very different meanings. Be sure to use the words that you mean.

principal/principle

Principal has three meanings.

- It refers to the leader of the school: Mrs. Cunningham is the principal of Ballast Point Elementary School.
- It means chief or main: My principal reason for leaving is clear.
- It refers to the money that generates interest: He spends only the interest, never the principal.

Principle has two meanings.

- It means a fundamental truth or law: The principles of gravity never change.
- It also means morals or standards for living: He is a man of high principles.

stationery/stationary

Stationery is writing paper: I wrote him a letter on my best stationery.

Stationary means *motionless:* The hunter remained stationary as the tiger approached.

then/than

Then is an adverb telling when: I drank my coffee, and then I paid the bill.

Than is a subordinating conjunction that introduces a comparison: Millie is smarter than Paco.

to/too/two	*To* has two uses:
	• To is a preposition: I followed him to the cafeteria.
	• To is also part of an infinitive: I don't want to insult you.
	Too can also be used in two ways:
	• Too is an adverb meaning *also*: Carson has a brother, too.
	• Too is also an adverb that adds intensity to adjectives: This sauce is too hot to eat.
	Two is a number: Owen has two missing teeth.
whether/weather	*Whether* is a subordinating conjunction that suggests a choice: We will hold the race whether it rains or not.
	Weather is a noun referring to atmospheric conditions: We held the race despite the bad weather.

Word Watchers Practice Set

Directions: Choose the correct word in parentheses.

1. The mourners remained (stationery/stationary) while the funeral procession passed.
2. It is (to/too) cold outside to wear short sleeves.
3. A new Lexus usually costs more (then/than) a new Chevy.
4. My (principal/principle) responsibility on this job is to assure product safety.
5. I have not yet told you (whether/weather) I intend to vote for you.
6. The rules for baseball and softball are different, but the (principals/principles) are the same.
7. The Chief Justice of the Supreme Court offered an opinion (to/too).
8. When you pay your mortgage, the interest is deducted before the (principal/principle).
9. After she moved, I gave her a box of (stationary/stationery) with her new address printed on it.
10. We should always live according to our (principals/principles).

CHAPTER 6

Word Order Variations

In most sentences the subject comes first, followed by the verb and then any complements. However, this word order has some important exceptions.

QUESTIONS

Questions may invert the subject/verb order or place the subject between two parts of the verb. Note what happens to the subject when the following statement changes to a question:

Jamal is singing a solo in the senior recital.

Is Jamal singing a solo in the senior recital?

The first sentence follows a common Subject/Verb/Direct Object sentence pattern, but the second sentence, now a question, places the subject *Jamal* between the two parts of the verb phrase *Is singing*. The subject and verb have not changed—only their positions have.

The best way to identify the sentence parts of a question is to turn the question into a statement.

Do we *have* something to contribute?

We *do have* something to contribute.

Will you *paint* the kitchen?

You *will paint* the kitchen.

Practice Set 6–1

Directions: Change the following questions into statements and underline the verbs twice and the simple subjects once.

Example: Do you remember my name?

You do remember my name.

1. Have we discovered a new technique? _____

2. Did the police officer issue him a ticket? _____

3. May I offer you a lift? _____

4. Has the mail arrived? _____

5. Should we practice before our performance? _____

THERE IS/ARE AND *THERE WAS/WERE*

When the word *there* introduces a sentence, it functions as an adverb or as an introductory word with no grammatical function—not as the subject. Words with no grammatical function are called **expletives**. The word *there* often causes the subject to follow the verb.

Always look beyond the *there* to find the subject because the word *there* is never the subject.

       V   S

There *are* three banana *muffins* in the refrigerator.

       V   S

There *was someone* in the car with her.

Practice Set 6–2

Directions: In the following sentences, underline the verbs twice and the subjects once.

    Example: There on the couch sat Henry.

1. There is no paper in the copier.

2. There were three officers on duty during the midnight shift.

3. There is the new girl from Nigeria.

4. There was an eerie silence after the crash.

5. There goes the last bus to the mall.

QUICK TIP

Whenever possible, avoid using *there is/there are* constructions. They usually add unnecessary words to the sentence.

    Wordy: There was a bug in my bed.

    Concise: A bug was in my bed.

Practice Set 6–3

Directions: On a separate sheet of paper, rewrite the following sentences, avoiding the *there is/there are* construction.

1. There are many people who refuse to wait in line for anything.

2. I am unhappy when there are too many choices.

3. I can see that there is no alternative.

4. The instructor remains after class whenever there are questions.

5. Please let me know if there is too much salt in the stew.

6. There is no good reason for his attitude.

7. Gavin will call me if there is a problem.

8. I noticed there were flaws in the plan.

9. Where there is smoke, there is fire.

10. I left early because there was a power outage.

COMMANDS AND REQUESTS

Commands and requests generally don't include an obvious subject. In these types of sentences, the subject is almost always the implied word *you*.

Take out the garbage. Who is being told to take out the garbage? *You:* (You) Take out the garbage.

Please forgive me. (You) Please forgive me.

The actual subject in these sentences is *you*, but the subject *you* is understood, not written.

Practice Set 6–4

Directions: Write the subjects and verbs of the following sentences in the appropriate blanks. Because the subject is understood, not stated, put it in parentheses.

Example: Please mail your payment on time.

Subject: (you)_____ Verb: mail_____

1. Never carry your wallet in your back pocket.

Subject: _____ Verb: _____

2. Always read the fine print before using a credit card.

Subject: _____ Verb: _____

3. Take your friend to the new theater in City Center.

Subject: _____ Verb: _____

4. After a workout, relax with a cool-down period.

Subject: _____ Verb: _____

5. Study the dates for the history test.

Subject: _____ Verb: _____

Practice Set 6–5

Directions: Underline the verb twice and the subject once.

Examples:

Will you attend the state fair?

(You) Sign your name on the dotted line.

1. There are no temples in the ruins of ancient Crete.

2. In which direction does the Nile flow?

3. Buy your passes for the dinner cruise before Tuesday.

4. There is never a good excuse for sloppy workmanship.

5. Carefully examine the diamonds for cracks or other flaws.

6. There is always hot coffee in the workroom.

7. Will this sudden rain solve the drought problem?

8. Volunteer an hour of your time at the homeless shelter.

9. Do video gamers make good computer programmers?

10. Do not scare the children with that silly mask.

Practice Set 6–6

Directions: Underline the subjects once and the verbs twice in the sentences that appear in bold. If the sentence is a command, add the understood *you*.

1.) **Hold on to your hats!** 2.) **Have you ever wondered if a story you have read about or heard on the news is true?** Conspiracy theorists frequently have such questions. 3.) **There are many famous conspiracy theories**. One of the most famous is the Roswell Conspiracy. 4.) **What crashed in Roswell, New Mexico, on July 2, 1947?** The United States Air Force contends that it was a balloon, but others believe that it was really a UFO. A local radio station planned to report the story, but before they could do so, they purportedly received a message from the FBI: 5.) **"Do not transmit this story!** 6.) **There is a matter of national security involved."** Perhaps the most famous modern conspiracy theories surround the death of President John F. Kennedy. 7.) **Who killed JFK?** 8.) **Was it a lone gunman, Lee Harvey Oswald?** The Warren Commission says so. 9.) **However, there are other possibilities.** 10.) Conspiracy theorists say, "**Open your eyes!** The evidence contradicts the official explanation."

TEST YOURSELF

Directions: In the following sentences, underline the verb twice and the simple subject once. If the sentence is a command, add the understood *you*.

Examples: Do you want fries with your order?

(You) Give me a dollar to pay the tip.

1. Were lighthouses the first land-based guidance systems for ships?

2. Read about the first true lighthouse, built in Alexandria, Egypt, under Ptolemy's rule, in approximately 280 BCE.

3. How did Ptolemy make his invention work without electricity?

4. There was a coal fire behind the lens inside the tower.

5. Do lighthouses still use fire as the main source of light?

6. There are many lighthouses in the United States today, all using electricity rather than fire.

7. Where are they found?

8. You can see them along most coastal states, especially Maine.

9. Find images of famous lighthouses online.

10. Would you include a visit to a lighthouse on your next trip to New England?

WRITE NOW

Directions: Write five sentences describing your classroom or a room in your house. Do not use a *there is* or *there are* construction in any sentence.

GrammarSpeak ⊢————▶

Sometimes people mispronounce words by incorrectly adding letters. Practice saying the correct pronunciation aloud. Then say each one in a sentence.

Instead of:	Say:
Athlete	ATH-lete
Dilate	DI-late
Electoral	elec-TOR-al
Jewelry	JEWEL-ry
Masonry	MASON-ry
Mischievous	MIS-cha-vus
Height	HITE
Sherbet	SHER-bet

WORD WATCHERS

Sometimes, instead of thinking hard to find precise, effective words to express ideas, writers may carelessly include trite, overused words or phrases that do not make sense. Choose your words carefully.

and etc.	*Et cetera* is a Latin phrase meaning *and others*. If you say "And etc.," you are really saying, "And and others." Do not use the *and* with *et cetera*. In fact, avoid using *etc.* in formal writing.
Hopefully	*Hopefully* is an adverb that means "in a hopeful manner": He bought his lotto ticket hopefully. It should not be used in place of "I hope," as in "Hopefully, it will not rain today."
since the beginning of time	Unless you are a physicist who is truly referring to "the beginning of time" or making a biblical reference, this is a poor phrase to use to express how long something has been going on. Everyone—biblical scholars and scientists— seem to agree that there were no people in the beginning of time.
in today's society	There is no one society of "today." Use just *today* or specify the society that you mean: Today, viewers can choose from many television channels.
very unique	*Unique* means "one of a kind." Something cannot be "very" one of a kind. Use *unique* without the qualifier *very*.

Word Watchers Practice Set

Directions: Rewrite the following sentences, improving any carelessly written phrases.

1. They have been dating since the beginning of the universe.

2. She is a little bit pregnant.

3. I'm dying to meet the drummer in that band.

4. Hopefully, the baby will go to sleep, and I will be able to watch the basketball game.

5. We packed just the important items: food, water, warm clothing, blankets, and etc.

6. He tried to interest her in the brushes he was selling, but she could have cared less.

7. In today's society, it is very important to keep abreast of world events.

8. Markie, who hadn't eaten since breakfast that morning, told his mother that he was absolutely starving.

9. This strange-looking bird is very unique.

10. She was very laid back in her attitude.

Clauses

A **clause** is a group of related words containing a subject and a verb. In this chapter you will learn about two basic kinds of clauses: independent and dependent clauses.

INDEPENDENT CLAUSES

An **independent clause,** also called a **main clause,** is another name for a complete sentence.

The motorcycle skidded across the road.

The plant on the front porch died.

DEPENDENT CLAUSES

A **dependent clause,** also called a **subordinate clause,** cannot stand alone as a sentence. Even though it has a subject and a verb, it is not complete. It depends on the rest of the sentence to make sense. The following clauses have subjects and verbs, but they are not complete sentences:

When the motorcycle skidded across the road . . .

After the plant on the front porch died . . .

. . . that confuse me

Whoever wants to leave early . . .

If I do not come back by noon . . .

Dependent clauses never stand alone as a sentence. Notice how these clauses fit into complete sentences:

When the motorcycle skidded, the driver steered it safely.

After the plant on the front porch died, I replaced it with an artificial one.

I will ask the professor about the two questions *that confuse me.*

Whoever wants to leave early must fill out a form.

If I do not come back by noon, you should leave without me.

Dependent clauses can function as adverbs, adjectives, or nouns.

QUICK TIP

Never punctuate a dependent clause as if it were a complete sentence. Doing so creates a sentence fragment.

dependent clause (fragment)

Ricky did his laundry. *Because all his socks were dirty*.

dependent clause (fragment)

Whenever the gardenias start blooming in the spring. My hay fever makes me miserable.

Adverb Clauses

Adverb clauses are dependent clauses that function as adverbs. They are easy to spot because they are introduced by **subordinating conjunctions**. The following box lists some common subordinating conjunctions that introduce adverb clauses.

after	before	so that	when
although	if	than	whenever
as (as if, as though)	once	unless	wherever
because	since	until	while

Adverb clauses function like single-word adverbs. They usually modify verbs, but they can also modify adjectives and adverbs.

Adverb clause modifying the verb:

adverb clause ⎯⎯⎯▶ verb

Since the chairman was absent, I ran the meeting.

Adverb clause modifying an adjective:

adjective ◀⎯⎯⎯⎯⎯ adverb clause

Hungry *because we hadn't eaten since breakfast*, we stopped at the roadside diner.

Adverb clause modifying an adverb:

adverb ◀⎯ adverb clause

My brother works harder *than I do*.

Adverb clauses can appear at the beginning or end of a sentence, and they tell the following:

When:	*While Lucy cleared the table*, Danny washed the dishes. (explains when Danny washed the dishes)
Where:	*Wherever you lead*, I will follow. (tells where I will follow)
Why:	I stayed late *because he needed my help*. (tells why I stayed late)

How: He cried *as though his heart would break*. (shows how he cried)

To what extent: He ran *as far as he could*. (indicates to what extent he ran)

Adverb clauses exhibit two important characteristics:

1. Adverb clauses always begin with a subordinating conjunction.

   adverb clause
   Because I am tired, I cannot think clearly.

2. Adverb clauses can often change position in a sentence without changing the meaning.

   adverb clause
   When I saw his face, I wept with joy.

   adverb clause
   I wept with joy *when I saw his face*.

Practice Set 7–1

Directions: Underline the adverb clauses and circle the word or words they modify.

Examples: If you follow the map, you (will find) the buried treasure.

(Frustrated) when he couldn't read the small print, Paolo threw the paper in the trash.

He is (older) than I am.

1. Whenever the telephone rings, I must stop my work to answer it.

2. The red peppers taste hotter than the yellow peppers do.

3. Winning at cards is easy when you know how to play.

4. They canceled the trip since he had lost his job.

5. He tried to stay as long as he could.

6. She played as if she didn't want to win.

7. Careful because the document was so old, the museum curator showed us the manuscript.

8. Andrew Johnson became president after Abraham Lincoln was assassinated.

9. Jax can type faster than I can.

10. You may leave as soon as you have finished your work.

QUICK TIP

A word can function as more than one part of speech. Many words can be subordinating conjunctions or prepositions, depending on how they are used in a sentence. A preposition is followed by its object—a noun or pronoun and any modifiers. A subordinating conjunction, however, is followed by an adverb clause, which contains a subject and a verb.

prepositional phrase
I studied *until dawn*.

adverb clause
I studied *until the sun rose*.

Practice Set 7–2

Directions: Indicate whether the words in boldface are prepositional phrases or adverb clauses.

Examples:

After the race, the runner collapsed.　　　prepositional phrase

After the race ended, the runner collapsed.　　adverb clause

1. You must turn in your work **before you leave class**.　　　_____

2. You must turn in your work **before Monday**.　　　_____

3. She has been unemployed **since June**.　　　_____

4. She has been unemployed **since she lost her sales job**.　　　_____

5. **Until I got my test results**, I was worried about my health.　　　_____

6. **Until last week**, I was worried about my health.　　_____

7. I will meet you **after the ceremony**.　　　_____

8. I will meet you **after the ceremony ends**.　　　_____

9. **Before the movie**, we went out to dinner.　　　_____

10. **Before we went to the movie**, we went out to dinner.　　　_____

Adjective Clauses

Like single-word adjectives, **adjective clauses** modify nouns and pronouns. Listed below are some words that introduce adjective clauses.

that	when	where	which
who	whom	whose	why

Adjective clauses show which one and what kind:

Which one: The church *where we were married* has an enormous pipe organ. (tells which church)

What kind: A cat *that scratches the furniture* should be kept outside. (tells what kind of cat)

Unlike adverb clauses, adjective clauses cannot change position in the sentence. They directly follow the noun or pronoun that they modify, and moving them will change the meaning of the sentence or make it confusing.

Confusing: The runner showed his medal to the coach *who won the race*.

Clear: The runner *who won the race* showed his medal to the coach.

Practice Set 7–3

Directions: Underline the adjective clauses. On the blank, write the word that the adjective clause modifies.

Example: The man who found my dog called me. man _____

1. The hamburgers that they served were overcooked. _____

2. I plan to visit the town where my father was born. _____

3. We always discuss the amazing experiences that we had on the trip. _____

4. My company once employed the woman whom the newspaper endorsed for political office. _____

5. I will never forget the time when we had two flat tires on a deserted highway. _____

6. Her attitude, which was extremely positive, aided her recovery from surgery. _____

7. Everybody loved the chocolate cake that I baked for the party. _____

8. My grandmother, who had never finished school, returned to earn her college degree. _____

9. The boxes in that closet belong to my nephew, who has moved away.

_____

10. The artist whose work is displayed here died in 1950.

_____

Noun Clauses

A **noun clause** is a dependent clause that functions as a noun. Noun clauses begin with one of the following words:

what	where	whichever	whomever
whatever	wherever	who	why
when	whether	whoever	how
whenever	which	whom	that

Noun clauses serve the same functions as single-word nouns or pronouns.

Subject:	*How he could speak three languages fluently* really amazed me.
Direct object:	Scott always says *whatever first comes into his mind.*
Indirect object:	He offered *whoever washed his car* a ticket to the game.
Subject complement:	The chairman will be *whomever the committee selects.*
Object of the preposition:	This dessert is for *whoever wants it.*

Because noun clauses serve as basic sentence parts, the sentences in which they appear are not complete without them. Examine the following sentence:

noun clause
Why he made that remark is unclear.

The noun clause *Why he made that remark* is the subject of the sentence. If you remove the clause, the sentence is incomplete.

Practice Set 7–4

Directions: Underline any noun clauses.

Example: I did not reveal <u>what you told me</u>.

1. I offered to trade my lunch for what she had brought.

2. Before President Roosevelt died, President Truman did not know that the United States was developing atomic weapons.

3. Until the mechanic examined the engine, he did not know whether he would be able to repair the car.

4. Where the *Titanic* rested remained a mystery for many decades.

5. We will promise whoever attends the gala a photo opportunity with the governor.

6. We can understand why you chose to accept our offer.

7. The restaurant gave gift certificates to whomever the server had insulted.

8. The Red Cross promised the flood victims whatever they needed.

9. Wherever he leaves his bike must be safe.

10. How she behaved was beyond belief.

Practice Set 7–5

Directions: Label the dependent clauses in boldface as adjective, adverb, or noun clauses.

Examples: The fifty years that followed the Civil War saw many great changes in **how people became wealthy in the United States**. Great advances in technology offered people **who had the vision to invest in the future** a chance to become fabulously wealthy. **Because there were no rules against monopolies**, some businessmen took advantage of the times.

1. They didn't care **how they made their money**.

2. These men, called robber barons, behaved **as though they ruled the world**.

3. Jay Gould, **who made his money in railroads and the stock market**, is often considered the model of the robber baron.

4. His first investments taught him **that trust is a dangerous thing**.

5. **Although his own actions often skirted the law,** he wound up losing money to people even more crooked **than he was.**

6. These early lessons, **which he would remember all of his life**, taught him to trust no one but himself.

7. Newspapers of his day carried terrible stories about **why he was so reviled**, but recent historians have revealed **that he really was not such a bad guy**.

8. The fact is **that he loved having a bad reputation**.

9. He actually donated generously to many charities, but **because he was a very private person**, he always did so anonymously.

10. His magnificent mansion, **which is now open to the public**, is located on the Hudson River, in Tarrytown, New York.

Practice Set 7–6

Directions: Underline the dependent clauses and label them as ADJ (adjective), ADV (adverb), or N (noun) clauses.

Examples: The story <u>that she read</u> was funny. [ADJ]

<u>Since I sold my car</u>, I have been riding the bus. [ADV]

After <u>what he said</u>, I will never speak to him again. [N]

1. My computer, which has a virus, should be repaired.

2. Richard trimmed the tree that blocked my view.

3. She always gets whatever she wants.

4. What you do tonight will decide your fate.

5. The puppy tickled my toes while I was sleeping.

6. The house that they painted was really ugly.

7. Dante lost his keys when he was playing tennis.

8. The house where Mark Twain lived is now a museum.

9. If you forget the timer, you will burn the roast.

10. She bought the car that I wanted.

Practice Set 7–7

Directions: Fill in the blanks with the appropriate type of clause. Introductory words have been supplied for you.

Example: *Adverb clause:* While _____ , we played cards in the basement.

Adverb clause: While <u>the storm raged outside</u> , we played cards in the basement.

1. *Adverb clause:* I left early **because** _____.

2. *Adverb clause:* **Although** _____ , she found time to help me.

3. *Adverb clause:* They close the door **whenever** _____.

4. *Adjective clause:* The team **that** _____ will be eliminated in the next round.

5. *Adjective clause:* They tore down the movie theater **where** _____ _____

6. *Adjective clause:* The handyman **whom** _____ completed the job without charge.

7. *Adjective clause:* A dancer **whose** _____ must rest for at least one month.

8. *Noun clause:* Natalie didn't agree with **what** _____ .

9. *Noun clause:* **Whoever** _____ will be responsible for turning out the lights.

10. *Noun clause:* I told her **that** _____ .

Practice Set 7–8

Directions: Label the clauses in boldface as independent (I) or dependent (D). The correct answer has been provided in the first sentence as an example.

D

What happens to professional athletes **when their careers have ended? Once they leave the spotlight,** some find other rewarding careers. Others spend their lives playing imaginary games before adoring fans **who exist only in memory**. For example, Alan Page is one athlete who knew from the start **that he did not want to sit on the sidelines of life.** An All-American defensive end for the Fighting Irish at Notre Dame in 1966, Page earned a degree in political science **before he became a first-round draft pick for the Minnesota Vikings in 1967.** Page was the first defensive player ever to be named the NFL's Most Valuable Player, and **he was inducted into the Pro Football Hall of Fame on July 20, 1988.** These achievements, however, are the least important of Alan Page's remarkable life.

Page began planning for his life after football **long before the Vikings released him in 1978.** That same year, he graduated from the University of Minnesota Law School. After he served for six years as an assistant attorney general for the state of Minnesota, **Page was elected Associate Justice of the Minnesota Supreme Court in 1993. Although he was rarely "benched" as a football player**, Justice Page is happy to be on a different kind of bench today.

Justice Page regularly speaks to groups of minority students about the importance of education. He often addresses athletes **who do not take advantage of the educational opportunities available to them because of their athletic abilities**. He has said of such students: "We are doing no favors to the young men if we let them believe **that a game shall set them free.**"

▼ TEST YOURSELF

Directions: Underline the dependent clauses and label them as adjective, adverb, or noun clauses. A sentence may have more than one dependent clause.

                                         ADV

Example: She answered him honestly <u>when he asked her about her absence</u>.

1. I don't appreciate what you are doing.

2. When Cassius Clay changed his name to Mohammed Ali, he surprised many Americans.

3. Aspen trees, which are common in Colorado, have heart-shaped leaves that shimmer in the sunlight.

4. Students are participating in service learning projects because they care about their community.

5. The Bay of Pigs invasion of Cuba, which took place on April 17, 1961, was actually planned by President Eisenhower, but it became a political liability for President Kennedy.

6. The troop leader gave whoever sold the most cookies a merit badge.

7. He doesn't know how he will complete his research paper on time.

8. Where you work determines the kind of uniform that you must wear.

9. The intersection where the parade began was crowded with spectators.

10. We will leave as soon as the lecture is over.

WRITE NOW

Directions: The exercise on Justice Alan Page tells the story of an extraordinary individual. He had two different but exceptional careers. Here are some other extraordinary individuals: Ronald Reagan, an actor who became President of the United States; Grandma Moses, a famous folk artist who didn't start painting until age 76; Miyam Bialik, an actress who is also a neuroscientist. Do a little research and choose one of them or someone extraordinary that you know and write a short essay explaining what makes him or her extraordinary. Your essay should include at least five dependent clauses. Underline each dependent clause, and label your dependent clauses as adverbs, adjectives, or nouns.

GrammarSpeak ▸━━━━━▶

The following exercise contains some commonly mispronounced words. Practice saying the correct pronunciations aloud.

Instead of:	**Say:**
candidate	CAN did date
[Electoral]	ee LEC tor al
escape	es CAPE
espresso	es PRESS o
LIbrary	lie BRER ee

WORD WATCHERS

Good writing is concise. Avoid using wordy expressions.

completely straight	By definition, something that is straight has no crooked parts. It is unnecessary to qualify *straight* with *completely*.
but yet	*But* and *yet* are coordinating conjunctions with the same meaning. Never use them together. Choose one or the other.
disappear from view or sight	Something that disappears can no longer be seen. Adding *from view* or *from sight* is redundant.
due to the fact that	wordy for *because*
self-inflicted suicide	*Suicide* is the act of taking one's own life. It must be self-inflicted, so adding the qualifier is unnecessary.
at this point in time	This is a wordy expression for *now*.
refer back to	When you *refer,* you are already going back. Adding *back* is redundant.

Word Watchers Practice Set

Directions: Shorten the following phrases, eliminating wordiness.

Example: circled around _circled_

1. green in color _____

2. made a motion _____

3. held a meeting _____

4. linked together _____

5. if it is at all possible _____

6. general consensus of opinion _____

7. made an announcement _____

8. arrived at the conclusion _____

9. at all times _____

10. came to a complete and total stop _____

Types of Sentences

CLASSIFYING SENTENCES ACCORDING TO STRUCTURE

There are several ways to classify sentences. Sentences may be classified as **simple, compound, complex,** and **compound-complex,** based on the number of independent and dependent clauses they have.

Simple Sentences

A **simple sentence** contains only one independent clause. It may be short or long, but it does not have any dependent clauses. Compare these two simple sentences:

   S V
The dog barks.

          S   V
The shaggy brown *dog* with the pretty pink ribbon around its neck *barks* noisily at the pesky squirrel climbing up the old oak tree in the park near the elementary school on Elm Street.

The second sentence has many modifying words and phrases, but because it has only one independent clause and no dependent clauses, it is a simple sentence.

Practice Set 8–1

Directions: In the following simple sentences, underline the verb twice and the simple subject once.

 Example: Jimmy Carter, the former governor of Georgia, served as president of
       the United States from 1977 to 1981.

1. Andrew Jackson, the seventh president of the United States, once killed a man in a duel.

2. Both John Adams and Thomas Jefferson died on July 4, 1826.

3. James Buchanan was President James Polk's secretary of state and President Franklin Pierce's minister to Great Britain.

4. Dwight Eisenhower served as president of Columbia University following World War II.

5. Calvin Coolidge's father, a notary public, administered the oath of office to his son in 1923.

Compound Sentences

A **compound sentence** contains more than one independent clause and no dependent clauses. The independent clauses are joined by semicolons or by commas and coordinating conjunctions (*and, but, or, for, nor, so, yet*). The comma is placed **before** the coordinating conjunction.

In the following examples, independent clauses are joined by a coordinating conjunction or a semicolon to form a compound sentence:

ind. cl   CC   ind. cl

Coordinating conjunction: I tried to fix my computer, but I was not successful.

ind. cl   ind. cl

Semicolon: Spring is my favorite season; the weather is usually quite beautiful.

QUICK TIP

Here are two tips for remembering the seven coordinating conjunctions.

- You can remember the list with the three that rhyme in the middle:

  and, but, or, for, nor, so, yet

- You can also use the acronym FANBOYS:

  For   And   Nor   But   **Or**   Yet   So

Compound Subjects and Verbs

Certain types of sentences may appear to be compound when they really are not, so you must examine the structure carefully. Is this a simple sentence or a compound sentence?

S   S   V

My algebra *teacher* and *Uncle Jack* are friends.

In this sentence, the coordinating conjunction *and* does not connect two independent clauses; it connects the two subjects of the sentence, *teacher* and *Uncle Jack*. This sentence contains a **compound subject**. It is a simple sentence, not a compound sentence. Now consider this sentence:

Manuel *stood* in line and *paid* for the popcorn.

In this sentence, the coordinating conjunction *and* connects the two verbs, *stood* and *paid*, but there is still only one clause. This sentence contains a **compound verb**. It is a simple sentence, not a compound sentence.

Practice Set 8-2

Directions: Underline the verb twice and the simple subject once. Then indicate whether the sentences are simple or compound.

Examples: Keith circled the building and stopped
at the front door.

simple _____

He withdrew $50 from his account,
but he was still $10 short.

compound _____

1. The sun, the nine planets and their moons,
   asteroids, comets, and meteors make up our
   solar system.   _____

2. Florida is the Sunshine State, but Georgia
   is the Peach State.   _____

3. Making money in the stock market requires
   much research and a lot of luck.   _____

4. Jenny Lind, the "Swedish Nightingale," toured
   the United States in 1850.   _____

5. The copier and the printer are both out
   of order.   _____

6. The poet Dante was really named Durante
   degli Alighieri; however, everyone
   remembers him simply as Dante.   _____

7. Manny and I were both going to the same
   place, so I offered him a ride.   _____

8. The clothes left on the ironing board and the
   jackets on the living room chair should be
   hung in the closet.   _____

9. Neither the letter nor the package has
   arrived yet.   _____

10. Gelsey Kirkland attended the American
    School of Ballet, for she wanted to become
    a prima ballerina.   _____

Complex Sentences

The term *complex sentence* has nothing to do with how complicated a sentence may appear. A **complex sentence** is simply a sentence that has only one independent clause and at least one dependent clause.

       dep. cl   **ind. cl**
Because I could not stop in time, I hit the garage door.

   ind. cl   **dep. cl**   **ind. cl**
Students *who like to read* usually do well in school.

     dep. cl   **ind. cl**
What you said is not true.

QUICK TIP

Of all the types of complex sentences, those with noun clauses may be the most difficult to spot because the noun clauses are main parts of the independent clauses. Don't overlook them.

noun clause as subject
When we meet does not matter.

noun clause as subject complement
The miracle was *that he survived*.

Practice Set 8–3

Directions: Underline all dependent clauses in these complex sentences.

Example: African American inventors, <u>who have contributed much to our modern civilization</u>, are frequently overlooked in the history books.

1. Even though you may not appreciate Garrett Morgan's invention, you see its modern-day versions every day.

2. When cars first began crowding the nation's highways, Garrett Morgan was one of the first to acquire a U.S. patent for a traffic signal.

3. Morgan, who also held Canadian and British patents, invented the gas mask as well.

4. When Lewis Latimer was a child, his father was arrested and tried as a runaway slave.

5. Latimer grew up to become the only African-American member of Thomas Edison's team that worked on the incandescent light bulb.

6. Latimer is credited with inventing the carbon filament, which is an important part of the light bulb.

7. Elijah J. McCoy, who was an Afro-Canadian inventor, held many U.S. patents.

8. McCoy's most famous invention was one that he invented in his home-based machine shop.

9. According to legend, although other people tried to copy McCoy's oil-dripping cup, no copy worked as well.

10. Customers who wanted the best began to ask for "the real McCoy."

Practice Set 8–4

Directions: Identify the following sentences as simple, compound, or complex.

Examples: Opera is very popular in Italy.   <u>simple</u>

Italian opera lovers know the stories by heart, and they sing along with the choruses.   <u>compound</u>

When the audience hears the solos, everyone is quiet.   <u>complex</u>

1. Giuseppe Verdi was one of the greatest opera composers of all time, and his work is still beloved today.   _____

2. He wrote for Italians, who loved his emotion-packed stories.   _____

3. One of his last operas, *Aida*, was commissioned by the king of Egypt.   _____

4. *Aida* was full of romance and spectacle.   _____

5. With its huge choir, ballet dancers, and elaborate stage sets (sometimes including elephants), *Aida* has become one of the world's most popular operas; in fact, it is the most performed opera today.   _____

6. It first opened in Egypt, and a year later it opened in Italy.   _____

7. The story centers on Egyptian General Redames and his love for the young Aida, a slave girl of the King's daughter, Amneris.   _____

8. Troubles arise because Amneris loves Redames.   _____

9. However, Redames chooses Aida over the King's daughter.   _____

10. The result is a very sad ending, which features some of the most beautiful and dramatic music in opera.   _____

Compound-Complex Sentences

A **compound-complex sentence** is just what the name implies: it contains two or more independent clauses and at least one dependent clause.

         dep. cl   **ind. cl**
While the storm raged outside, Bert completed his homework,

      ind. cl
and Elizabeth took a nap.

Practice Set 8–5

Directions: Add words to the following sentences to make them compound-complex.

> **Example:** When <u>we heard the siren</u> , we ran for cover, for we were very scared.

1. The people who _____ may receive a refund, or they may cancel their order.

2. While _____ , some volunteers distributed water bottles, and others served food.

3. The bank requested that _____ , but I couldn't remember my password.

4. She didn't know all the technical terms, yet since _____ , she is going to take the test anyway.

5. They telephoned whoever _____ , so there is no reason to worry.

Practice Set 8–6

Directions: Underline the verbs twice and the simple subjects once in all of the independent clauses.

> **Example:** The alarm was sounding, so I ran outside.

1. If you want to learn Spanish, you should study with Maria.

2. What she gave him was more than enough.

3. Tech magnates Sergey Brin and Larry Page, who started Google at age 25, are among the world's youngest billionaires.

4. Diet and exercise are important for maintaining good health.

5. If you snore, you could be suffering from sleep apnea.

6. He plays several brass instruments, including the trumpet, the trombone, and the tuba.

7. Chocolate doesn't cause acne, but some studies indicate that dairy products do.

8. How you study is often more important than what you study.

9. I want to buy a hybrid car because gasoline prices have skyrocketed.

10. When you paid for dinner, you forgot to leave a tip, so I left some money on the table.

Practice Set 8–7

Directions: After determining the number and kind of clauses in each of the following sentences, label the sentences as simple (S), compound (C), complex (CX), or compound-complex (CC).

Example: When you adopt a pet, you must consider your family's needs.   complex

1. Today many pet owners choose to adopt cats because they are easy to care for and can be kept indoors.

2. One of the most popular breeds is the Siamese, descendants of the sacred temple cats of Siam.

3. In the late 1800s, the cats were exported to England from Siam, now called Thailand.

4. What most distinguishes Siamese cats is their coloration.

5. All Siamese have a creamy base coat with colored points on their faces, ears, paws, and tails; however, these points can vary from dark brown to gray or lilac.

6. Siamese are also characterized by their almond-shaped blue eyes.

7. These cats have loud voices, which are often compared to a baby's cries for attention.

8. Siamese cats are very intelligent, and they are curious and playful animals.

9. Since they enjoy human companionship, Siamese cats are quite social, and they usually make affectionate pets.

10. The unique characteristics of the Siamese have led to many starring roles in movies, television shows, and books.

COORDINATION AND SUBORDINATION

Understanding the four sentence types is important because it will enable you to add variety to your writing. You can use these variations to combine ideas effectively.

Compound sentences **coordinate** ideas, meaning that they express ideas that are about equal in importance:

I stood at attention, and I saluted the flag.

This sentence simply says that both actions occurred. Readers don't know if one action occurred because of the other or before or after the other. Since both ideas are equal in importance, we express both in independent clauses.

Complex sentences **subordinate** ideas, meaning that one idea is the major focus of the sentence while the other idea contributes some extra information—maybe why or when the major idea happened:

While I stood at attention, I saluted the flag.

The main point is the main clause, *I saluted the flag.* The word *while* makes the other idea subordinating. It's not as important to know that I stood at attention as it is to know that I saluted the flag.

You probably could express your ideas using all simple sentences, but as you learn to vary your sentences and include compound, complex, and compound-complex sentences, your writing style will improve. Examine the following simple sentences:

Aisha cleared the table.
Aisha washed the dishes.
Aisha did not clean the counter.

We could use coordination to combine the ideas like this:

Aisha cleared the table and washed the dishes, *but* she did not clean the counter.

Here is another example:

Franklin fell out of that tree. Franklin broke his arm.

We could use subordination to combine ideas, at the same time letting the reader see the importance of time in the two events:

Franklin broke his arm *when* he fell out of that tree.

Practice Set 8–8

Directions: Using coordination or subordination, combine the following simple sentences to make one compound, complex, or compound-complex sentences.

> **Example:** The food truck comes to our campus for lunch. I'm no longer bringing my lunch from home.
>
> The food truck comes to our campus for lunch, so I'm no longer bringing my lunch from home. (coordination)
>
> Because the food truck comes to our campus for lunch, I'm no longer bringing my lunch from home. (subordination)

1. Luis enjoys watching football on television. He has never seen a live game in a stadium. _____

_____

2. Tim took this picture of a beautiful sunrise. He developed the picture himself. _____

_____

3. The department's holiday party was held last Saturday. I had the flu. I couldn't go.

   _____

   _____

4. Several fans wanted the rock star's autograph after the concert. They stormed the stage. The performer feared for his life. _____

   _____

5. Not all taxpayers can compute their own taxes. The laws are complicated. Some taxpayers must pay an accountant or tax service for help._____

   _____

6. Snow and rain covered most of the West this morning. Travelers were stranded for hours. Several airports have now reopened. _____

   _____

7. Music companies have taken a strong position on copyright theft. They file suits against people who do not pay for downloads. _____

   _____

8. Amazon.com is one of the world's largest shopping markets. You can buy any-thing from a used book to a new car. _____

   _____

9. The best movies are released in December. People have time to see films dur-ing holiday vacations. Producers want their films to be eligible for the year's Academy Award nominations. _____

   _____

10. Americans like a lot of personal space. They don't like to speak to people who stand too close. _____

    _____

▼ TEST YOURSELF

Directions: Identify the following sentences as simple, compound, complex, or compound-complex.

Example: When the bell rings, I always gather my books, for I don't want to be late for my next class.

compound-complex
_____

1. We put on our raincoats and ran outside.

   _____

2. Before I answered her question, I scratched my head and cleared my throat.

   _____

3. You should never hang wind chimes that disturb the neighbors.

   _____

4. Winston Churchill faced many hardships,
   yet he never gave in to defeat.   _____

5. I closed my eyes when I heard the crash,
   so I would not be a very good witness.   _____

6. Chicken chow mein is made with chicken,
   onions, celery, and bean sprouts.   _____

7. She couldn't see the board, nor could she
   hear what the professor was saying.   _____

8. Camels, which have two humps, are often
   mistaken for dromedaries.   _____

9. I don't know what you paid, but it was
   probably too much.   _____

10. The cradle of civilization lay between the
    Tigris and the Euphrates rivers.   _____

WRITE NOW

Directions: Imagine that you have just won a million dollars. Use coordination and subordination to do the following:

1. Write two **compound** sentences about what you would buy for yourself.

2. Write two **complex** sentences about where you would travel.

3. Write two **compound-complex** sentences about whom you would help.

GrammarSpeak ⟶

The following exercise is a list of commonly mispronounced words. Practice saying the correct pronunciations aloud to help you develop better oral language habits.

Instead of:	**Say:**
prescriptions	pre SCRIP shuns
probably	probably
pronunciation	pronunciation
supposedly	supposedly
caramel	caramel

WORD WATCHERS

Some words are misspelled so frequently that you may think the incorrect spelling is correct simply because you are used to seeing the words spelled that way. Listed below are some words that you should learn to spell correctly.

athlete	(not athelete) Tip: Pronounce it correctly—ATH lete.
congratulations	(not gradulations) Tip: Don't confuse this with graDuation.
grammar	(not grammer) Tip: You'll get an *A* if you remember to spell grammar with an *a*.
mathematics	(not mathmatics) Tip: Look for *them* in mathematics.
writing	(not writting) Tip: Doubling the consonant *t* shortens the vowel *i*. *Writting* would rhyme with *sitting*.
a lot	(not alot) Tip: Always two words.
convenience	(not convience) Tip: Sound this one out to include each sound—con VEN i ence.

Word Watchers Practice Set

Directions: Circle the word that is spelled *incorrectly* in each sentence.

1. The coach congradulated the athlete on beating the record time.
2. My mathematics class is much easier than my creative writting class.
3. You can't make alot of grammar mistakes if you want to receive a good grade on your paper.
4. Writing an outline should not be considered an inconvience.
5. A world-class athlete can excel in a lot of different sports.

Putting the Basics to Work

PART 2

Sentence Fragments and Run-On Sentences

You have probably already learned "the rules" about constructing sentences. At some point in your study of English grammar, somebody undoubtedly taught you that a sentence is a "complete thought." If you had trouble understanding what that meant, you probably were not alone. Some grammatically correct sentences do not seem to express complete thoughts:

It is.

They did.

He might.

Any word grouping that is an independent clause is a sentence. Complete thought or not, the examples above are sentences because they are independent clauses.

As you study this chapter, use the lessons you have learned about phrases, clauses, and sentence construction to help you identify sentence fragments and run-on sentences.

SENTENCE FRAGMENTS

A **sentence fragment** is an incomplete sentence—something is missing. Length cannot determine whether a grammatical construction is a sentence or a fragment. A sentence is an independent clause containing a subject and a verb; it can stand by itself to express a complete thought. A fragment may have a subject and a verb, but it is not an independent clause and cannot stand alone as a sentence.

Sentence: It is late.

Fragment: Since it is late.

Sentence fragments can occur for many different reasons:

- The subject may be missing.

    Fragment: Went to the mall to buy a birthday gift.

    Sentence: *My friend* went to the mall to buy a birthday gift.

- The verb or part of the verb phrase may be missing.

  Fragment: The car sputtering and shaking at every red light.

  Sentence: The car *was* sputtering and shaking at every red light.

- The independent clause may be missing.

  Fragment: Because the power went out in our building.

  Sentence: Because the power went out in our building, *everyone left early.*

  Fragment: Feeling tired after a long day at the office.

  Sentence: *He was* feeling tired after a long day at the office.

Be sure to distinguish between subordinating conjunctions and transitional words and expressions. Some common transitional words are *therefore, thus, however, in addition, for example,* and *on the other hand.*

A subordinating conjunction introduces a *dependent* clause.

    subordinating conjunction
Fragment: *Since*   he failed his driving test.

Transitional words or phrases introduce an *independent* clause.

    transitional expression
Sentence: *In fact,*   he failed his driving test.

    transitional word
Sentence: *Therefore,*   he failed his driving test.

Beginning a sentence with subordinating conjunctions like *although* and *whereas* is fine, as long as the dependent clause they introduce is followed by a comma and an independent clause. If you have followed *although* or *whereas* with a comma, you have likely created a fragment.

Incorrect: She invited several friends for dinner. *Although, she had to work early the next morning.*

Correct: She invited several friends for dinner although she had to work early the next morning.

If you begin a sentence with *such as,* you will automatically have a fragment.

Fragment: Hurricane winds have caused destruction in several coastal states. *Such as Florida, Mississippi, and Texas.*

Correct: Hurricane winds have caused destruction in several coastal states, such as Florida, Mississippi, and Texas.

QUICK TIP

Occasionally, sentence fragments are acceptable:

For emphasis:	Not a day passes without tears. *Not a day!*
To answer a question:	Will the president run for a second term? *Absolutely.*
Dialogue:	"I'm tired of waiting for the weather to cool off." "*Me, too.*"

In formal writing, however, you should avoid using sentence fragments.

Practice Set 9–1

Directions: In the blanks provided, label the following word groups as sentences or fragments.

Example: Until I find the prescription for my allergy pills. _____fragment_____

1. To offer an apology for mispronouncing his name. _____

2. His former coach and mentor. _____

3. Who tried to prepare for the storm that was brewing. _____

4. It is always dangerous to add more salt. _____

5. The second hand on the clock on my desk at home. _____

Correcting Sentence Fragments

Depending on the situation, there are many ways to fix sentence fragments.

Add Words.

This method works well when a basic sentence part, like the subject or the verb, is missing.

Fragment: Quickly threw a blanket over the smoldering fire on the stove.

Sentence: *The babysitter* quickly threw a blanket over the smoldering fire on the stove.

Fragment: The truck broken down by the entrance ramp on the freeway.

Sentence: The truck *had* broken down by the entrance ramp on the freeway.

Change or Eliminate Words.

Fragment: Although rain had been predicted for days.

Sentence: Rain had been predicted for days.

OR

However, rain had been predicted for days.

Attach the Fragment to the Sentence That Comes Before or After It.

Fragment: The coach assigned the starting position to Carolyn. The fastest sprinter on the relay team.

Sentence: The coach assigned the starting position to Carolyn, the fastest sprinter on the relay team.

Practice Set 9–2

Directions: Make each of the following sentence fragments into a complete sentence.

Example: Because the room was too noisy.

I couldn't concentrate because the room was too noisy.

1. If I ever need help with algebra.

   _____

2. For example, another snowstorm on the way tonight.

   _____

3. Such as the Brooklyn Bridge, the Golden Gate Bridge, and the Mackinac Bridge.

   _____

4. In music, a whole note followed by two half notes and a quarter note.

   _____

5. When the story of the missing aircraft appeared on the news.

   _____

6. To answer his questions truthfully and without hesitation.

   _____

7. Whom we told about the problem.

   _____

8. Whereas anyone could have taken this photograph.

   _____

9. Because no one can be sure what the future may bring.

   _____

10. While the children were playing in the courtyard.

   _____

QUICK TIP

As you may have noticed, identifying isolated groups of words as fragments is much easier than finding fragments in your own writing. To solve this problem, you must learn to proofread effectively. One effective way to find sentence fragments in your writing is to read each sentence aloud slowly, stopping at every end punctuation. Ask yourself if this sentence makes sense, as if it were the only thing written on the page. If the sentence doesn't make sense, then it is a fragment.

Practice Set 9–3

Directions: Correct the fragments in the following paragraphs by adding words, changing or eliminating words, or attaching the fragments to make complete sentences as shown in the example.

Most people who have lived or traveled in the southern United States are familiar with kudzu. The leafy green vine that covers trees, drapes over shrubbery, and engulfs entire landscapes. Kudzu, described as "the vine that ate the South," imported from Asia one hundred years ago to beautify the landscape and prevent soil erosion. Since 1970, however, it has been considered an invasive weed. And a harmful one at that.

Like kudzu, invasive weeds running rampant across the North American continent. They are responsible for the decline of innumerable plant and animal species. Which are either threatened or endangered by extinction. According to a recent study. These weeds are a leading danger to the world's ecology. The Interior Department claims that invasive weeds infest more than 100 million acres in the United States. The damage caused to agriculture, rangeland, and recreational areas amounting to billions of dollars annually.

While environmental problems, such as chemical pollution or hazardous waste, can be cleaned up or may disappear with time. Weeds present a more difficult dilemma. Biological invasions reproduce themselves and can last forever. What has caused this colossal environmental problem? The answer is that we live in a much smaller world than ever before. Today, global travel and trade enable invasive weeds to move easily from one continent or ecosystem to another. Sometimes intentionally, sometimes not.

One of the major difficulties involved in solving this ecological problem is that the weeds cross so many boundary lines. It is not a situation that governments designed to handle. Nevertheless, numerous local, state, and federal agencies involved in the crusade against invasive weeds. Before he left office in 2001, President Clinton ordered the creation of a National Invasive Species Council and increased funding to solve the problem. Although this is a relatively small step. It is important in alerting Americans to the threat. Since spraying and weeding are solutions that create problems of their own. Perhaps early detection and prevention are our only hope.

RUN-ON SENTENCES

Run-on sentences have various names. Fused sentences incorrectly join independent clauses with no punctuation. Comma splices incorrectly join independent clauses with a comma. You may hear these kinds of run-on sentences called by other names, such as run-togethers or blended sentences. The name doesn't really matter. All of these labels refer to the same error: the incorrect joining of independent clauses.

Run-on sentences are not necessarily long. Even short independent clauses strung together create a run-on.

Run-on: Kenny loves photography he bought a new camera.

Run-on: Kenny loves photography, he bought a new camera.

These two sentences are faulty because two independent clauses are joined incorrectly, one with no punctuation, and one with just a comma.

Correcting Run-on Sentences

There are four simple ways to fix run-on sentences.

1. Create Separate Sentences.

Divide independent clauses into separate sentences, using a capital letter and appropriate end punctuation.

Run-on: Our aging cat has diabetes we have to give him an insulin shot daily.

Correct: Our aging cat has diabetes. We have to give him an insulin shot daily.

This method works well if the independent clauses are long or are of different sentence types and need different end punctuation.

Run-on: Many Americans lack medical insurance, where can they go for help?

Correct: Many Americans lack medical insurance. Where can they go for help?

Practice Set 9–4

Directions: Correct the following run-ons by dividing them into separate sentences.

Example: I can't balance my account will you help me find my mistakes?

I can't balance my account. Will you help me find my mistakes?

1. The United Nations started in 1945 it had 51 members.

   _____

2. The leaders aim to preserve peace and social well-being economic independence is also an important goal.

   _____

3. New York City is the site of the UN Headquarters John D. Rockefeller donated $8.5 million for the site, which is near the East River.

   _____

4. The UN site is an international zone it has its own post office and stamps.

   _____

5. Most visitors like to see the General Assembly room flags of UN members fly in front of the complex.

   _____

2. Coordinate the Sentences.

Join the two independent clauses with a comma followed by a coordinating conjunction (*and, but, or, for, nor, so, yet*). This method is effective if the clauses are closely related and fairly short.

Run-on:	The grass grows rapidly in the summer we mow it weekly.
Correct:	The grass grows rapidly in the summer, *so* we mow it weekly.
Run-on:	My car is brand-new it is always in the repair shop.
Correct:	My car is brand-new, *but* it is always in the repair shop.

Practice Set 9–5

Directions: Correct the following run-ons by adding a comma and a coordinating conjunction to each sentence.

Example: Mr. Wilson mowed his lawn he edged the sidewalk and the flower beds.

Mr. Wilson mowed his lawn, and he edged the sidewalk and the flower beds.

1. We could see the storm approaching we gathered our towels and left the beach.

   _____

2. The airplane returned to the terminal a warning light indicated a problem with the landing gear.

   _____

3. Tonight the temperature will drop below freezing the farmers will cover all of the strawberry plants.

_____

4. We can go out to dinner with friends we can stay home and relax.

_____

5. Felipe has a high grade point average he is also an outstanding baseball player.

_____

3. Use a Semicolon.

A **semicolon (;)** separates independent clauses that are short or closely related in meaning; a complete sentence must stand on each side. However, the clause following the semicolon does *not* begin with a capital letter. Using a semicolon is an effective way to join fairly short and closely related independent clauses.

> **Run-on:**   The boat has finally been repaired, we can go water-skiing next weekend.

> **Correct:**   The boat has finally been repaired; we can go water-skiing next weekend.

Often, semicolons are followed by conjunctive adverbs (words like *however* and *therefore*) or transitional expressions (like *in fact* or *for example*). These linking words or phrases emphasize the relationship between the two independent clauses.

> The boat has finally been repaired; *therefore*, we can go water-skiing next weekend.

> The boat has finally been repaired; *in fact*, we can go water-skiing next weekend.

Note that a semicolon precedes the transition *therefore* or *in fact*, and a comma follows it.

QUICK TIP

If a transition comes in the middle of one independent clause, you can't use a semicolon; you must use two commas.

The repair costs, *however*, were extremely high.

The repair costs, *in fact*, were extremely high.

Practice Set 9–6

Directions: Use semicolons to correct the following run-on sentences. If a sentence is already correct, write "correct" in the margin.

> **Example:** Many children watch too much television often the TV functions as a babysitter.

> Many children watch watch too much television; often, the TV functions as a babysitter.

1. The sunset, however, has never been more spectacular.

2. Jen concentrates on taking notes in class, therefore, she has little trouble when studying for a test.

3. Flannery O'Connor's short stories are set in the South, they contain unusual characters and unexpected violence.

4. One candidate was concerned about health care and education reform, however, his opponent worried about the economy and international politics.

5. Organ transplants have become very successful, in fact there are many more patients waiting for surgery than there are organ donors.

4. Change One of the Independent Clauses into a Dependent Clause.

Another effective way to join independent clauses and avoid run-ons is to change one of the independent clauses into a dependent clause. To make this change, you must add a subordinating conjunction to create an adverb clause (like *because, since, although*) or a relative pronoun to create an adjective clause, (like *who, which, or that.*)

> **Run-on:** Juvenile obesity is a major cause of physical and emotional illness, parents must address this problem.

> adverb clause
> **Correct:** *Because juvenile obesity is a major cause of physical and emotional illness,* parents must address this problem.

> adjective clause
> **Correct:** Parents must address the problem of juvenile obesity, *which is a major cause of physical and emotional illness.*

Practice Set 9–7

Directions: Correct the following run-on sentences by turning one independent clause into a dependent clause. In this exercise, add a subordinating conjunction or relative pronoun to create an adverb clause or adjective clause.

> **Example:** Termites cause serious problems for homeowners these pests have become resistant to many pesticides.

Because termites have become resistant to many pesticides, they cause serious problems for homeowners.

OR

Termites, which cause serious problems for homeowners, have become resistant to many pesticides.

1. Marvel Comics began in 1939 under a different name these superheroes have been given new life in movies and television shows.

2. Joseph forgot to pay his utility bill the electric company turned off his power.

3. Lucia Jimenez is a very successful realtor, she is sincere, honest, and hard-working.

4. The antique cabinet was badly damaged in the move a restoration expert should appraise it.

5. School uniforms have positive effects on students many public schools now require them.

We have reviewed the four most common ways to repair run-on sentences: (1) Create separate sentences by adding a period, a capital letter, and appropriate end punctuation; (2) join the two independent clauses with a comma and a coordinating conjunction; (3) use a semicolon to join short and closely related sentences; (4) add a subordinating conjunction to one of the independent clauses to make it a dependent clause. You can also rework a sentence by changing the word order, adding words, or eliminating words, as long as doing so doesn't change the meaning.

Run-on: Teaching children to dance improves their coordination it also gives them self-confidence.

Correct: Teaching children to dance *improves* their coordination *and gives* them self-confidence. (compound verb)

Run-on: Miss Kissinger was my high school French teacher, she sparked my desire to visit Paris.

Correct: Miss Kissinger, *my high school French teacher*, sparked my desire to visit Paris. (appositive)

Run-on: Otis sped down the highway, he barely avoided a collision with a slow-moving tractor.

Correct: *Speeding down the highway*, Otis barely avoided a collision with a slow-moving tractor. (verbal phrase)

QUICK TIP

Be careful about the conjunctive adverb *then*. Although it looks like a subordinating conjunction, it is not. You are likely to create a run-on if a clause beginning with *then* is not written properly as an independent sentence.

Run-on: I washed the dishes, then I settled down to watch my favorite TV show.

Correct: I washed the dishes. Then I settled down to watch my favorite TV show.

Correct: I washed the dishes, and then I settled down to watch my favorite TV show.

Correct: I washed the dishes; then I settled down to watch my favorite TV show.

Practice Set 9–8

Directions: Correct the following run-on sentences. Vary the correction methods, using each method at least once. You can change words, eliminate words, add words, or change word order. If a sentence is correct, write "correct" in the margin.

Examples: You must proofread carefully for sentence errors, grammar mistakes weaken your writing.

You must proofread carefully for sentence errors. Grammar mistakes weaken your writing.

OR

You must proofread carefully for sentence errors, for grammar mistakes weaken your writing.

OR

You must proofread carefully for sentence errors; grammar mistakes weaken your writing.

OR

You must proofread carefully for sentence errors because grammar mistakes weaken your writing.

OR

You must proofread carefully for grammar mistakes that weaken your writing.

1. Some states require motorcyclists to wear helmets others do not.

    _____

2. Sharks have an incredibly keen sense of smell in fact they can smell blood in the water from miles away.

    _____

3. White chocolate isn't really chocolate at all it contains cocoa butter, sugar, and milk but no cocoa solids.

    _____

4. Cutting back on sugary drinks, for example, is a good way to lose weight.

    _____

5. Daylight Savings Time creates many problems with sleep patterns, travel, even health therefore some people favor staying on Daylight Savings Time all year.

    _____

6. Monday is a federal holiday however I have to work all day.

    _____

Practice Set 9–9

Directions: Correct the run-ons in the following paragraphs by using a variety of the methods discussed in this chapter. We have made the first correction for you.

S
Nearly all human beings experience stress. some people deal with it better than others. As a response to danger, stress enables a human being to channel physical resources of strength and speed for protection. A certain amount of stress is,

therefore, necessary for survival, but chronic stress—stress experienced over a long period of time—weakens the body physically and mentally. Emotional stress can weaken the immune system, it increases the chances of coronary disease and viral infection. Stress can even affect one's body shape the chemical reactions connected to the stress response may cause fat cells to accumulate in the abdomen.

Not everyone responds in the same way to particular stressors, for example, there are significant gender differences. Although women's blood pressure appears to be less affected by stress than men's, women react to a greater range of stressors and feel stress more often. Events of early childhood also influence how adults handle stress, children in unstable homes exhibit stronger reactions to adult stresses than do children raised in stable, supportive environments. Unfortunately, childhood stress seems to be an ever-increasing aspect of modern life.

Since totally eliminating stress from our lives is impossible, we must learn to handle it effectively. We can try to develop more stress-resistant behaviors. People who cope well with stressful situations tend to concentrate on immediate problems rather than on long-range ones, they are able to rationalize their troubles in a positive way, they have an optimistic outlook toward life and themselves. Meditation and other relaxation techniques, massage, exercise, and a strong support system also help to relieve stress. Finally, expressing our emotions—whether aloud to others or in written form—will contribute to a more functional, relaxed, stress-free life.

Practice Set 9-10

Directions: Correct faulty fragments or run-ons in the following sentences. If a sentence is correct, just write "correct" in the blank.

Example: Most visitors to India want to see the Taj Mahal it is a UNESCO World Heritage site.

Correction: Most visitors in India want to see the Taj Mahal. It is a UNESCO World Heritage site.

1. Taj Mahal several decades in the making, beginning in 1592.

   _____

2. The Mogul Emperor Shah Jahan built the Taj for his wife Mumtaz she was his favorite wife.

   _____

3. Mumtaz died bearing their fourteenth child in 1631.

   _____

4. Shah Jahan promised his dying wife a beautiful tomb; made of white marble.

   _____

5. "A poem in stone" referring to the amazing structure in Agra, India.

   _____

6. The exterior walls covered in intricate mosaics.

   _____

7. Many of the walls and floors are studded with precious gemstones.

   _____

8. More than 20,000 laborers and artisans built the tomb. And the surrounding gardens and fountains.

   _____

9. Two graves are in the building, Shah Jahan and Mumtaz both buried there.

   _____

10. A wonder of the modern world.

    _____

▼ TEST YOURSELF

Directions: Many sentences in the following paragraphs contain fragments and run-ons. Correct them by changing punctuation and capitalization. You do *not* need to add, change, or delete words.

One of the most intriguing figures of the Civil War was Major General George McClellan. A graduate of West Point. McClellan suffered from an inflated ego and an inability to take action. So much so that some even accused him of cowardice. When McClellan took command of the Army of the Potomac, the recruits were a ragtag bunch of farmers. Who were inexperienced in the ways of war. He was an outstanding leader, organizing the troops and turning them into confident soldiers, however, he frequently showed a lack of respect for Lincoln, his commander-in-chief. He was nicknamed "The Young Napoleon." Not only for his leadership skills, but also for his conceited and arrogant behavior.

McClellan's abilities did not extend to the battlefield, however. Often incorrectly convinced that his troops were vastly outnumbered and unwilling to put them in harm's way. He angered Lincoln by his refusal to engage the Army of the Potomac in battle. Or to push forward when they were close to victory. Lincoln's frustration showed in a famous letter he once wrote to McClellan. The letter, addressed to "My Dear McClellan," said, "If you are not using the army, I should like to borrow it for a short while," it was signed, "Yours respectfully, Abraham Lincoln." Lincoln finally relieved McClellan of his command in 1862, nevertheless, Lincoln had to tangle with him again when McClellan became the Democratic Party's candidate for president in the 1864 election.

WRITE NOW

Directions: Imagine that you have just won $10 million in a lottery game. Write a 10-12 sentence paragraph about what you would do with the money. Include the following: a sentence beginning with *although*; a sentence containing the phrase *such as*; two independent clauses joined by a semicolon; two independent clauses joined by *however* and the appropriate punctuation; two related sentences, the second one starting with *then*.

GrammarSpeak ⟼ ➞

Some words are so commonly used that many speakers don't realize that they are slang or made up words. Practice saying the proper words below aloud.

Instead of:	Say:
Ain't	Isn't
Theirself	Themselves
Gonna	Going to
Irregardless	Regardless
Thunk (past tense of think)	Thought
Tooken	Taken
Flustrated	Flustered OR frustrated
A nother	Another
Swang	Swung

WORD WATCHERS

Some words are misspelled so frequently that you may think the incorrect spelling is correct simply because you are used to seeing the words spelled that way. Listed below are some words that you should learn to spell correctly.

develop	(not develope) Tip: Adding the *e* on the end lengthens the *o* vowel. Develope would rhyme with cantaloupe and envelope.
judgment	(not judgement) Tip: Some dictionaries list *judgement* with an *e* as an acceptable secondary spelling, but that spelling is really the British spelling. If you are not using other British spellings (like *colour* and *honour*) in your writing, you should not use this one either.
license	(not lisence) Tip: C comes before *s* in the alphabet.
occasion	(not occassion) Tip: Two *c*'s, one *s*.
separate	(not seperate) Tip: Keep your spelling skills up to **par** when you spell separate.
definitely	(not definately) Tip: Pronounce it correctly. There is an "it" in *definitely*.

Word Watchers Practice Set

Directions: Circle the word or words that are spelled *incorrectly* in each sentence.

1. You must develop good judgement if you are going to have a driver's license.
2. I am definately going to separate my white clothes from my colored ones the next time I do the laundry.
3. On this special occasion, I will take poetic lisence and wish you all the joy your heart can hold.
4. It is my judgment that this is an appropriate occasion for celebration.
5. I do not want to develope a crush on Maurice, even though he and Felicity have gone their seperate ways.

Commas

Commas separate, combine, emphasize, and clarify. Even the most skilled writers have comma questions. However, comma usage can become less confusing if you follow three important guidelines:

1. Use a comma only when there is a grammatical reason to use it.

2. Do not overuse commas. Inserting a comma where it does not belong is just as wrong as omitting a comma where it does belong.

3. Learn the comma rules, apply them, and save the exceptions for later. Following the rules consistently will make you right most of the time.

Understanding basic sentence structure simplifies comma usage. Students sometimes insert commas where there are pauses in oral reading or where "it sounds right." These practices often cause comma errors. It is best to follow the specific comma rules.

INDEPENDENT CLAUSES JOINED BY A COORDINATING CONJUNCTION

Use a comma before a coordinating conjunction that separates independent clauses.

Coordination occurs when a comma and a coordinating conjunction join two or more independent clauses. The coordinating conjunctions are *and, but, or, nor, for, so, yet*. You can use the mnemonic FANBOYS to help you remember this list:

For

And

Nor

But

Or

Yet

So

QUICK TIP

Remember that words can function as more than one part of speech. *For* is a coordinating conjunction only if it means *because;* otherwise, it is a preposition.

Coordinating conjunction: I left, *for* the meeting was over.

Preposition: I left *for* the meeting.

But is usually a conjunction, but it can be a preposition if it means *except,* as in the following example:

Everyone *but* me got a new uniform.

Since every independent clause has a subject and a verb, a subject/verb construction must appear on each side of the coordinating conjunction.

S V   CC S   V
We left for the airport two hours early, but we still missed our flight.

If a subject and a verb do not appear on both sides of the coordinating conjunction, do not use a comma.

S V   CC   V
We left for the airport two hours early but still missed our flight.

This sentence does not have a subject and verb on both sides of the coordinating conjunction. The sentence simply has a compound verb, so no comma is needed.

If a coordinating conjunction joins two dependent clauses, do not use a comma.

Cassie said *that I should meet her at two o'clock* and *that we could drive to the party together*.

These are two noun clauses, not independent clauses. The word *that* tells you that the clauses are dependent, not independent.

QUICK TIP

The most effectively coordinated sentences are relatively short and closely related in meaning.

Ineffective coordination: I am a college freshman, and my girlfriend is from Indiana.

Effective coordination: I am a college freshman, and I want to major in elementary education.

Practice Set 10–1

Directions: In the following sentences, add commas where needed. If the sentence is correct as it is, just write "correct."

Example: Americans love watching professional sports, and millions of fans enjoy sports trivia.

1. Many siblings have played professional sports but not all of them have become famous.

2. Peyton and Eli Manning are both quarterbacks in the NFL and both have earned Super Bowl rings.

3. Wayne Gretzky was an outstanding hockey player but his brother Brent Gretzky scored only one goal in his thirteen games in the NHL.

4. Baseball has had over 350 sets of brothers so one could call it the sport of brotherly love.

5. Cal and Billy Ripkin had 451 home runs between them yet Billy accounted for only 20 of them.

6. Cal Ripkin played for the Baltimore Orioles and is considered one of the best shortstops ever to play the game.

7. Ripkin earned the nickname "Iron Man" because he did not miss a game nor did he ever leave the lineup for sixteen consecutive seasons.

8. Trios of brothers in professional baseball include the DiMaggios and the Alous.

9. Identical twins Tiki and Ronde Barber both played in the NFL but never for the same team.

10. Sisters Serena and Venus Williams are successful professional tennis players but they do not hesitate to compete against each other.

ITEMS IN A SERIES

Commas to Separate Items in a Series

A **series** is a list.

If more than two items appear in a list, put commas between the items and before the conjunction.

These items may consist of single words, phrases, or clauses.

> **A series of nouns:** We served *chicken*, *rice*, and *asparagus* at the wedding.

> **A series of prepositional phrases:** The defense attorney mailed the documents *to her client*, *to the prosecutor*, and *to the judge*.

> **A series of clauses:** Parents usually care about *what their teenagers do*, *where they go*, and *how much money they spend*.

QUICK TIP

Sometimes, for emphasis, the conjunction appears between every item in the series. In this case, do not use any commas.

The villain was irrational and greedy and cruel.

Practice Set 10–2

Directions: In the following sentences, add commas where needed. If the sentence is correct as it is, just write "correct."

> **Example:** She ran into the kitchen, opened the refrigerator door, and searched for something to eat.

1. I offered the angry customer the choice of a refund an exchange or a store credit.

2. Slade looked for his keys on his dresser behind the desk and under the cushions.

3. He bought a car with a hybrid engine leather seats and a sun roof.

4. She loves to photograph athletes engaged in their sport babies sleeping in their mothers' arms and young children playing games.

5. The car salesman understood what his customer wanted when he needed it and how much he could afford to pay.

COORDINATE ADJECTIVES

Coordinate adjectives are equal adjectives that modify the same noun.

If adjectives are coordinate, place a comma between them.

In order to decide if adjectives are coordinate, you must apply two tests:

1. Can the adjectives be reversed and still make sense?

2. Do the adjectives make sense with an *and* between them?

If both tests work well, the adjectives are coordinate, and you use a comma between them. If both tests don't work well, assume that the adjectives are not coordinate and omit the comma.

> He lives in an *old, neglected* house. (*A neglected, old house; an old and neglected house*—both of these phrases make sense. The adjectives are coordinate, so you use a comma between them.)

> The *famous plastic* surgeon operates on Hollywood celebrities. (*The plastic famous surgeon, the famous and plastic surgeon*—neither of these phrases makes sense. The adjectives are not coordinate, so you do not use a comma.)

Practice Set 10–3

Directions: In the following sentences, add commas where needed. If the sentence is correct as it is, just write "correct."

> **Example:** The sly, greedy fox attacked the chickens.

1. The sad disillusioned student considered withdrawing from college.

2. The tall distinguished gentleman in the front row of the auditorium is a successful software manufacturer.

3. She needed to polish the two silver candlesticks.

4. The wealthy businessman was wearing a dark blue sports jacket.

5. The dark depressing film was based on a disastrous Antarctic expedition.

INTRODUCTORY ELEMENTS

Use a comma after an introductory element.

An **introductory element** is a grammatical construction that appears at the beginning of a sentence and cannot stand alone. Many types of phrases and clauses introduce sentences and are followed by commas.

Comma after an Introductory Prepositional Phrase

When a sentence begins with an introductory prepositional phrase, use a comma to separate it from the main clause.

After the game, we hurried to the movie.

Because of his positive attitude and extensive product knowledge, the salesman earned high commissions.
(This long prepositional phrase begins with a prepositional expression, *because of*, and has a compound object, *attitude and knowledge*.)

If a sentence begins with more than one prepositional phrase, a comma should follow the last one.

prepositional phrases
In the middle of the professor's lecture on commas, the student fell asleep.
(This sentence begins with three prepositional phrases.)

QUICK TIP

Some writers omit the comma after an introductory prepositional phrase if the phrase is very short. Either way is correct.

At noon we take a lunch break.

OR

At noon, we take a lunch break.

Comma after an Introductory Adverb Clause

If an adverb clause comes at the beginning of a sentence, put a comma after it. If the adverb clause comes at the end of the sentence and follows the independent clause, do not use a comma.

introductory adverb clause
Because we had overslept, we rushed to get to work.
(This introductory adverb clause is followed by a comma.)

adverb clause

We rushed to get to work *because we had overslept.*
(This adverb clause follows the independent clause and requires no comma.)

Comma after a Verbal Phrase

Since participles are adjectives and can never be the subjects of sentences, a participial phrase at the beginning of a sentence is always followed by a comma. With introductory gerund and infinitive phrases, comma use varies. If the gerund or infinitive phrase is the subject of the sentence, no comma follows it. If the gerund or infinitive phrase is not the subject, a comma follows it.

participial phrase

Coming home late from the party, Shannon faced her angry parents.
(A comma follows the introductory participial phrase.)

gerund phrase

Coming home late from the party created a problem for Shannon.
(No comma follows the gerund phrase used as a subject.)

infinitive phrase

To understand commas well, you must study hard.
(A comma follows the introductory infinitive phrase used as an adverb.)

infinitive phrase

To understand commas well is crucial for good writers.
(No comma follows the infinitive phrase used as the subject.)

Comma after Transitional Words or Phrases

A **transition** is a word or phrase that shows the relationship between two sentences or paragraphs. Various kinds of transitions show different relationships. For example, some transitions show cause and effect (*thus, therefore, as a result, consequently*), and others show time (*first, second, next, finally*). If a single word or a short prepositional phrase is transitional and comes at the beginning of a sentence, a comma should follow it.

Therefore, John got a job at an advertising agency.

In fact, he was hired after only one short interview.

Comma after a Mild Interjection

An **interjection** is a word that expresses feeling or emotion and plays no grammatical role in the sentence. If the expression of feeling is strong, an exclamation point follows it. However, a mild interjection at the beginning of a sentence takes a comma. This rule also applies to the words *yes* and *no* when they are interjections.

Oh, that's nice.

Yes, I would like some salsa with my tortilla chips.

Ouch! You're really hurting me.

Practice Set 10–4

Directions: In the following sentences, add commas where needed. If the sentence is correct as it is, just write "correct."

Example: During the final week of the semester I have three exams.

Correction: During the final week of the semester**,** I have three exams.

1. Looking closely at the order form the manager could see the error.

2. We turned off the water heater when we left on our summer vacation.

3. Paying a bill before the due date will save money on finance charges.

4. No I cannot attend my cousin's wedding in March.

5. If you do not hand in your paper on time your professor will deduct ten points from the final grade.

6. On the other hand traveling during peak season can be expensive.

7. At the beginning of the piano recital the music teacher introduced the performers.

8. To lose weight you must monitor your diet and exercise several times per week.

9. The fireworks were difficult to see because the fog was so thick.

10. Before hiking on mountain trails you must apply sunscreen and insect repellent.

RESTRICTIVE AND NONRESTRICTIVE ELEMENTS

Don't be intimidated by the terms *restrictive* and *nonrestrictive*. **Restrictive** simply means "essential," and **nonrestrictive** means "nonessential." When deciding whether to use commas, you must determine how important a clause or phrase is to the meaning—not the structure—of the sentence. This rule applies to adjective clauses, participial phrases, and appositives, and it is one of the most difficult rules for writers to understand. Specific grammar rules dictate most comma placement; however, this comma decision depends on the writer's intent.

Adjective Clauses

Adjective clauses can be restrictive (essential) or nonrestrictive (nonessential). Ask yourself this question: Is the adjective clause needed to make the meaning of the sentence clear, or is it adding extra information not essential to the meaning?

If an adjective clause is essential to make the meaning clear, it is restrictive, or essential, and does not require commas.

Examine this sentence:

A woman *who is the director of a company* earns a high salary.

Who is the director of a company is an adjective clause. If you leave it out, you still have a structurally complete sentence: *A woman ~~who is the director of a company~~*

earns a high salary. However, the meaning of the sentence is not clear. You need the clause to tell *which* woman. Since the clause is essential to the meaning, don't put commas around it.

On the other hand,

If the adjective clause simply gives extra, added information and is not essential to make the meaning of the sentence clear, it is nonrestrictive, or nonessential, and you must set it off with commas.

Maria Ortiz, ~~who is the director of a company~~, earns a high salary.

Who is the director of a company is an adjective clause, but if you leave it out, your reader still knows you are talking about Maria Ortiz.

Maria Ortiz, *who is the director of a company*, earns a high salary.

The clause is not essential to make the meaning clear, so you do set it off with commas. Now compare these two sentences:

The city *where he went to college* is in Georgia.

The adjective clause *where he went to college* is essential to identify the city and make the meaning of the sentence clear. Therefore, you do not set it off with commas.

Atlanta, *where he went to college*, is in Georgia.

The adjective clause *where he went to college* is added, nonessential information, so you set it off with commas.

Participial Phrases

Restrictive and nonrestrictive participial phrases apply the same comma rules as adjective clauses:

If the phrase is essential to the meaning of the sentence, do not use commas. If the phrase offers extra information and removing it would not alter the meaning of the sentence, do use commas.

A restaurant *located near a college campus* is sure to be popular.

If we take out *located near a college campus*, the sentence suggests that any restaurant is sure to be popular. The writer means that a particular restaurant—one located near a college campus—is sure to be popular.

Max's Pizza Palace, *located near State College*, is very popular.

This sentence makes the point that Max's Pizza Palace is very popular. *Located near State College* adds information. If we took out that phrase, the sentence would make the same point, so we surround it with commas.

Appositives

Appositive are also restrictive or nonrestrictive. Remember that an appositive is a noun that follows another noun and renames it.

Most appositive phrases are nonrestrictive and are set off by commas. However, if the phrase is very short, closely related to the noun, or essential to the meaning, consider it restrictive and do not use commas.

Billy Crystal, *the director of the play*, is a famous actor and comedian.

I enjoyed reading *A Tale of Two Cities, a novel by Charles Dickens*.

The novel *A Tale of Two Cities* is set during the French Revolution.

My son *Adam* has two children.

With restrictive and nonrestrictive clauses, comma usage is usually an all-or-nothing proposition. Use either two commas or none.

Incorrect: Mark Twain, who wrote *Huckleberry Finn* traveled extensively in Egypt.

Correct: Mark Twain, who wrote *Huckleberry Finn*, traveled extensively in Egypt.

Incorrect: The raccoon, that sneaked into the garage was frightened.

Correct: The raccoon that sneaked into the garage was frightened.

One comma will set off a nonrestrictive clause or phrase only when the clause or phrase comes at the end of the sentence.

Tonight we are going to see *Cabaret*, which is a play set in Germany before World War II.

Some additional hints will help you decide if a clause is restrictive or nonrestrictive.

1. Usually, clauses or phrases that modify proper nouns are nonrestrictive and take commas. Because the specific names appear, you do not need the clause or phrase to identify the nouns.

   Hillsborough Community College, *which is located in Tampa*, has five campuses.

2. Clauses or phrases beginning with the relative pronoun *that* are always restrictive; therefore, they never require commas.

   The suit *that he bought for the conference* was very expensive.

Practice Set 10–5

Directions: In the following sentences, add commas where needed. If the sentence is correct as it is, just write "correct."

Example: My Uncle Mike, who speaks Spanish, is going to work in Mexico.

1. John Fitzgerald Kennedy the thirty-fifth president of the United States was assassinated in 1963.

2. The landscapers who planted the Botanic Garden received an award from the governor's office.

3. Denzel Washington whose movies range from action thrillers to serious drama is a versatile performer.

4. The story "The Most Dangerous Game" is set on a fictitious island in the Caribbean Sea.

5. Most people celebrated the end of the twentieth century in the year 2000 which was not really the end of the millennium.

6. Colleges that offer a flexible course schedule usually attract nontraditional students.

7. My neighbors moved to Black Mountain a small town in North Carolina.

8. *Fences* which was written by August Wilson is a play about barriers of all kinds.

9. Luis and his brother lived in the town where the mudslide destroyed several neighborhoods.

10. This Renoir painting is the one that was sold for $10.00 at a yard sale.

INTERRUPTING EXPRESSIONS

Use commas to set off interrupting expressions.

Interrupting expressions are words and phrases that are not part of the main idea of the sentence. They are always set off by commas, and they can appear at the beginning, the middle, or the end of a sentence. Several types of expressions are interrupters.

Commas around Parenthetical Expressions

Parenthetical expressions are true interrupters, for they are comments (words or phrases) inserted into the middle of a sentence, interrupting the flow of the thought. Whenever you have a parenthetical expression that interrupts the flow of the sentence, place commas before and after it.

The dishonest employee is, *I am sure*, not working there anymore.

You are in trouble, *I think*, because of your irrational behavior.

Commas to Set off Transitions

Transitions are words or phrases that show the relationship between two sentences or paragraphs. If a transition comes at the beginning of a sentence, it is an introductory element, and you must follow it with a comma. If it comes in the middle of an independent clause, set it off with commas. If it comes at the end of a sentence, put a comma before it.

However, the judge is an extremely impatient individual.

The judge, *however*, is an extremely impatient individual.

The judge is an extremely impatient individual, *however*.

Commas to Set off Names of Direct Address

Direct address is speech directed to a person, using that person's name or title. A noun of direct address never has a grammatical function in the sentence, such as subject or object. A name of direct address can come at the beginning, middle, or end of the sentence.

> *Sam*, please open the door.

> I do not know, *Mother*, if I can meet you at the mall today.

> Here is my assignment, *Professor Curtis*.

Commas to Set off Echo Questions

Echo questions echo declarative statements and turn them into questions. Sometimes called **tag questions**, echo questions come in the middle or at the end of a sentence.

> Your birthday is next week, *isn't it?*

> If the echo question comes in the middle of the sentence, surround it with commas.

> You're coming with me, *aren't you*, when I leave for the hospital?

Commas to Separate Negative Contrasts

Expressions of negative contrast always involve a negative word, like *not* or *unlike*, and two different ideas. Sometimes these constructions are called **contradictory phrases** or **contrasted elements**. A negative contrast can come in the middle or at the end of a sentence and will require one or two commas, depending on its location.

> Mr. Stein's daughter is moving to New York, *not Chicago*.

> An ophthalmologist, *never an optician*, can prescribe medication.

Practice Set 10–6

Directions: In the following sentences, add commas where needed.

> **Example:** You know, of course, that the rebate deadline has expired.

1. The professor never the teaching assistant turns in the final grades.

2. Dr. Lewis is it true that you are going to retire next year?

3. The conference will take place in Rome not Venice.

4. This medication according to recent laboratory studies may have severe side effects.

5. The alarm clock should be reset however before you go to sleep.

6. Tell me Dr. Daniel when the scholarship applications must be completed.

7. The movies that are nominated for Academy Awards are worth seeing aren't they?

8. The candidate I honestly believe has no chance of winning her party's nomination.

9. Put the toys away after you have finished playing Ellie.

10. We ordered soup and salad not hamburgers and French fries.

ABSOLUTE CONSTRUCTIONS

Use commas to set off absolute constructions.

An **absolute construction** is a phrase consisting of a noun plus a participle or participial phrase. The absolute construction adds meaning to a sentence without specifically connecting to any sentence part. The entire phrase is a unit and may appear anywhere in a sentence. If the absolute construction appears at the beginning of a sentence, use a comma after it; if it appears at the end of a sentence, put a comma before it. If it appears in the middle of a sentence, surround it with commas.

Her long hair blowing in the breeze, the young girl looked like a model.

The teenager left for the game, *his poor test grade quickly forgotten*.

The kitten, *its head buried in the blanket*, was sound asleep.

DIRECT QUOTATIONS

Use commas to set off direct quotations.

Direct quotations repeat someone's exact words. Use a comma after words, such as *said*, *stated*, or *exclaimed*, that announce a direct quotation.

His father said, "I am very proud of your performance in the game."

When the quotation appears before the announcing words, use a comma after the quotation unless it is a question or exclamation. Note that the comma goes *inside* the closing quotation, not outside. Question marks and exclamation points take the place of commas.

"I am having a bad day," the child whimpered to her grandfather.

"What time does the bus leave?" the tourist asked.

When the announcing words interrupt a one-sentence quotation, set them off with commas.

"My husband has not felt well," the woman told the doctor, "since we returned from our cruise."

When the quotation consists of more than one sentence, be sure to use a period between the sentences. Otherwise, you will create a run-on sentence.

Incorrect: "Let's go home now," Elena said, "I am getting very tired."

Correct: "Let's go home now," Elena said. "I am getting very tired."

Remember that commas and periods always go inside quotation marks; semicolons and colons always go outside quotation marks. Question marks and exclamation points vary according to the particular situation.

Be careful about confusing direct quotations with indirect quotations. An indirect quotation paraphrases what a person has said, but it does not use the exact words. Indirect quotations do not require quotation marks or commas.

Indirect quotation:	Arthur's professor said that she would give him an extension on the paper.
Direct quotation:	Arthur's professor said, "I will give you an extension on the paper."

Practice Set 10–7

Directions: In the following sentences, add commas where needed. Write "correct" next to sentences that need no commas.

Example: "Pay at the door," the usher announced.

1. "I can't finish this chapter" Grace complained.

2. My daughter says that she wants to leave early on Monday morning.

3. I was unable to cash my check the bank having closed for Presidents' Day.

4. "What do you think of this fabric?" the designer asked her client.

5. Her eyes shining with happiness the bride walked slowly down the church aisle.

6. "We can leave" Aaron whispered "before the game is over."

7. The football player his uniform caked with mud felt frustrated and angry over the penalty.

8. The professor warned "Make sure you study your notes for the grammar test."

9. "Watch out!" the crane operator yelled to the pedestrians below.

10. "The movie starts at five o'clock" he said. "I'll meet you in the lobby."

CONVENTIONS

Commas with Dates and Addresses

Dates and addresses having two or more parts take commas *between* and *after* the parts.

I was born on Monday, March 29, 1985, in Springfield, Ohio.

Note these important exceptions. Do *not* put commas between the following:

Month/Day:	June 3 is my birthday.
Month/Year:	He graduated in June 2014.

Day/Month/Year: Our last day of school was 3 June 2014.

Number/Street: We lived at 510 Lake Avenue.

State/ZIP Code: They sent money to a post office box in Atlanta, Georgia 30338.

On Monday, June 12, 2012, the young attorney opened his first office at 600 Jackson Street, Suite 200, Tampa, Florida 33602, and began practicing criminal law.

Commas with Names and Titles

If a title or an abbreviation follows a name in a sentence, put commas *between* the name and title and *after* the title.

I met Joseph Bartlett, MD at the conference on infectious diseases.

Dr. Martin Luther King, Jr., was deeply inspired by the teachings of Mohandas Gandhi.

Comma after a Salutation in a Letter or E-mail

A comma follows the salutation in an informal letter.

Dear Santa,

Commas with Numbers and Statistics

It is common practice to place commas within numbers over three digits to make them more readable. Start at the right, and place a comma after every third digit.

The bankrupt business was liquidating over 3,500,000 novelty items at vastly reduced prices.

Commas separate certain kinds of information and statistics. Note the following examples:

five feet, four inches

six pounds, eight ounces

QUICK TIP

With easy-to-read numbers of four digits, a comma is usually optional.

The club members sold 2500 boxes of cookies.

Also, certain large numbers never take commas: social security numbers, telephone numbers, driver's license and credit card numbers, and long addresses.

98430 Fletcher Avenue

In any case, consistency in the handling of numbers is important.

AVOIDING A MISREADING

Use a comma to avoid a misreading of a sentence.

This final comma rule does not give permission to place commas anywhere you please. You should not add commas to sentences because the commas look good, sound good, or seem to reflect a pause. However, if a sentence simply does not make sense without a comma or if the comma clarifies the meaning, you may add the comma. Be careful, however. The comma must clearly prevent sentence confusion. Also, remember that adding a comma will never fix a poorly constructed sentence.

Unclear:	To Jane Robinson seemed handsome and brave.
Clear:	To Jane, Robinson seemed handsome and brave.
Unclear:	Those who can act quickly and decisively.
Clear:	Those who can, act quickly and decisively.
Unclear:	When angry camels spit.
Clear:	When angry, camels spit.

Practice Set 10–8

Directions: In the following sentences, add commas where needed. If the sentence is correct as it is, just write "correct."

Example: She used to live in Macon, Georgia.

1. The Nobel Peace Prize is always awarded in Stockholm Sweden.

2. According to the *Denver Post* Janet Harwig DDS is closing her dental office in Aurora Colorado.

3. The young couple moved to 6405 Shadow Mountain Drive Apartment B-3 Austin Texas 80421 and began to decorate their apartment.

4. The fifth grader is already five feet three inches tall.

5. At six fifteen musicians entered the recording studio.

6. The earth is over 93000000 miles away from the sun.

7. In summer thunderstorms occur frequently.

8. My best friend finished medical school in June 2014.

9. When depressed veterans should seek psychiatric counseling.

10. He registered on August 23.

Practice Set 10-9

Directions: In the following sentences, add commas where needed. Write "correct" next to sentences that need no commas.

Example: Not all best sellers were written by modern writers.   correct

Example: *Pride and Prejudice,* written by Jane Austen, is one of the most popular best sellers of all time.

1. Jane Austen an early nineteenth-century English novelist was born on December 16 1775 in Hampshire England.

2. Because her novels often focus on women's independence they have found an eager audience today.

3. Austen herself never married yet her heroines are always in search of "Mr. Right."

4. A man worth marrying should have money good looks and especially good character.

5. Mr. Darcy who is the love interest in *Pride and Prejudice* possesses all three.

6. However his haughty proud demeanor masks his true nature and makes him appear unworthy.

7. In the beginning of the novel Elizabeth Bennet the second of five daughters hates Mr. Darcy but she eventually realizes his true character and therefore returns his love.

8. Austen's novel *Emma* tells the tale of a young woman who sees herself as a matchmaker and a doer of good deeds.

9. People have recently become aware of Austen's work because of the release of movies based on three of her works: *Pride and Prejudice Emma* and *Sense and Sensibility*.

10. In addition the movie *Clueless* is a modern adaptation of *Emma* but is set in Beverly Hills California rather than in England.

 ## TEST YOURSELF

Directions: In the following sentences, add commas where needed. If the sentence is correct as it is, just write "correct."

Example: During the final act of the play everybody dies.

Correction: During the final act of the play, everybody dies.

1. A person who doesn't understand financial matters shouldn't try to run a business.

2. Her nephew is a rude obnoxious child.

3. People who need to should leave the show at intermission.

4. Bill Gates for example supports many charitable causes.

5. I didn't read the book nor did I see the movie.

6. She bought two new bathing suits.

7. All my cat does is eat sleep and make a mess.

8. The governor took office on January 10 2010 in Raleigh North Carolina.

9. Although he is my twin brother we do not look at all alike.

10. "I am leaving now" the nurse said quietly to the patient.

11. The driver his cell phone ringing loudly was easily distracted.

12. Speaking in a very low voice the politician admitted that he had lied in his campaign ads.

13. Students who do not study usually do poorly in college.

14. I need your raincoat not your umbrella.

15. My father who owns a dry cleaning business was able to get the spot out of my dress.

16. New York my favorite city is very crowded in the spring.

17. He needed a haircut but didn't get one.

18. Meredith you are going to Los Angeles on business aren't you?

19. She analyzed the poem "Mending Wall" for her English assignment.

20. You know of course that she is not coming to the seminar.

21. In fact their credit card balance was far too high.

22. Marcella said that the Writing Center needed additional assistants.

23. His term lasted from January 2013 to January 2015.

24. The basketball center for our college team is 7 feet 3 inches tall.

25. In the middle of a huge project at work the manager resigned.

WRITE NOW

Directions: Write a sentence requiring commas for each of the rules listed below. Be sure to punctuate each correctly.

1. Use a comma before a coordinating conjunction that separates independent clauses.

2. Use commas to separate items in a series.

3. Use a comma after an introductory element.

4. Use commas appropriately for restrictive and nonrestrictive clauses and phrases.

5. Use commas to set off interrupting expressions.

6. Use commas to set off an absolute construction.

7. Use commas to set off a direct quotation.

8. Use commas when appropriate for dates and addresses, names and titles, informal salutations, large numbers, and statistics.

GrammarSpeak ➡

Some speakers incorrectly insert "at" when inquiring about location. Practice asking about locations correctly by repeating aloud the correct sentences below.

Instead of:	Say:
Where is the meeting at?	Where is the meeting?
Where is my brother at?	Where is my brother?
Where are we at on this project?	Where are we on this project?
Where was he born at?	Where was he born?
Where were you at when the storm hit?	Where were you when the storm hit?

WORD WATCHERS

Some words are considered substandard and should never be used in writing.

hisself/theirself	Nonstandard for *himself* and *themselves*.
irregardless	Nonstandard for *regardless*.
should of/would of/ could of	The *of* in these phrases should be *have:* I should have saved my money (not *I should of saved my money*).
use to/suppose to	Nonstandard for *used to* and *supposed to*. Don't drop the *d:* He used to be my friend. He is supposed to be in class.
anywheres/nowheres	Nonstandard for *anywhere* and *nowhere*.

Word Watchers Practice Set

Directions: Choose the correct word in parentheses.

1. We will hold the picnic (regardless/irregardless) of the weather.
2. I would (of, have) become a famous singer if I could (of/have) sung on key.
3. The actors created the stage sets and costumes (theirselves/themselves).
4. She was (suppose/supposed) to meet me at the mall by lunchtime.
5. Scientists have not found life (anywhere/anywheres) on Jupiter.
6. She should (of/have) listened to the directions more closely.
7. (Nowhere/Nowheres) in this building can I find an elevator.
8. Felix told me about the car crash (hisself/himself).
9. Pluto (use/used) to be considered a planet.
10. They gave (theirselves/themselves) a bonus for achieving their sales quota.

Other Punctuation and Capitalization

SEMICOLONS (;)

Separating Independent Clauses

Semicolons can join two sentences that are relatively short and closely related in meaning. Basically, the semicolon takes the place of the comma and the coordinating conjunction. The second independent clause begins with a lowercase letter rather than a capital.

Independent clause   coordinating conjunction   independent clause

This fern is drooping,   *so*   it must need water and fertilizer.

OR

independent clause   independent clause

This fern is drooping; it must need water and fertilizer.

Transitional expressions often follow semicolons. Such expressions emphasize the type of relationship between the two independent clauses. Note that a comma always follows the transitional expression.

The following sentences show three different ways of punctuating independent clauses:

Comma + conjunction: The water is quite calm now**, but** a storm may be approaching later.

Semicolon: The water is quite calm now**;** a storm may be approaching later.

Semicolon + transitional expression + comma: The water is quite calm now**; however,** a storm may be approaching later.

Be careful, though. Not every transitional expression requires a semicolon. If the transitional expression appears in the middle of one independent clause, set it off with commas:

Incorrect: The building; however, has been condemned.

Correct: The building, however, has been condemned.

Study the following list of transitional expressions so that you can use them effectively for sentence variety.

> **Transitional expressions to indicate addition:** *again, also, besides, equally important, finally, first, further, furthermore, in addition, last, likewise, moreover, next, second, third*
>
> **Transitional expressions to indicate cause and effect:** *accordingly, as a result, consequently, hence, in short, otherwise, then, therefore, thus*
>
> **Transitional expressions to indicate contrast:** *although true, for all that, however, in contrast, nevertheless, notwithstanding, on the contrary, on the other hand, still*
>
> **Transitional expressions to indicate similarity:** *likewise, similarly*
>
> **Transitional expressions to indicate special features or examples:** *for example, for instance, incidentally, indeed, in fact, in other words, in particular, specifically, that is, to be exact, to illustrate*
>
> **Transitional expressions to indicate summation:** *in brief, in conclusion, in short, on the whole, therefore, thus, to conclude, to summarize, to sum up*

QUICK TIP

Be careful not to create sentence fragments when you start sentences with transitional words and phrases like *for example, for instance, whereas, such as,* and *like*.

Fragment: For example, my parents and my children.

Correct: For example, my parents and my children like the same movies.

Fragment: Whereas George's goals are rather unclear.

Correct: Whereas George's goals are rather unclear, he still wants to move to New York.

Practice Set 11–1

Directions: Add commas and semicolons where needed in the following sentences.

Example: My son is a great baseball player; thus, he hopes to get an athletic scholarship.

1. I forgot to pack a bathing suit and towel consequently I chose not to go to the beach.

2. Waking up early to exercise however gives you more energy during the day.

3. Justin is an outstanding writer in fact he won second place in the school's essay contest.

4. Mr. Jennings reminded Nick to pay the cable bill nevertheless he forgot to mail it before the due date.

5. Your first assignment for English therefore will be to study the comma rules in Chapter 10.

Separating Items in a Series

When the items in a series contain commas, use a semicolon to separate the items.

This summer, we are planning to visit Atlanta, Georgia; Miami, Florida; and Dallas, Texas.

Here, the use of the semicolon makes the meaning of the sentence clear.

Practice Set 11–2

Directions: Add semicolons and commas where needed.

Example: Danny needs some new shoes; however, he can't afford them right now.

Example: We sent invitations to my parents, Brian and Debbie Berg; your parents, Mike and Robin Schorr; and Ella's parents, Tom and Melissa Jones.

1. Spring semester ends early this year graduation is scheduled for May 2.

2. The following professionals spoke at the conference: Elise Garcia an architect Dave Brewster a space planner and Kathy Coleman an engineer.

3. I would like to meet him in fact I would like to meet his entire family.

4. Baby boomers are those people born between 1946 and 1964 seventy-eight million Americans fall into this category.

5. The best cities in the United States to find a job are Boston Massachusetts Austin Texas and Baltimore Maryland.

6. She approached the podium and carefully arranged her notes then she began to speak.

7. The identical twins grew up in separate families nevertheless their habits and attitudes were very similar.

8. The broadcast tonight will contain a story about several area chefs, including Maya Rivera Executive Chef of Jardinière Lou Wilde owner of Lou's Fabulous Food Truck and Madison Reynolds the head baker at Sweet Cupcakes.

9. My girlfriend wants to go to the concert thus I stood in line for hours to buy tickets.

10. The electric bill is much higher therefore in the hot summer months.

COLONS (:)

Use **colons** in these special situations.

Use colons to separate independent clauses from other words, phrases, or clauses that rename or define the independent clauses.

The colon must be preceded by an independent clause (a complete sentence), but it does not have to be followed by one.

Colon followed by an independent clause: The young man had one major goal: he wanted to go to college.

Colon followed by a phrase: The young man had one major goal: to go to college.

Colon followed by a single word: The young man had one major goal: college.

All of these sample sentences are correct because an independent clause comes before the colon and what comes after the colon defines or clarifies this clause.

Use colons to introduce lists or long series preceded by an independent clause.

We need several items at the grocery store: eggs, milk, bread, and laundry detergent.

Often, expressions like *the following* or *as follows* introduce this list.

Stock dividends will be issued on the following dates: February 15, May 15, August 15, and November 15.

Be careful about the phrases *such as* and *like*. These are never followed by a colon.

Incorrect: I read several fashion blogs, such as: *Brooklyn Blonde, Closet Freaks, and Dapper Lou.*

Correct: I read several fashion blogs, such as *Brooklyn Blonde, Closet Freaks, and Dapper Lou.*

QUICK TIP

A colon never separates a verb from its direct object or subject complement, or a preposition from its object.

        verb   direct objects

Incorrect: We ordered: a new sofa, dining room chairs, and a coffee table.

Correct: We ordered a new sofa, dining room chairs, and a coffee table.

Correct: We ordered some new furniture: a sofa, dining room chairs, and a coffee table.

        preposition   objects

Incorrect: Richard has lived   in: Florida, Missouri, Pennsylvania, and Texas.

Correct: Richard has lived in Florida, Missouri, Pennsylvania, and Texas.

Correct: Richard has lived in the following states: Florida, Missouri, Pennsylvania, and Texas.

Use colons to introduce long or formal quotations.

In his inaugural address in January 1961, President John Fitzgerald Kennedy issued the following challenge to the American people: "Ask not what your country can do for you. Ask what you can do for your country."

Use colons to separate titles and subtitles, chapters and verses of biblical citations, hours and minutes. Also use a colon after the greeting of a formal letter.

A User's Guide to the Millennium: Essays and Reviews

Matthew 5:17

6:00 PM

Dear Professor Forbes:

Practice Set 11–3

Directions: Insert colons where needed in the following sentences. If a sentence is correct, write "correct" in the margin.

Examples: We volunteered for three different jobs: painting, cleaning, and driving.

1. The editor was correct in her prediction the novel would be a best seller.

2. Rabbi Berger's favorite quotation comes from Isaiah 2 4. It reads as follows "They will beat their swords into plowshares and their spears into pruning hooks. Neither will they learn war anymore."

3. A non-stop flight from Chicago to Salt Lake City leaves at 8 40 in the morning.

4. A wise hiker carries water, food, bandages, and insect repellent.

5. In addition to a uniform, volunteers receive the following equipment a two-way radio, maps, and a first aid kit.

6. Dear Dr. Shames

7. You can see some successful musicals, such as *Wicked* and *Jersey Boys*, in performing arts centers throughout the United States.

8. I received a notice from the library that the book *Hollywood and Broadway A Study in Contrasts* is a week overdue.

9. There are two words he always misspells *definitely* and *judgment*.

10. During the famous March on Washington on August 28, 1963, Dr. Martin Luther King, Jr., spoke some of his most memorable words "I have a dream that my four little children will one day live in a nation where they will not be judged by the color of their skin but by the content of their character."

END PUNCTUATION

Use end punctuation marks, including periods (.), question marks (?), and exclamation points (!), to end a sentence.

Periods

Use periods (.) at the end of statements, commands, or requests.

Statement: The baby is sleeping in the cradle near the fireplace.

Command: Answer his question.

Request: Please shut the door.

Use periods within and after certain abbreviations.

Mr., *Mrs.*, and *Ms.* are followed by a period. *Miss* is not followed by one since it is not an abbreviation. Styles are changing regarding the use of periods with degrees and time periods. Most style manuals no longer require the periods for degrees, such as *PhD* or *MD*, or with *AM* and *PM* and *BC* and *AD*. You may also see AM, PM, BC, and AD properly written in small capital letters without the periods.

The abbreviations for the names of many organizations and government agencies no longer require periods.

AAA	DEA	FDA	NAACP	OPEC
ACLU	EPA	HUD	NATO	PTA
ASPCA	FBI	IRS	NOW	UNICEF

Standard postal service abbreviations for state names do not contain periods.

FL, GA, NC, NY, CA, AZ, TX, TN, CO

If you are unclear about a particular abbreviation, consult a current dictionary. Another mark of punctuation, such as a comma or a question mark, may follow a period after an abbreviation, but a sentence can end with only one period.

Since the assassination of Dr. Martin Luther King, Jr., many streets in the United States bear his name.

Does he work for the Mackintosh Corp.?

Let's meet today at noon on Main St.

Question Marks

Use a question mark (?) at the end of a sentence that asks a question, whether it is a direct question or an echo question.

Direct question: Can you babysit on Saturday evening?

Echo question: You can babysit on Saturday evening, can't you?

Use a period, not a question mark, after an indirect question.

An indirect question isn't really a question at all. It is a statement that suggests that there is a question about something, but it does not directly ask the question, so it is followed by a period.

Indirect question: Jamie wondered whether she would be able to find an apartment for the summer.

Exclamation Points

Use an exclamation point (!) at the end of a statement expressing strong feeling or after an interjection showing intense feeling or emotion.

Statements expressing strong feeling: I most certainly will not marry you!

How wonderful!

Interjection showing intense emotion: Wow!

The expression *What a(n)* at the beginning of a sentence or word group usually indicates an exclamation.

What a terrific party that was!

What an exciting trip to take!

QUICK TIP

Avoid overusing exclamation points in formal writing. They lose their effectiveness very quickly. Never use more than one exclamation point to end a sentence.

I cannot believe that he gave her an engagement ring!!!!!

Practice Set 11–4

Directions: Punctuate the following sentences using periods, question marks, and exclamation points. If a sentence is correct, write "correct" in the margin.

Example: Are Tatiana and Rudy going ice-skating at the new rink downtown**?**

1. Do you know if all of the supplies were included in the most recent shipment

2. What a fantastic summer vacation

3. The kindergarten teacher wondered if the child knew how to read.

4. Most US bank accounts are insured by the FDIC, aren't they

5. I am truly shocked by your crude language in class

PUNCTUATION WITH QUOTATIONS

Quotations use various kinds of punctuation, including double quotation marks, single quotation marks, ellipsis, and brackets.

Quotation Marks

Use quotation marks to set off a direct quotation.

A **direct quotation** repeats someone's exact speech. Using other punctuation with quotation marks varies according to the placement and type of the quotation. Use the following examples as a guide:

- **Quotation follows introductory material:** My friend Kristin said, "Mark and I would like you to come for dinner on Sunday."

- **Quotation comes before the explanatory material:** "Mark and I would like you to come for dinner on Sunday," my friend Kristin said.

- **Quotation includes question mark or exclamation point:** "May I borrow two cups of flour?" my neighbor asked.

  "I can't wait until graduation!" the excited student told her parents.

- **Quotation and sentence are both questions or exclamations:** Did Shannon ask her father, "Can we go fishing this weekend?"

  He shouted from the balcony, "I love you!"

- **Sentence is a statement, but ends with a quotation that is a question or exclamation:** MacKenzie asked, "How are you?"

- **Sentence is a question or exclamation but quotation is not:** Did Merrill say, "You are fired"?

- **Single sentence quotation divided by explanatory words:** "I bought a microwave," Russell said, "because I never have time to cook." (Note that the first word of the second half of the quotation does not get capitalized.)

- **If the quotation itself is more than one sentence, separate the sentences with end punctuation to avoid creating a run-on sentence:**

  Incorrect: "I'm going to bed early tonight," Nell said, "I was up late all weekend."

  Correct: "I'm going to bed early tonight," Nell said. "I was up late all weekend."

Be careful to distinguish direct quotations from indirect ones. An **indirect quotation** simply paraphrases someone's words and does not require quotation marks.

Direct quotation: My doctor said, "Take two aspirin and call me in the morning."

Indirect quotation: My doctor told me to take two aspirin and call him in the morning.

Use quotation marks around the titles of short works, such as poems, songs, articles, short stories, speeches, episodes of television shows, and chapters in a book.

> The English professor's favorite short story is "The Lesson," by Toni Cade Bambara.

> "Smoke Gets in Your Eyes" was the first episode of the television series *Mad Men*.

> I quoted from the chapter titled "The Etruscans" in the book *The History of Italy*.

Do not use quotation marks around the title of your own paper on the original manuscript. These titles are not direct quotations and are not set off by commas.

Use quotation marks to set off words used in a special sense.

> Is this band playing what my grandparents call "swing" music?

> "Freedom" doesn't mean the right to do whatever you want.

Placement Rules for Quotation Marks Used with Additional Punctuation

Always place periods and commas inside closing quotation marks.

> Ricky has easily memorized Carl Sandburg's short poem "Fog."

> "I can't wait here any longer," the frustrated client said to the receptionist.

Always place semicolons and colons outside quotation marks.

> His favorite hymn is "Amazing Grace"; he especially loves hearing it played on bagpipes.

> There are two main characters in Poe's famous story "The Tell-Tale Heart": the murderer and the victim.

Single Quotation Marks

Use single quotation marks to enclose a quotation within a quotation.

> The apostrophe functions as a single quotation mark.

> My daughter reminded me, "Remember Dad's favorite saying, 'You always get what you pay for.'"

Ellipsis

Use an ellipsis to show that some material has been omitted from a direct quotation.

An ellipsis is three spaced periods appearing together. This punctuation is effective in condensing a long quotation that contains more information or words than the writer wants to quote. If the omission appears at the end of the quotation, use four periods—three for the ellipsis and one for the end of the sentence. After the ellipsis, the rest of the quotation must be logical and grammatically correct.

The following quotations are excerpts from Abraham Lincoln's "Gettysburg Address." The first one is a complete quotation. The second one contains several ellipses marking the omission of words.

Complete quotation: "We are met on a great battlefield of that war. We have come to dedicate a portion of that field, as a final resting place for those who here gave their lives that that nation might live."

Quotation containing omissions: "We are met on a great battlefield . . . to dedicate a portion of that field, as a final resting place for those who here gave their lives. . . ."

Brackets

Use brackets [ ] to insert words of your own into quotations for explanation, clarity, or grammatical correctness.

"We are met on a great battlefield [Gettysburg] of that war."

ITALICS

Use italics to note certain titles. With a computer, creating italics is easy. If you are writing by hand, underlining substitutes for italicizing.

Italicize the titles of long works: books, plays, long poems, long essays, pamphlets, newspapers, magazines, operas, movies, television series, radio programs, albums, paintings, and sculptures.

Books: *Wuthering Heights, Huckleberry Finn*

Plays: *The Piano Lesson, Six Degrees of Separation*

Long poems: *Beowulf, Song of Roland*

Essays: *Self-Reliance, A Defense of Poetry*

Pamphlets: *Common Sense, Ten Early Warning Signs of Cancer*

Newspapers: *Atlanta Journal, Detroit Free Press*

Magazines and journals: *Better Homes and Gardens, Journal of Modern Psychiatry*

Operas: *Carmen, Aïda*

Movies: *The Sound of Music, Citizen Kane*

Television series: *Law and Order, Dancing with the Stars*

Radio programs: *All Things Considered, Prairie Home Companion*

Musical recordings—albums or CDs: *Born This Way, Money*

Paintings: *Starry Night, Guernica*

Sculptures: *The Thinker, Venus de Milo*

Do not italicize or underline the title of your own paper on the original manuscript.

Do not italicize the names of sacred books or their sections.

Koran, the Bible, Luke, Psalms, Torah, Vedas

Do not italicize the names of legal documents.

Constitution, Declaration of Independence, Bill of Rights

Italicize the names of particular ships, planes, trains, and spacecraft.

Titanic, Spirit of St. Louis, City of New Orleans, Challenger

Italicize foreign words that have not become a standard part of contemporary English.

She committed a *faux pas* by not acknowledging the wedding gift.

Italicize words, phrases, letters, and numbers used in a special context.

In a dictionary with small print, distinguishing a dotted *i* from a lowercase *l* is often difficult.

Students often confuse the spelling of *there, their*, and *they're*.

In today's society is a meaningless, overused expression.

Practice Set 11–5

Directions: Punctuate the following sentences, using whatever kind of punctuation is needed. Underline words or phrases that require italics.

Example: "Let's go to the zoo tomorrow afternoon," LeAnne suggested.

Example: I have read Mark Twain's <u>Huckleberry Finn</u> many times.

1. Would you like pancakes for breakfast Mr. Lunsford asked his children

2. I need some help with my research paper the student said to the librarian I can't find anything on my topic

3. Flannery O'Connor once wrote The peculiar problem of the short-story writer is how to make the action he describes reveal as much of the mystery of existence as possible

4. Andrew asked, Have you ever read Robert Frost's poem Fire and Ice

5. My car has a dead battery the frustrated driver reported to the AAA operator and I need a jump-start immediately

6. Andre Dubus's short story Killings describes a grieving father's act of revenge

7. Help me the frightened man screamed from the balcony of the burning building

8. One of the most shocking episodes of Breaking Bad is entitled Dead Freight

9. Did you hear the pharmacist ask When do you want to pick up your prescription

10. In the Beatles' tribute show, the quartet opened with Love Me Do and closed with Let It Be

HYPHENS

Hyphens (-) are used to separate. In most instances, the use of a hyphen is a spelling consideration rather than a grammatical one. If you have questions about hyphen use, consult a current dictionary. However, there are some rules that you should apply consistently.

Use hyphens in fractions.

Management fired one-half of the staff.

Use hyphens for compound numbers.

Hyphenate compound numbers, such as *thirty-seven* or *fifty-three*. Do not hyphenate numbers like *one hundred*, *five thousand*, or *ten million*.

three hundred fifty-four dollars

Use hyphens between two words used together to form a compound adjective only when the compound adjective comes before the noun it modifies.

Rod Stewart, Elton John, and Mick Jagger are *world-famous* rock singers.

The rock singers Rod Stewart, Elton John, and Mick Jagger are *world famous*.

Do not use hyphens between adverbs ending in -ly and adjectives.

I posted a *clearly written* notice on the employee bulletin board.

Use hyphens with prefixes such as ex, self, and all and the suffix elect.

My *ex-wife* is *president-elect* of the garden club.

Use hyphens with prefixes before proper nouns or adjectives.

He testified before the House *Un-American* Activities Committee in *mid-July*.

QUICK TIP

Many writers use hyphens to divide words of two or more syllables at the end of a line if the completed word extends beyond the margin. This practice can cause confusion and spelling errors. If you must divide a word, use a dictionary to divide by syllables correctly. Fortunately, computers usually eliminate this problem.

DASHES

Dashes (—) are used to link information. A dash is two hyphens typed together with no space between, before, or after. In formal writing, use dashes sparingly. However, using a dash is appropriate for appositives or other parenthetical expressions that contain internal commas or that should be set off for strong emphasis.

> Three members of my family—Aunt Loretta, Uncle Marshall, and Cousin Francine—were born in Chicago.

> Rich desserts, snack foods, and alcohol—these are a dieter's downfall.

PARENTHESES

Parentheses are used to enclose information. In informal writing, writers use parentheses to enclose information that is extra, humorous, or out of logical order. Avoid parentheses in formal writing. However, parentheses are required in the following situations:

Use parentheses to enclose birth and/or death years following a person's name.

> Rose Kennedy (1890–1995), the matriarch of the Kennedy family, outlived four of her nine children.

Use parentheses to enclose publication dates, page numbers, or other documentation information.

> *Dr. Jekyll and Mr. Hyde* (1886), a short novel by Robert Louis Stevenson, is also a film and a musical play.

Use parentheses around numbers that list a series.

> Mrs. Rodriguez wants to sell her home because (1) it is too large for one person, (2) it is too expensive to maintain, and (3) the property taxes have doubled in the last five years.

Place commas, periods, semicolons, and colons outside the parentheses unless the parenthetical material is a complete sentence that requires its own end punctuation.

> "A large income is the best recipe for happiness I ever heard of," according to Jane Austen (1775–1817).

> I had to borrow Natasha's jacket when it turned cold. (I had left mine at the restaurant.)

Practice Set 11–6

Directions: Punctuate the following sentences using hyphens, dashes, parentheses, and underlining (italics).

Example: Henry David Thoreau (1817–1862) wrote the essay <u>Civil Disobedience</u> (1849) to explain his refusal to pay a government poll tax.

1. Roses, azaleas, and begonias all of these plants are on sale at Plant World this weekend.

2. Charles Lindbergh 1902 1974 is remembered for 1 his solo flight across the Atlantic Ocean, 2 his highly conservative politics, and 3 the kidnapping and murder of his infant son.

3. South Pacific, Miss Saigon, and M. Butterfly these contemporary plays have certain similarities to the Puccini opera Madame Butterfly.

4. You can now subscribe to People magazine online.

5. Telemarker is a term used to describe a skier who skis downhill using cross country style equipment.

6. If you want to apply for financial aid, you must turn in all forms by mid June.

7. We will board our three pets the cat, the dog, and the hamster when we leave on vacation.

8. The snowboarder's brightly colored hair makes him a well known figure on ESPN.

9. On Thanksgiving Day, the volunteers at the soup kitchen served seventy five breakfasts, ninety two lunches, and two hundred dinners.

10. In The Seven Habits of Highly Effective People 1989, Stephen Covey suggests that character changes are more important than personality fixes.

APOSTROPHES

An **apostrophe** looks like a single quotation mark. Use apostrophes in the following situations:

Use apostrophes to show possession or ownership.

Jennifer found *Keisha's wallet* under the front seat of the car. (The wallet belongs to Keisha.)

We stacked the *children's games* in the closet. (The games belong to the children.)

While it is easy to see possession when something *belongs* to someone, possession also means that something is *of* something else.

Tomorrow's lecture will be about apostrophes. (the lecture *of* tomorrow)

He deserves a *day's pay* for a *day's work*. (the pay *of* a day for the work *of* a day)

Water from the flowers spilled onto the antique *book's cover*. (the cover *of* the book)

Apostrophes also show ownership with some indefinite pronouns.

someone's raincoat, everybody's business, another's theory

Use apostrophes to form the plurals of letters, numbers, symbols, and words used as words.

> A dyslexic individual often confuses *b*'s and *d*'s.

> My Social Security number has five *6*'s in it.

> You should not use *&*'s in formal writing.

> Be careful about using too many *and*'s in a sentence.

Notice that the *s* is not italicized in these plural forms.

QUICK TIP

Using a lowercase *s* without an apostrophe for numbers and abbreviations is also acceptable.

> TVs appeared in many homes in the 1950s.

If omitting the apostrophe causes confusion, leave it in.

Confusing:	I made three As last term. (Without the apostrophe, *As* looks like the word *as*.)
Clear:	I made three A's last term.

Use apostrophes to take the place of missing letters in contractions or dates.

cannot = can't	does not = doesn't
he is = he's	would not = wouldn't
they are = they're	1993 = '93

One of the difficulties with apostrophes is deciding whether to place them before the *s* or after the *s*. Note the following rules:

- **For plural possessives, make the noun plural before adding the apostrophe.**

Possessive Noun	Rule	Examples
singular, does not end in s	add apostrophe + *s*	• one girl's project • the baby's toys
singular, ends in s	add apostrophe + *s* or just apostrophe*	• Yeats's poetry or Yeats' poetry
plural, ends in s	add apostrophe	• four girls' projects • both families' tents
plural, does not end in s	add apostrophe + *s*	• children's music • women's lounge

*Most authorities recommend going by pronunciation: if you say the extra syllable in the possessive, then you add s.

- **With compounds, showing possession and number varies.**

Compound	Rule	Examples
single words showing joint possession	add apostrophe + *s* or just apostrophe to final noun	• Elaine and Amir's adventure • Kim and James' wedding
single words showing separate possession	add apostrophe + *s* or just apostrophe to each noun	• Ray's and Scott's video games • James' and Charles' homes
compound words showing possession	add apostrophe + *s* to the final word	• my brother-in-law's car • the attorney general's argument
plural compound words	add *s* to the first word	• two brothers-in-law • two attorneys general
plural compound words showing possession	add s to the first word and apostrophe + *s* to the last word	• two brothers-in-law's cars • two attorneys general's arguments

Learn when not to use apostrophes.

Do not use an apostrophe to form the possessives of personal pronouns.

Incorrect: The book is her's.

Correct: The book is hers.

Incorrect: That picnic spot is our's.

Correct: That picnic spot is ours.

Do not use an apostrophe in the word *its* if you mean *belonging to it*. *It's* means *it is* or *it has*.

Incorrect: The zebra lost it's stripes.

Correct: The zebra lost its stripes.

Incorrect: Its going to rain.

Correct: It's going to rain.

Do not add apostrophes to verbs ending in *s*.

Incorrect: Megan cook's us breakfast.

Correct: Megan cooks us breakfast.

Do not use apostrophes to make nouns plural.

    Incorrect: I bought several bathing suit's.

    Correct: I bought several bathing suits.

Do not make titles possessive.

    Incorrect: "Reunion's" setting is New York City.

    Correct: The setting of "Reunion" is New York City.

Practice Set 11–7

Directions: Add apostrophes where needed.

    Example: For the parade, the trainer braided the horse's mane and tail with colorful ribbons.

1. Next month the book club will meet at Jean and Kennys house.
2. How many *is* are there in the word *Mississippi*?
3. We are hanging the mens coats in the childrens playroom.
4. Its always a struggle to put the dog in its cage for the night.
5. My father-in-laws closet is full of old fishing equipment.
6. The last time we visited Disney World was in 08.
7. The four chefs aprons are hanging in the kitchen.
8. Shaina bought five dollars worth of chocolate candy.
9. I found someones laptop in the trunk of my car.
10. Mickis and Federicos jobs require many hours of overtime.

CAPITALIZATION

Capitalization is making the first letter of a word uppercase.

Capitalize the first word of any sentence, question, or exclamation.

    We should replace the carpet in the dining room.

    Is it still raining?

    What a brilliant idea!

Capitalize the first word of a direct quotation if the quotation is a complete sentence.

    The dean replied, "Classes begin on January 8."

Capitalize all proper nouns—the names of specific persons, places, or things.

Jane Doe	Lowry Park	Plaza Hotel
Plant High School	Lake Lure	Majestic Theater
Rome, Georgia	Asia	Brooklyn Bridge
Bay Way Drive	Indian Ocean	Medal of Honor

Capitalize titles that appear before names and the titles of heads of state.

Chancellor Gwendolyn Stephenson	Doctor Seth Mabry
Judge Christine Nguyen	Chairman Mao Zedong
Uncle Dave	President Thomas Jefferson

Capitalize a title if it substitutes for a name.

We will meet Mom and Dad at 6:30 for dinner, and my grandfather will probably join us.

Capitalize the personal pronoun I.

The mechanic did not seem to understand what I was telling him.

Capitalize the names of all sacred books and of races, nationalities, languages, and religions and their followers.

New Testament	African-American	British	Farsi
Koran	Buddhism	Caucasian	Korean
French	Muslims	Hispanic	Judaism
Hindi	Vietnamese	Islam	Latin

Capitalize the names of deities.

People worship God in various ways. The Romans worshipped Jupiter as their primary deity.

Capitalize the titles of specific courses of study.

Do not capitalize a general school subject (algebra, biology, economics, history) unless it is a language or is the title of a specific course. Do not capitalize an academic major unless it is a language.

This semester, I am taking Linguistics 1670, Ideas of the Western World, sociology, and French.

Capitalize the names of historical documents and periods of historical significance.

Renaissance	Industrial Revolution	Magna Carta
Ice Age	Civil War	Treaty of Versailles
Paleozoic Era	World War II	Bill of Rights

Capitalize the first word and all important words in a title.

Do not capitalize the articles (*a*, *an*, *the*) or short prepositions and conjunctions unless they appear first in the title.

> *A Shot in the Dark*, *The Grapes of Wrath*, *In the Heat of the Night*, *Of Mice and Men*, *The Hunt for Red October*, "A Good Man Is Hard to Find"

Capitalize the names of specific businesses, organizations, and teams.

Target	Girl Scouts of America
The Critter Shop	Chicago Cubs
Red Cross	University of Texas Longhorns
National Organization for Women	Atlanta Falcons

Capitalize brand names but not the item.

> Kleenex tissue, Colgate toothpaste, Quaker oatmeal, Nabisco graham crackers

Capitalize the days of the week, the months of the year, and the names of holidays and special events.

Monday	Memorial Day	Mother's Day
Saturday	Fourth of July	Super Bowl
June	Easter	Winter Olympics

Do not capitalize the names of the seasons unless they are part of the name of a particular event.

> We cut back our rosebushes in winter.

> In March or April, students at the University of Pennsylvania celebrate Spring Fling.

Capitalize the names of the planets.

> Mercury, Venus, Earth, Mars, Jupiter, Saturn, Uranus, and Neptune revolve around the sun in the Milky Way Galaxy.

> If Earth is listed specifically as a planet, as in the sentence above, capitalize it. If it is otherwise mentioned, do not capitalize it.

> Many parts of the earth have become overpopulated and polluted.

Capitalize the names of particular areas of the United States.

> People born in the South usually have strong feelings of regional loyalty.

Do not capitalize directions.

> To reach the mall, drive south on Westshore Boulevard.

Practice Set 11–8

Directions: Add capital letters where needed. Cross out any incorrect lowercase letters and write the correct capital letter directly above it.

Example: when grocery shopping at albertson's, peter usually buys tropicana orange juice and breakstone sour cream.

1. many people who live in switzerland speak french, german, and english.

2. in april, i spoke with mayor bob buckhorn at the annual fundraiser for metropolitan ministries of hillsborough county.

3. in *a tale of two cities*, charles dickens describes the year 1775, prior to the french revolution, as follows: "it was the best of times, it was the worst of times."

4. recently, droughts and floods in the west have had disastrous consequences.

5. to complete his science and humanities requirements, jonathan has registered for applied physics 102 and art history 203.

6. we gave grandma and grandpa a family photograph for the jewish holiday of hanukkah.

7. on friday gabrielle is going to tile world of italy to select a new kitchen floor.

8. during registration, my advisor urged me to check with professor chambers about my english grade.

9. the scholarship is designated for hispanic females who want to major in business at the university of south florida.

10. in the summer of 2014, reverend and mrs. miller, who lived in the northeast, drove west toward the sierra mountains of california.

ABBREVIATIONS, SYMBOLS, AND NUMBERS

Abbreviating Words

Abbreviations are shortened forms of words.

Common abbreviations for titles used with names are acceptable in formal writing.

Mr., Mrs., Dr., Rev., Gen., Sr., Jr., JD., Esq., MD., PhD., DO.

Commonly understood abbreviations (acronyms) for organizations, departments of government, and technical terms are acceptable in formal writing.

YMCA	NYSE	NCAA	NFL
NBA	UN	FDA	LED
NBC	CIA	FCC	GPS

RCA	NLRB	VA	CD
GOP	FAA	AIDS	TV

If you want to use a more obscure abbreviation in a paper, write out the full name the first time that you mention it and put the abbreviation in parentheses after it. Then you can use the abbreviation alone for subsequent references.

Senator Graham's assistant will attend the next meeting of the Southwest Florida Water Management District (SWFWMD).

In formal writing, avoid most abbreviations of names, amounts, dates, and places.

Incorrect: During Xmas vacation in NY, Jos. gained ten lbs. because he ate dinner late in the P.M. and had no time to exercise in the AM.

Correct: During Christmas vacation in New York, Joseph gained ten pounds because he ate dinner late in the evening and had no time to exercise in the morning.

Although Latin abbreviations, such as *i.e.*, *e.g.*, and *etc.*, are acceptable in documentation and informal writing, avoid them in formal writing.

Incorrect: Gardeners must replant petunias, pansies, marigolds, *etc.* every spring.

Correct: Gardeners must replant annuals like petunias, pansies, and marigolds every spring.

Writing Symbols

Use only acceptable symbols in formal writing.

- Use a dollar sign with dollar amounts that are too long to write out.

  Incorrect: I paid five hundred thirty-six dollars and twenty cents for my computer.

  Correct: I paid $536.20 for my computer.

- Be consistent with percentages throughout a paper. Write out *percent* or use % every time.

- Do not use an ampersand (&) or a cent sign (¢) in formal writing.

Writing Numbers

Write all numbers under one hundred, and any number that begins a sentence.

Three starlings have built a nest in the eaves of the porch.

If this situation is awkward because the number beginning the sentence is long, rephrase the sentence. More than two words is too long.

Incorrect: 119 errors appeared in the accountant's tax records.

Correct: The accountant's tax records contained 119 errors.

Be consistent in form when using numbers in the same sentence, particularly when some numbers would normally be spelled out while others would not.

Last week, Randy sold only 20 candy bars, but this week he has sold 127.

Use numbers in dates, times using AM and PM, addresses, telephone listings, fractions, percentages, decimals, scores, statistics, money, divisions of books and plays, and identification numbers.

The baby was born at 10:01 AM on February 8, 2014, and weighed 7 pounds, 1 ounce.

The final game of the World Series was tied 4–4 at the beginning of the ninth inning.

The protagonist dies in act 1, scene 3 of the play.

Practice Set 11–9

Directions: Correct the errors in abbreviations and numbers by crossing out the incorrect word or number and writing the correction above it.

Example: ~~Chas.~~ Simone owns 6 different homes.
(*above:* Charles ... six)

1. 50 people tried out for the 10 vacancies on the team.

2. My mother always serves apple pie & ice cream at family dinners.

3. My son is a Dr., and he is interning at MA General Hosp. in Boston.

4. The study showed that fifty percent of the law school class were females and that 25% of the class were minority students.

5. On our drive from GA to WY, we spent five hundred seventy dollars and fifteen cents on gas.

Practice Set 11–10

Directions: There is an error or errors in punctuation or capitalization in each of the following sentences. Find and correct these mistakes. Cross out the incorrect lower-case letter and write the capital letter directly above it.

Example: The short story "the lady or the tiger" is always popular with students.
(*corrections:* T L T)

1. The concert lasted for two hours, then the band played some songs that the audience requested.

2. Shakespeare's play "Romeo and Juliet" is often the basis for modern productions about ill-fated lovers.

3. Mushroom, pepperoni, and cheese; these are the boys' favorite kinds of pizza.

4. Professor Tidwells Economics classes will be limited to business majors only.

5. The possum hid it's babies under the deck in our backyard.

6. We bought emergency supplies, such as: batteries, bottled water, candles, and canned food.

7. The librarian asked if Kristin wanted to check out the book she was reading?

8. "Will dinner be ready soon," Max asked his grandmother.

9. *Theme for English B*, a poem written by Langston Hughes, explores the relationship between student and teacher.

10. The mens' locker room is located at the end of the hall.

▼ TEST YOURSELF

Directions: Add all punctuation marks and capitalization needed. You may add any punctuation *except* commas. Correct any abbreviation errors as well.

The march 1975 issue of ms. magazine published an article written by African-American novelist Alice Walker. Entitled in search of Zora Neale Hurston, this article awakened interest in the work of an artist who had died in poverty and obscurity, and it led to a Hurston revival. Born in january 1891 in alabama, Hurston moved to eatonville, FL, at a young age, and its eatonville that lies at the heart of her work. Her short stories and novels are filled with childhood memories, characters, and vivid descriptions of life in eatonville, chartered as an all black town in 1887. Hurston left eatonville at thirteen, but she returned home for visits throughout her life. She began college at howard university and finally graduated with a degree in anthropology from barnard college in 1927. Hurstons interest in anthropology was evident in her work as she documented african american folklore and created fiction filled with authentic dialect. Even before entering barnard, Hurston had become active in the literary movement known as the harlem renaissance. Her well known book their eyes were watching god was published in 1937.

For several decades, however, Hurston's work was ignored and underappreciated due to her conservative political views. She spent her last ten years working as a freelance writer, newspaper columnist, librarian, substitute teacher, and, occasionally, a maid. After a stroke, Hurston died in a charity nursing home in 1960. her public obscurity ended in 1973 when alice walker, who loved her writing, went to fort pierce, florida, found her pauper's grave, and bought her a tombstone, calling her "A Genius of the south." Today Hurstons work is studied in english classes throughout the United States, and her life is celebrated at the zora neale hurston national museum of fine arts and the annual zora neale hurston festival of the arts and humanities in eatonville.

WRITE NOW

Directions: What do you know about your name? Does it have a special meaning? Were you named after someone special? Write an 8–10 sentence paragraph about your name, following the directions of at least five of the prompts below. Be sure to punctuate all of your sentences properly.

1. Write a sentence using a semicolon to separate two independent clauses.
2. Write a sentence using a colon to introduce a list.
3. Write a sentence using the phrase "such as" to introduce a list.
4. Write a sentence ending with a period and quotation marks.
5. Write a sentence containing a comma and quotation marks.
6. Write a sentence in which a quotation is part of a question.
7. Write a question ending with a quotation that is not part of the question.
8. Write a sentence containing an indirect quotation.
9. Write a sentence spelling out a fraction.
10. Write a sentence containing a compound adjective that comes before the word it modifies.

GrammarSpeak ┠──────▶

Here is another exercise to help you establish better oral language habits. The following exercise contains some common words that are mispronounced when speakers add letters incorrectly. Practice saying the correct pronunciation aloud.

Instead of:	Say:
Acrossed	a CROSS
Fillum	film
Flounder (a fish)	FOUND er
Realator	REAL tor
Triathalon	tri ATH lon

WORD WATCHERS

Pronouns can be confusing. Choose them carefully.

it's/its	*It's* is the contraction *it is:* It's true that my father is remarrying.
	Its is a possessive pronoun meaning *belonging to it:* The puppy wagged its tail.
there/their/they're	*There* has two uses. It is an adverb telling where: My book is over there.
	It is an expletive, part of the *there is/there are* construction: There is no excuse for that behavior.
	Their is a possessive pronoun meaning *belonging to them:* They paid for their own meals.
	They're is the contraction of *they are:* They're leaving for home tomorrow.
who/which/that	*Who* refers to people.
	Which and *that* refer to things and sometimes groups or classes of people. Don't use *which* to refer to a person: The student *who* (not *which*) plagiarized the paper was expelled.
who's/whose	*Who's* is the contraction of *who is:* Who's knocking at the door?
	Whose is a possessive pronoun meaning *belongs to whom:* Whose jacket is this?
which/witch	*Which* is a relative pronoun: My watch, which is broken, tells the correct time twice a day.
	A *witch* is a follower of Wicca or a woman with magical powers: In Arthur Miller's play *The Crucible,* Rebecca Nurse is accused of being a witch.
you're/your	*You're* is the contraction of *you are. Your* is a possessive pronoun: You're correct in your assumption.

Word Watchers Practice Set

Directions: Choose the correct word in the parentheses.

1. (It's/Its) true that the two celebrities will be married in May.
2. Jordan's new car, (witch/which) she received on her sixteenth birthday, is usually parked in the driveway.
3. I found a doctor (who's/whose) younger than I am.
4. (There/Their/They're) was a keypad outside the garage, so we didn't need a key to get into the house.
5. If (your/you're) certain that the dog is healthy, I will adopt him from the Humane Society.
6. Babysitters (who/which/that) have more than three years of experience can command high salaries.
7. This morning Lindsay and Calvin left for San Francisco in (there/their/they're) camper.
8. The company filed for (it's/its) tax exemption before the deadline.
9. The partner (who's/whose) name is on the door commands the most respect.
10. (There/Their/They're) the ones who will be responsible if the measurements are incorrect.

Pronoun Usage

PRONOUN/ANTECEDENT CONNECTION

A pronoun is a word that takes the place of a noun or another pronoun. Without pronouns, our writing would sound repetitive:

After the *doctor* spoke, the *doctor* waited for the patient to ask questions.

The **antecedent** is the word that the pronoun is replacing:

antecedent   pronoun

After the *doctor* spoke, *she* waited for the patient to ask questions.

The antecedent must be a noun or another pronoun. It can also be a noun substitute, such as a gerund or a noun clause.

gerund antecedent   pronoun

Running is good exercise because *it* raises the heart rate.

noun clause antecedent   pronoun

I didn't purchase *what he made* because *it* won't fit in my room.

Often, writers have problems with pronouns because they forget to make the necessary connection between the pronoun and the word or words it replaces. Sometimes writers use so many pronouns that the original antecedent becomes unclear. Other times, there is no specific antecedent at all.

This, That, Which, and It

This, *that*, *which*, and *it* should refer to a specific antecedent, not to an entire sentence. An entire sentence cannot be a noun or a noun substitute.

Incorrect: Austin volunteered to clean the garage. *This* made his parents happy.

What made his parents happy? The pronoun cannot refer to the entire sentence. One way to correct the problem is to change the vague pronoun *this* to an adjective modifying the specific noun *offer*.

Correct: Austin volunteered to clean the garage. *This offer* made his parents happy.

You can also use your coordination skills to combine sentences. The coordinating conjunction *so* will join the two ideas effectively.

Correct: Austin volunteered to clean the garage, *so* his parents were happy.

Recasting the sentence using subordination can also eliminate the pronoun problem:

Correct: *When* Austin volunteered to clean the garage, his parents were happy.

Practice Set 12–1

Directions: Rewrite the sentences below, eliminating any pronouns that do not refer to specific antecedents.

Example: Jaden bought the most expensive pair of shoes in the store. That made her husband really angry.

Jaden bought the most expensive pair of shoes in the store. That purchase made her husband really angry.

OR

Jaden bought the most expensive pair of shoes in the store, so her husband was really angry.

OR

When Jaden bought the most expensive pair of shoes in the store, her husband was really angry.

1. Certified radiation therapists are always in demand. That makes finding a job in the field fairly easy.

   _____

2. Positions may require a bachelor's degree, an associate's degree, or a certificate, which means there are many avenues of training available.

   _____

3. Radiation therapy is used to treat cancer. This can be rewarding, but it can also be quite stressful.

   _____

4. Therapists work around radioactive materials, which means they must be very careful to observe strict safety regulations.

   _____

5. When those who work in this field watch their patients recover, it makes all of their training and hard work worthwhile.

   _____

Mistaking Possessives for Antecedents

Since possessives are adjectives, they cannot serve as antecedents.

Incorrect: During President Johnson's administration, *he* initiated many social reforms.

The possessive *President Johnson's* cannot serve as the antecedent for *he* because possessives are adjectives.

Correct: During President Johnson's administration, *President Johnson* initiated many social reforms.

Correct: President Johnson initiated many social reforms during his administration.

Although the first correction works grammatically, the repetition sounds awkward, so the second revision works better.)

Practice Set 12–2

Directions: Rewrite the sentences below, eliminating any pronouns that do not have proper antecedents.

Example: At Dustin's pool party, he hired a rock band.

Dustin hired a rock band to play at his pool party.

1. On the side of Marshall's car, he put his company's website address.

_____

2. When the emperor's plan was revealed, he made the crowd angry.

_____

3. After Shelbi's big lottery win, she bought her family members new cars

_____

4. When I filled the car's gas tank, it started right away.

_____

5. After the center's winning three-point shot, she received a loud cheer.

_____

Establishing Clear Antecedents

The antecedent must be clear. Be sure that the pronoun refers to a specific antecedent.

Incorrect: *They* said that insurance rates in Florida should be changed.

Who is *they*? Is *they* a newspaper columnist? A television reporter? An insurance executive? A home owner?

Correct: *An editorial writer in the Tampa Tribune* said that insurance rates in Florida should be changed.

Remember that *you* has a specific meaning. Don't use it when you mean people in general.

Incorrect: I hate to go to a theater where *you* can't buy popcorn.

Do I care if *you* can't buy popcorn? No, I care only if *I* can't buy popcorn.

Correct: I hate to go to a theater where *I* can't buy popcorn.

Sometimes rewriting the sentence to eliminate the incorrect pronoun fixes the problem.

Correct: I hate going to a theater that doesn't sell popcorn.

Practice Set 12–3

Directions: Rewrite the sentences below, correcting any pronoun errors.

> **Example:** Instructors should always include the story of the Sphinx on your reading list.
>
> Instructors should always include the story of the Sphinx on *their students'* reading lists.

1. They say that the Sphinx was a very odd character in Greek mythology.

   _____

2. I like reading stories that tell you about strange characters.

   _____

3. The sphinx had a lion's body and a woman's head, and it blocked a mountain by asking a question you could not answer.

   _____

4. They told Oedipus that if you answered the riddle correctly, you would be made King of Thebes.

   _____

5. The Oedipus legend is mentioned by several Greek poets, but they say that the most popular version comes from Sophocles' plays *Oedipus Rex, Oedipus at Colonus*, and *Antigone*.

   _____

Avoiding Ambiguous Antecedents

The antecedent must be specific. The pronoun must clearly refer to the word for which it stands. Sometimes writers include two possible antecedents, making the pronoun ambiguous.

Incorrect: Janet told Andrea that *she* needs to see a therapist.

Who needs to see a therapist? Does *she* refer to Janet or Andrea? The pronoun is ambiguous.

Correct: Janet told Andrea that *Andrea* needs to see a therapist.

Now the answer is clear: Janet was referring to Andrea. Although this revision repairs the pronoun problem, repeating the noun *Andrea* sounds awkward. You may need to recast the sentence for a better result:

Correct: Janet told Andrea to see a therapist.

Another way to correct the ambiguous pronoun is by using dialogue:

Janet told Andrea, "You need to see a therapist."

OR

Janet told Andrea, "I need to see a therapist."

Avoiding Repetitious Pronouns

The pronoun should not be repetitious. Sometimes writers needlessly include a pronoun immediately after the subject when the pronoun isn't needed.

Incorrect: The Olympic runner *he* finished the marathon in a little over two hours.

The *he* following *Olympic runner* is unnecessary. Correct this problem by eliminating the unnecessary pronoun.

Correct: The Olympic runner finished the marathon in a little over two hours.

Practice Set 12–4

Directions: Cross out unclear, ambiguous, or repetitious pronouns, and if necessary, write in a correction above the errors.

Superstitious people
Example: ~~They~~ say that walking under a ladder causes bad luck.

1. She had to work late, which meant that she missed the bus.

2. Dr. Santos told Jim that he needed to get more rest.

3. John Wayne he was the star of many classic Hollywood westerns.

4. In Freudian psychology, he defines the id, the ego, and the superego.

5. They say that genetics is as important as environment in determining personality.

6. I received a ticket, but it was clearly the other driver's fault.

7. Asheville it is a beautiful city in the mountains of North Carolina.

8. On the radio it said that we should get rain by the end of the week.

9. When Tamara's car was in the shop, she asked me for a ride.

10. Robert was struck by lightning while he was playing golf. This made him cautious.

PRONOUN CASE

Another problem area involves the case of personal pronouns. **Case** means "form." The personal pronouns have three cases or forms: subjective, objective, and possessive. Pronouns must be in the appropriate case. Study the chart below to familiarize yourself with these forms:

Person	Subjective	Objective	Possessive
First person (the person speaking)	I, we	me, us	my, mine, our, ours
Second person (the person spoken to)	you	you	your, yours
Third person (the person spoken about)	he, she, it, they	him, her, it, them	his, her, hers, its, their, theirs

The **subjective case** includes the pronoun forms used as subjects and subject complements.

Subject of the sentence: *We* are tired of waiting for the doctor.

Subject of a clause: Natalie is happy because *she* won the lottery.

Subject complement: It was *he* who made the announcement.

The **objective case** is used for objects—direct object, indirect object, object of a preposition.

Direct object: The detective saw *them* at the crime scene.

Indirect object: The chef gave *me* a new recipe.

Object of a preposition: At the campsite, giant ants crawled over *us*.

The **possessive case** shows ownership or possession and can function as adjectives or pronouns.

The neighbors sold *their* house. (adjective describing *house*)

Those books are *mine*. (pronoun serving as subject complement)

Usually, English speakers use the correct case forms instinctively. For instance, most speakers know to say, "I am going to a movie," not "Me am going to a movie." Several areas do cause some case problems, though.

Pronouns as Subject Complements

Pronouns used as subject complements must always be in the subjective case. Many speakers incorrectly use the objective case after a linking verb. For example, when answering the telephone, people mistakenly say, "This is him" instead of "This is he."

It was John who complained about the cost.

Incorrect: It was *him* who complained about the cost.

Correct: It was *he* who complained about the cost.

Incorrect: The person who recommended the restaurant was *me*.

Correct: The person who recommended the restaurant was *I*.

Although using *I* may sound awkward, the pronoun *I* is correct because it is a subject complement.

Avoiding Case Errors Caused by Compounds

Compounds may involve two or more pronouns (*she and I*) or a pronoun and a noun (*Jane and I*). Compounds often cause case errors. Many writers incorrectly use the subjective pronoun *I* in every compound involving the first person.

While it is correct to say, "Robert and I left early" (subjects), it is not correct to say, "Cameron gave the package to Mike and I" (object of the preposition) or "Megan left you and I her phone number" (indirect object).

One of the most frequent errors with the subjective case *I* is in the expression *between you and I*. *Between* is a preposition, so it should be followed by the objective pronoun *me*. *Between you and me* is always correct.

Just between *you and me*, I think he knows about the surprise party.

QUICK TIP

To determine which pronoun case form to use, separate the compound and test it out loud. Whatever form the pronoun takes alone is the same form it takes as part of a compound. When there are two pronouns of different persons and one is first person, think about being polite and put yourself (first person) last. Say *"him and me," "you and I," "they and we."*

He is going to the game. *I* am going to the game.	*He and I* are going to the game.
We saw *Mary* at the mall. We saw *him* at the mall.	We saw *Mary and him* at the mall.
Give the dessert to *him*. Give the dessert to *me*.	Give the dessert to *him and me*.

Comparisons with *Than* or *As*

When a subordinate clause uses *than* or *as* to introduce a comparison followed by a pronoun, case confusion often results. Remember that the subjective case pronouns are used as the subjects of subordinate clauses. Comparisons with *than* or *as* require careful analysis.

dependent clause

James is smarter *than I am*.

The subject of the subordinate clause *than I am* is the subjective case pronoun *I*. To say, "James is smarter *than me am*" sounds wrong. You can also write this sentence leaving out the verb *am*. This type of clause is called an **elliptical clause** because something has been left out. Even without the verb, the subordinate clause needs a subject in the subjective case form, so you must say, "James is smarter than *I*," not "James is smarter than *me*."

Often, the pronoun that you choose determines the meaning of the sentence. Examine these sentences:

He paid her more than I.

He paid her more than me.

Which is correct? The answer depends on the writer's meaning.

"He paid her more than *I*" means "He paid her more than I (paid her)."

"He paid her more than *me*" means "He paid her more than (he paid) me."

It is easy to figure out the correct pronoun case with *than* or *as* by finishing the comparison. The sound and the meaning will tell you which pronoun is correct.

Try this one:

We left the party as late as (they/them).

We left the party as late as *they* did. The answer is *they*.

Pronouns as Appositives

An appositive renames the noun that it follows. If the appositive is a pronoun, use the same case for the pronoun as you do for the noun. If the noun is in the subjective case, the pronoun should also be in the subjective case. If the noun is in the objective case, the pronoun should also be in the objective case.

Appositive to the subject: The *winners* of the contest, *John and he*, received a trophy and a check.

Appositive to the direct object: We saw two *people, Nicole and her*, sitting in the empty train station.

Note: If a pronoun comes before a noun that renames or clarifies it (*we* students, *us* fathers), ignore the noun and put the pronoun in its proper case according to its use in the sentence.

Subject:	*We* ~~students~~ enjoy having Fridays free.
Indirect object:	The counselors gave *us* ~~students~~ another chance.

Practice Set 12–5

Directions: Circle the correct pronoun form in parentheses.

Example: The social worker mailed (they/(them)) and (we/(us)) some forms to complete.

1. His sister earned a higher grade on the English test than (he/him).

2. The neighbors and (we/us) are having a barbecue to celebrate Memorial Day.

3. The manager told James and (I/me) to come back the next day for a discount.

4. After Jenny and (she/her) arrived at the party, everyone started dancing.

5. Their friends do not ski as well as (they/them).

6. Between you and (I/me), studying every night helps a lot.

7. Please deliver the pizza to (she/her) and (he/him).

8. The winners of the contest are the Watsons and (we/us).

9. The doctor gave my brother and (I/me) a physical exam before camp.

10. The director offered a raise to two employees, Elsie and (he/him).

Pronouns Preceding Gerunds

Gerunds are verbals (words formed from verbs but acting as a different part of speech). They always end in *-ing*, and they always act as nouns. Although you often hear people incorrectly using objective case pronouns before gerunds, it is correct to use possessive case pronouns.

> **Incorrect:** The teacher resents *him* being late to class so often.

> **Correct:** The teacher resents *his* being late to class so often.

Try this one yourself:

> (I/me/my) studying every afternoon for three hours has certainly made this class easier.

The possessive *my* precedes the gerund *studying*.

> *My studying* every afternoon for three hours has certainly made this class easier.

Practice Set 12–6

Directions: Circle the correct pronoun form in parentheses.

> **Example:** I don't appreciate (him/his) following me home.

1. (They/Them/Their) turning back the clock confused everyone.

2. Can you believe (she/her) working overtime for so many days straight?

3. (I/Me/My) asking for a second helping of meatloaf pleased the chef.

4. The problem is (we/us/our) staying out too late during the week.

5. (You/Your) helping me find a job has been crucial to my success.

Who and *Whom*

Determine whether to use *who* or *whom* (and *whoever* and *whomever*) by its function in the sentence.

Who and *whoever* are subjective case.

Subject of the sentence: *Who* is coming to my party?

Subject of a clause: *Whoever* parks on the grass will get a ticket.

In this sentence, the entire noun clause *whoever parks on the grass* is the subject of the sentence, but that fact is not why we use *whoever*. *Whoever* is the **subject** of that noun clause, so we need a pronoun in the subjective case.

Whom and *whomever* are objective case.

Direct object: They interviewed *whomever* the board suggested.

In this sentence the noun clause *whomever the board suggested* is the direct object of the sentence, but this fact does not affect the choice of pronoun in the clause. *Board* is the subject of the clause, and *suggested* is the verb. The board suggested *whomever*, so *whomever* is the direct object within the noun clause. Since it is an object, the pronoun must be in the objective case.

Object of the preposition: The child for *whom* they have been searching has been found.

In this sentence *whom* is the object of the preposition *for*. Since it is an object, it must be in the objective case.

When a sentence contains a pronoun like *who* or *whom* within a dependent clause, isolate the clause and then determine how the pronoun functions within the clause itself. How the pronoun functions in the dependent clause determines the case. How the dependent clause functions in the sentence is *not* important and has no effect on the case of the pronoun within it.

dependent clause
The man *who wrote the book* is speaking tonight.

First isolate the clause from the rest of the sentence.

S   V   DO
who wrote the book

When you see the clause by itself, you can see that *who* is the subject of the clause, so the subjective case is correct. The dependent clause itself is used as an adjective to modify *man*, but this fact has no bearing on the case of the pronoun.

The man *whom he wrote about* is speaking tonight.

Isolate the dependent clause:

whom he wrote about

He is the subject of the clause; *wrote* is the verb. *About* is a preposition, and *whom* is its object. Since the pronoun is an object of the preposition, we use the objective case, *whom*.

QUICK TIP

A way to check for the correct case form of relative pronouns in questions is to answer the question with a personal pronoun. The case of your answer should be the same as the case of the relative pronoun.

> *Who* is in charge? *She* is in charge.

> *She* is in the subjective case, so *who* is correct.

> *Whom* did you see? I saw *him*.

> *Him* is in the objective case, so *whom* is correct.

QUICK TIP

In current American usage, many speakers have stopped using the pronoun *whom* altogether, but in formal speech and all writing, the case forms should be used correctly.

> **Formal usage:** The child whom she tutored received a college scholarship.

> **Informal usage:** The child she tutored received a college scholarship.

Practice Set 12–7

Directions: Circle the correct form of the pronoun in parentheses. If there is a subordinate clause in the sentence, make sure to isolate it before making your choice.

Examples: (Who)/Whom) is in charge here?

One of the clerks (who/whom) the judge had hired) left her position to work for a large law firm.

1. For (who/whom) did the officer write the ticket?

2. (Who/whom) did you see at the meeting?

3. (Who/Whom) did the judges choose as the winner of the annual essay contest?

4. Datacall allows counselors to talk to (whoever/whomever) needs them on campus.

5. Because the doors were locked, (whoever/whomever) was in the building couldn't leave.

6. According to Greek myth, the Sphinx devoured those (who/whom) could not answer her riddles.

7. The editor by (who/whom) they have been criticized is preparing a formal apology.

8. (Who/Whom) is responsible for emailing that computer virus to so many people?

9. I will vote for (whoever/whomever) promises to reduce taxes.

10. The defendant, (who/whom) seemed guilty, was freed for lack of evidence.

Other Relative Pronouns

Who, whom, whoever, and *whomever* fall into a larger category of pronouns called relative pronouns. Relative pronouns introduce adjective or noun clauses. Here are some rules about relative pronouns:

1. Some relative pronouns do not have case forms. *That, which,* and *what* are the same in the subjective and the objective case and do not have possessive forms.

   S   O

   What matters most is *what* you do.

2. *Who, whoever, whom, whomever,* and *whose* refer to people. *Which* refers to objects and animals. *That* is appropriate for people, animals, or objects.

   The plumber *who* fixed my sink works for my brother.

   The bank, *which* usually closes at noon, will remain open until six o'clock today.

   The dog *that* barked all night annoyed my neighbor.

Practice Set 12–8

Directions: Circle the correct form of the relative pronoun in parentheses.

Example: President John Kennedy, (who/which) was our youngest elected president, was known for his eloquent speech and keen sense of humor.

1. The raccoon (that/who /whom) lives in my yard comes out at night.

2. We discovered the hacker (who/whom/which) is responsible for the computer virus.

3. The electrician (who/which) wired the house did not have a license.

4. The girl (whom/which) we hired has worked for us before.

5. We caught the snake (who/that) was hiding in the garage.

Practice Set 12–9

Directions: Find and correct twelve pronoun errors in the following passage. The first sentence has already been corrected.

In 1958, the new National Aeronautics and Space Agency, NASA, named seven men
who
~~which~~ were to become instant American heroes: the Mercury Seven astronauts.

It's goal was to send a man into orbit around the earth and bring him back safely. Alan Shepherd, John Glenn, Scott Carpenter, Gus Grissom, Gordon Cooper, Wally Schirra, and Deke Slayton were all expert test pilots, and each was determined to prove himself worthy of being part of the team. Shepherd, an expert Navy pilot, was the first to fly, but him flying into outer space was a first only for the United States. Twenty-three days earlier, the Soviet Union had sent cosmonaut Yuri Gagarin into space, and it was him who was first.

Gus Grissom, the second American in space, flew a perfect mission but lost their space capsule when it sank during recovery. He did not receive the praise lavished on Alan Shepherd, whom had been first. Grissom perished several years later, along with astronauts Ed White and Roger Chaffee, while training for what was to be the first manned Apollo flight. Grissom and them were killed in a fire, believed to have been caused by a short circuit that ignited the pure oxygen atmosphere. Their's was not the only mission to end in tragedy, of course, and many critics questioned us sending people into space. Grissom hisself accepted the risk. Perhaps foretelling his own demise, he expressed his hope that the program would not be delayed because of any casualties.

Practice Set 12–10

Directions: Add an appropriate pronoun in the blanks below.

   Example: I couldn't decide ____whom____ to vote for.

1. A. J. and _____ have requested a hearing.

2. I have no idea _____ they wish to hire.

3. My father disapproves of _____ coming home past midnight.

4. _____ students must work together on the service learning project.

5. We carefully laid the blanket on top of _____.

6. Adam and Dana invited Scott and _____ to their wedding.

7. _____ wrote this letter has some explaining to do.

8. I can't understand _____ wasting your time.

9. There was no response from the applicant to _____ they sent the offer.

10. Megan gave her old toys to Owen and _____.

TEST YOURSELF

Directions: Circle the correct form of the pronoun in parentheses.

Example: I am delighted about (you/your) finding a new job.

1. The elephant (who/that) had a tracking device in its ear was easy to locate.
2. Coach Chapman warned (we/us) cyclists about the sharp rocks on the trail.
3. My friend and (she/her) will be coming to the graduation party.
4. The manager gave the new employee and (she/her) an excellent evaluation.
5. Everyone began arguing when Donald and (we/us) left the meeting.
6. My assistant is not as efficient as (I/me).
7. (He/Him/His) leaving town after the robbery certainly looks suspicious.
8. The committee will choose (whoever/whomever) will represent our college at the conference.
9. The counselor (who/whom) they contacted about the child's behavior problems offered helpful suggestions.
10. The engineer (who/whom/which) is a consultant on the drilling project once worked in Saudi Arabia.

WRITE NOW

Directions: Write an 8-10 sentence paragraph about a relationship you have with a friend or someone close to you. Include the following:

1. A sentence using compound personal pronouns as the subjects.
2. A sentence containing the pronoun *whom*.
3. A sentence containing a possessive pronoun before a gerund.
4. A sentence containing a pronoun used as an appositive.
5. A sentence with a prepositional phrase that contains a personal pronoun as the object of the preposition.

GrammarSpeak ⊢——————▶

In everyday speech, we have a tendency to use the incorrect pronoun case—especially in compound constructions. For example, we may think that the following sentence is correct: "It is more convenient for you and I to ride together." However, the *I* should be *me* after the preposition *for*.

Either with two partners or speaking all the parts yourself, practice the dialogue below between a project manager and her team of Neil and Emma so that you can become accustomed to hearing proper pronoun case usage.

PM: Just between you and me, I think this project will be a big success.

Neil: I appreciate your offering Emma and me this opportunity.

PM: I think that you and she will do a great job.

Emma: Neil said that you asked specifically for him and me.

Neil: Emma and I will ask Jacob and Anne to join the team.

Emma: Our best workers so far have been he and she.

WORD WATCHERS

The tone of your writing should depend on the assignment and the audience. Avoid overly formal or informal words and phrases.

amongst	This is the British way to say *among*. In American English, it sounds old fashioned and overly formal.
firstly, secondly	These are pretentious beginnings. They begin to sound even worse as the list progresses: *fourthly, fifthly, sixthly, seventhly*. Use *first, second, third*.
male, female	*Male* and *female* are too technical when used to refer to a man and a woman unless you are writing a scientific or technical work: The man and woman (not *male and female*) sat on the bench and watched the sun set.
laid-back	This is colloquial for *casual*. You should not use any slang in your writing because not everyone will understand it; also, slang changes over time, so your meaning may be unclear.
okay	This is colloquial for *all right* or *acceptable*. Do not use it in formal writing.
didn't/can't/wouldn't	Contractions are appropriate in informal writing, but they are out of place in formal essays.

Word Watchers Practice Set

Directions: Change the inappropriate word in bold print to one that better suits the tone or eliminates the slang.

1. Her **laid-back** attitude will get her in trouble with her boss.
2. As we arrived at the basketball court, we realized that several **males** had already started to play.
3. My girlfriend says that if she wins the lottery, she will divide the money **amongst** everyone at work.
4. I have several reasons for changing my mind. **Firstly**, the situation has changed.
5. You will have fifteen minutes to complete this portion of the test. Using a pencil rather than a pen is not **okay**.
6. Mario tried to explain his situation to the landlord, but the landlord just **dissed** him.
7. The **dude** in the yellow shirt is the pastor at my church.
8. The pharmacy is open **24/7**.
9. It was **my bad** that the letter was not sent in time.
10. It was **so not like him** to forget to call.

Agreement

When we talk about *agreement* in grammar, we are usually talking about making our subjects and verbs agree and making our pronouns and their antecedents—the words that they replace—agree. Many of the rules are the same for both areas of agreement, so looking at both areas together can make the rules a little easier to understand.

SUBJECT-VERB AGREEMENT

Subject-verb agreement means that the subject and the verb match in number. Singular subjects take singular verb forms, and plural subjects take plural verb forms.

The -*s* ending

Subject-verb agreement begins with an understanding of the -*s* ending. If you were asked, "How do you make a word plural?" you might be tempted to answer, "Add an *s*." While adding an *s* works for most nouns, it does not work for verbs. In fact, adding an *s* to a verb creates a singular form. Look at these two sentences:

Singular form: The dog *barks*.

Plural form: The dogs *bark*.

In the first sentence, the subject is singular and matches a singular verb form. Notice that only the verb ends in *s*. In the second sentence, the plural subject matches the plural verb form; note that the plural verb does *not* end in *s*. Generally, only one of the words ends in *s*, either the subject or the verb. However, there are some important exceptions to this rule. Sometimes a singular noun ends in *s*:

          S V

The *glass falls* on the floor.

Other times, plural nouns don't end in *s*: *children, women, sheep*. Then, neither the subject nor the verb ends in *s*.

          S V

The *children play* in the park.

QUICK TIP

Most agreement errors occur with third-person present tense verbs, so here is a rule to keep in mind: With third person present tense verbs, singular verbs always end in *s*.

Singular	**Plural**
She is	They are
He does	They do

Practice Set 13–1

Directions: Circle the correct verb in parentheses.

Example: The builder (thinks/think) that the project will take a week to complete.

1. I know that the dancers (competes/compete) this week.
2. The chicken soup (tastes/taste) really salty.
3. The baker (offers/offer) his customers free cupcakes on Tuesdays.
4. The commuter (rushes/rush) to catch the bus.
5. After the meeting, she (has/have) to meet him for lunch.
6. The two jackets (costs/cost) more than the two dresses.
7. Happiness (comes/come) in many forms.
8. Three salad plates (is/are) missing from the set.
9. She thinks the movie (lasts/last) until midnight.
10. This driver (goes/go) faster than he should on the rain-soaked highway.

Words Between the Subject and Verb

Words that come between the subject and the verb do not change subject-verb agreement.

The verb must always agree with the subject, no matter where the subject comes in the sentence. Pay particular attention to prepositional phrases. The subject of the sentence is never part of a prepositional phrase. To avoid confusion, cross out all prepositional phrases before you identify the subject.

The *basket* (of apples) *falls* (on the floor).

One (of the flashlights) *needs* new batteries.

Certain prepositions consist of more than one word. These can be especially confusing because they make the sentence sound as if it has a plural subject. These prepositions include *along with*, *as well as*, *in addition to*, and *together with*. Remember that these are not the same as *and*. Cross out these prepositional phrases as you would any prepositional phrase.

The *cat*, (~~along with the kittens~~), *sleeps* (~~by the fireplace~~) (~~in the den~~).

The *boat*, (~~in addition to the automobiles~~), *requires* insurance.

In fact, no intervening words, phrases, or clauses change subject-verb agreement.

subordinate clause

My *mother*, (~~who loves to give instructions~~), *is* usually right.

verbal phrase

The *train* (~~carrying the secret documents~~) *is* late.

appositive

Sophia Ramirez, (~~the treasurer and parliamentarian~~), *enjoys* attending club activities.

Practice Set 13–2

Directions: Put a line through any prepositional phrases, subordinate clauses, verbal phrases, or appositives that come between the subject and the verb. Then circle the correct verb in parentheses.

Examples: The paintings ~~on that wall~~ (costs, (cost)) millions.

His house~~, as well as his car,~~ ((was), were) damaged in the flood.

Babe Ruth, ~~who played for several baseball teams,~~ ((is)/are) most known for his years as a New York Yankee.

The nurse ~~helping the surgeons~~ ((makes)/make) many of the decisions regarding my care.

Quentin Tarantino~~, the famous writer and director,~~ ((has won), have won) two Oscars.

1. These recipes, which all come from this cookbook, (uses/use) no flour or sugar.

2. The flights over the Grand Canyon (takes/take) about an hour.

3. Penn and Teller, the illusionists with a comic twist, frequently (performs/ perform) in Las Vegas.

4. Construction workers completing the Crosstown Expressway (makes/make) overtime when they work on the weekend.

5. My coupon, along with your employee discounts, (saves/save) us about $25.00.

6. Our new CEO, who had dinner with four managers last week, (is/are) trying to get to know his employees.

7. The police officers working the parade (tries/try) hard to keep the crowds under control.

8. Tony Dungy, former head coach of the Tampa Bay Buccaneers and the Indianapolis Colts, (explains/explain) his philosophy of life in his book *Quiet Strength: The Principles, Practices, and Priorities of a Winning Life.*

9. The cost of two tickets from New York to Chicago (changes/change) from day to day.

10. A strong marketing plan, in addition to a dedicated sales force, (means/mean) the difference between success and failure.

Compound Subjects

Compound subjects that are joined by and are usually plural.

> S   V
> *Francie and Murray* ski in Colorado in the winter.

> S   V
> *Honesty and integrity* work together to build character.

Practice Set 13–3

Directions: Underline the compound subjects and circle the correct verb in parentheses.

Example: His wavy hair and his charm with the ladies (makes/make) him the perfect choice.

1. The governor's humble beginnings and his experience in the corporate world (enables/enable) him to understand the problem.

2. Northern Florida and Southern Georgia (shares/share) many common attributes.

3. A change in the weather and the delay of our flight (has made/have made) our trip to the Grand Canyon impossible.

4. Your supervisor and my department head (is/are) both planning to skip the meeting.

5. Life and its burdens sometimes (gets/get) me down.

Exceptions to the Compound Rules

Some compounds joined by *and* appear plural but really refer to a single unit, like *ham and cheese* or *president and chief executive officer*. These compounds are singular.

>   S   V
> My *best friend and traveling companion is* Elizabeth.

>   S   V
> *Macaroni and cheese goes* well with hot dogs.

When *each* or *every* appears before a compound subject, the sentence takes a singular verb form.

> S   V
> *Each test score and lab report counts* toward the grade in the course.

> S   V
> *Every man, woman, and child participates* in the lifeboat drill.

When *each* follows a compound subject, the subject takes a plural verb form.

S   V

*Robin and Jeffrey **each** want to go on a cruise.*

Sometimes a compound subject is joined by *either/or, neither/nor, not only/but also* or by *or* or *nor*. In this case, the verb agrees with the subject nearer to it.

nearer subject verb

***Either** Katherine **or** Don plays* tennis for the college team.

nearer subject   verb

*Buses, vans, **or** limos transport* the hotel guests to the airport.

nearer subject verb

***Neither** Tien **nor** her sisters attend* school at night.

QUICK TIP

When using singular and plural subjects together, try to place the plural subject closer to the verb.

nearer subject verb

Awkward: *Neither the kittens nor the cat sleeps* on the bed.

The verb of this sentence, *sleeps*, agrees with *cat*, the subject nearer to it, but placing the singular subject second is awkward.

nearer subject   verb

Better: *Neither the cat nor the kittens sleep* on the bed.

Practice Set 13–4

Directions: Circle the correct verb in parentheses.

Examples: Either Brianna or her brothers (sells /(sell)) hot dogs at the ballpark.

Every brush and comb ((has been)/have been) sterilized before use.

1. Each representative and senator (has/have) agreed to participate in the program.

2. His only companion and friend (has been/have been) his golden retriever, Max.

3. Every dish, bowl, and glass (needs/need) to be washed carefully.

4. Neither the printer nor the computers (works/work) properly.

5. Louisa and Natalia each (wants/want) to leave for New York this evening.

6. Lemonade, iced tea, or apple juice (tastes/taste) good on a hot summer day.

7. Not only the newspaper but also the radio bulletin (warns/warn) of the approaching hurricane.

8. Spaghetti and meatballs (appears/appear) on the menu in most Italian restaurants.

9. Each car seat, stroller, and high chair (was/were) carefully tested for safety.

10. Both Elvis Presley and John Lennon (is/are) still mourned by millions of music fans.

Indefinite Pronouns

Indefinite pronouns are those that do not refer to specific persons, places, or things. They can be singular or plural. Because some are singular and some are plural, writers often make agreement errors using them. To help in this area, study the following chart closely.

Always Singular	Always Plural	Singular or Plural
one, each, another	both	some
either, neither	few	none
everyone, everybody, everything	several	any
someone, somebody, something	many	all
anyone, anybody, anything		more
no one, nobody, nothing		most

Singular Indefinite Pronouns

The pronouns that are always singular include words that end in *-one*, *-body*, and *-thing*: *anyone, anybody, anything, someone, somebody, something, no one, nobody, nothing*.

       S   V

Anybody has the option to retake the quiz.

The pronouns that are always singular also include *each, either, neither, another, one*.

       S   V

Neither wants to cook dinner this evening.

QUICK TIP

Remember to ignore prepositional phrases that come between the subject and the verb:

          S   V

    Neither (of the roommates) *wants* to cook dinner this evening.

The subject of the sentence is neither, not roommates. Neither is always singular, so the verb must match.

Plural Indefinite Pronouns

Pronouns that are always plural include *both*, *few*, *several*, and *many*.

> S   V   S   V
> *Many are* called, but *few are* chosen.

Indefinite Pronouns that Are Singular or Plural

Some indefinite pronouns can be singular or plural, depending on how they are used in the sentence. These pronouns include *all*, *any*, *more*, *most*, *none*, and *some*. The verb agrees with the antecedent, which is usually the object of the preposition in the phrase that follows the pronoun.

> S   V
> *All* of the wine *is* chilled.

(In this sentence, *All* refers to the singular object of the preposition, *wine*.)

> S   V
> *All* of the hamburgers *are* hot.

(In this sentence, *All* refers to the plural object of the preposition, *hamburgers*.)

Practice Set 13–5

Directions: Circle the correct verb in parentheses.

> **Example:** Many of the animals (was/were) evacuated during the hurricane.

1. Some of the high-tech sound systems (confuses/confuse) the average buyer.

2. Each of the accused students (pleads/plead) individually before the council.

3. Anyone under the age or height limits (is/are) not permitted to enter the ride.

4. In the event that nobody (shows/show) up, we will cancel the meeting.

5. Most of the water (has/have) evaporated.

6. Everyone carrying packages (walks/walk) through a metal detector.

7. None of the stores (was/were) open before 10 AM.

8. When something breaks at home, no one ever (takes/take) the blame.

9. One of the student nurses (attends/attend) the conference in Seattle each year.

10. Because everyone (has/have) to prove citizenship, no one (is/are) exempt from submitting a passport.

Collective Nouns

A **collective noun** names a group of people or animals; words like *team*, *faculty*, *class*, *band*, *committee*, *jury*, *audience*, *herd*, *flock*, and *council* are collective nouns. Collective nouns are usually singular because the members of the group are acting as a single unit.

> S   V
> The *committee votes* on the issue tomorrow

S   V
The *flock* of geese *flies* south for the winter.

QUICK TIP

Sometimes the sentence suggests that the members of the group are acting sepa-
rately as individuals rather than together as a unit. In such a case, a plural verb form
is correct. However, using a collective noun in this way usually sounds awkward. Try
recasting these awkward sentences, using a plural subject:

S   V
Awkward: The *audience were rattling* their programs.

S   V
Better: The *members* of the audience *were rattling* their programs.

Practice Set 13–6

Directions: Circle the correct verb in parentheses.

Example: The city council (appoints / appoint) the mayor.

1. The jury (meets/meet) in the room to the right of Courtroom A.

2. The class (leaves/leave) when the bell rings.

3. A herd of cattle (crosses/cross) the highway in the blinding snowstorm.

4. I want to be present when the band (practices/practice) the song I wrote.

5. Our team never (loses/lose) at home.

Word Order Variations

Variations in word order do not change subject/verb agreement.

In most sentences in English, the subject comes before the verb:

S   V
The *winner* of this prize *is* lucky.

S   V
During intermission, the *parents buy* a drink and a snack.

In sentences in which the verb comes before the subject, the standard rules of
agreement remain the same. Word order does not change agreement.

There is/There are Constructions

Word order changes in sentences beginning with *there is* or *there are*. In the following sentences, *there* is not the subject of the sentence.

V   S
There *is* no *excuse* for your behavior.

V   S
There *are differences* of opinion within this group.

Questions Change Sentence Word Order

To find the subject and verb in a question, try turning the question into a statement.

V S   S V
Is he a freshman? *He is* a freshman.

V ⌐—— S ——⌐   ⌐—— S ——⌐ V
Are Alexis and Roberto seniors? *Alexis and Roberto are* seniors.

Practice Set 13–7

Directions: Underline the simple subject(s); then circle the correct verb in parentheses.

Examples: (Does/**Do**) Main Street and Grand Avenue intersect at the light?

There (was/**were**) no problems with the new instructions.

1. When (has/have) your neighbors decided to move?

2. Although the actor won many awards, there (is/are) several movies in which he took a minor role.

3. How (does/do) this cleaner work on delicate fabrics?

4. There (seems/seem) to be no end to his extraordinary talents.

5. (Is/Are) the designs of the house ready for approval?

6. Why (has/have) the producer of those plays quit?

7. Where (does/do) Sierra and Nassim plan to live after the wedding?

8. There (is/are) no peanuts left in the bag.

9. What (does/do) George Eliot and George Sand have in common?

10. There (is/are) a coaches' meeting taking place on the second floor.

Linking Verbs and Subject Complements

The Subject/Linking Verb/Subject Complement sentence pattern can pose a problem. Sometimes the subject is singular and the subject complement is plural, or vice versa, but the rule is always the same:

Linking verbs agree with the subject, not the subject complement.

Consider this sentence:

          S   V   SC
The funniest *part* of the play *was the mistakes.*

Some writers may be tempted to use a plural verb form to agree with the plural word *mistakes*. However, *mistakes* is not the subject; *part* is. Because the verb must agree with *part*, the singular verb form is correct.

Practice Set 13–8

Directions: Circle the correct verb in parentheses and underline the subject.

Example: Her only <u>excuse</u> (is/are) her time management issues.

1. His only responsibility (is/are) his two part-time jobs.
2. Porcelain dolls (is/are) my favorite collectible.
3. The reason for her laughter (was/were) his silly jokes.
4. A bandage and a kiss (is/are) the cure for this skinned knee.
5. The most important clue in the mystery (is/are) the fingerprints.
6. The response to the reports (was/were) a dozen phone calls.
7. The problem (seems/seem) to be the many spelling errors in the report.
8. Her only source of income (is/are) her two part-time jobs.
9. The cause of this erosion (seems/seem) to be the many storms we have had this year.
10. High salaries (is/are) not a cure for an unhappy workforce.

Words that Appear Plural but Are Really Singular

Titles, diseases, amounts, words used as words, and gerund phrases are singular.

Many titles of works of art such as books, poems, movies, television shows, paintings, and songs contain plural parts, but they are singular.

     S   V
Friends often *takes* place in a coffeehouse in New York.

      S   V
Sunflowers is a famous painting by Van Gogh.

Although the names of diseases often end in s, they are singular.

     S   V
Measles is a dangerous disease for pregnant women.

     S   V
AIDS touches the lives of people worldwide.

Amounts of time, weight, money, and distance are usually singular.

        S   V
Ten dollars is too much to pay for a hamburger.

S ⎯⎯⎯ V
Twenty-six miles makes a marathon.

Words or phrases used as words are always singular.
Possessions contains two sets of double letters.

⎯⎯⎯ S ⎯⎯⎯ V
"Politics makes strange bedfellows" is certainly true.

Gerunds used as subjects are singular, even though the phrase itself may contain plural words.

⎯⎯ S ⎯⎯ V
Finding my own errors was hard.

⎯⎯ S ⎯⎯ V
Pursuing your dreams takes diligence.

Many single objects that have two parts, such as trousers, scissors, tweezers, jeans, eyeglasses, and pliers, are plural.

S V
My *jeans are* too tight.

S V
The *pliers grasp* the nut easily.

The Number and A Number

The phrase *the number* is singular. The phrase *a number* is plural.

⎯⎯ S ⎯⎯ V
The number of letters to answer seems overwhelming.

A number of people have already left for the convention.

Directions: Circle the correct verb in parentheses.

Example: The clippers (needs/*need*) to be sharpened.

1. A number of mistakes (appears/appear) in the treasurer's report.

2. Watching late-night movies on television (makes/make) me sleepy.

3. His pants (is/are) so long that he keeps tripping on them.

4. Diabetes often (causes/cause) vision problems in older adults.

5. Six weeks (was/were) a long time to be away from home.

6. Keeping the files in order (requires/require) careful attention to detail.

7. Fifty dollars (seems/seem) to be what everyone is donating to the memorial fund.

8. *Cats* (is/are) a modern stage musical based on the poetry of T.S. Eliot.

9. The scissors (was/were) so dull that they hardly cut paper.

10. "Time heals all wounds" (does/do) not always prove true.

Practice Set 13–10

Directions: Check your understanding of all of the subject-verb agreement rules by circling the correct verb in parentheses.

Example: Each of the hockey players ((scores)/score) in the first period.

1. Lance's major writing problem (was/were) sentence fragments.

2. There (is/are) a clarinet and a saxophone on sale at the music store at the mall.

3. Our family (celebrates/celebrate) holidays together several times a year.

4. The piano, in addition to the dining room table and chairs, (comes/come) from my grandparents' house.

5. Every computer and copy machine in the office (needs/need) to be replaced.

6. Either coffee, tea, or milk (is/are) served with breakfast.

7. Everybody in the neighborhood (brings/bring) a covered dish to the annual block party.

8. Some of the cookies (contains/contain) chocolate chips and walnuts.

9. Knitting children's sweaters (has/have) become Sonia's favorite leisure activity.

10. Bacon and eggs (appears/appear) on the breakfast menu at most restaurants.

PRONOUN-ANTECEDENT AGREEMENT

Now that you have learned the rules for subject/verb agreement, **pronoun-antecedent agreement** should not be difficult. Use the same rules to take the agreement process one step further.

An antecedent is the word that a pronoun stands for. Consider the following sentences:

Jim cut *his* finger, and *he* had to get stitches.

Because the roof was leaking, the homeowner had to repair *it*.

In the first sentence, the pronouns *his* and *he* stand for the noun *Jim*, the antecedent. In the second sentence, the pronoun *it* stands for the antecedent *roof*.

Although the possessives *my, our, your, his, her, its,* and *their* function as adjectives, they are also personal pronouns and must have antecedents. Look at the following sentence.

The dog wagged *its* tail.

Its stands for the noun *dog*, the antecedent.

Practice Set 13–11

Directions: In the following sentences, underline the pronouns and draw an arrow to their antecedents.

Example: President Lincoln was born in Kentucky, but he grew up in Illinois.

1. Janice felt herself blush with embarrassment.

2. The angry citizens voiced their opinions loudly at the city council meeting.

3. Eric testified that the wet conditions had contributed to his accident.

4. Mr. Fuentes himself gave the welcome address.

5. Shannon left work early, but she didn't go straight home.

6. The old building has maintained its grand appearance over the years.

7. Laya sat on her bed, and she opened the letter.

8. When Mr. Donovan arrived at the airport, he realized that he had forgotten his suitcase.

9. The program allows the directors to reward themselves for their hard work.

10. The old woman realized that she needed to hang up her keys.

Pronouns and Antecedents

The most basic rule of pronoun/antecedent agreement is that the pronoun always agrees with its antecedent in number.

Therefore, a singular pronoun refers to a singular antecedent, and a plural pronoun refers to a plural antecedent.

	Singular Forms	Plural Forms
First Person	I, me, my, mine, myself	we, us, our, ours, ourselves
Second Person	you, your, yours, yourself	you, your, yours, yourselves
Third Person	he, him, his, himself, she, her, hers, herself, it, its, itself	they, them, their, theirs, themselves

Practice Set 13–12

Directions: In the blanks, write the appropriate pronoun from the chart above. Make sure that all pronouns agree with their antecedents.

Example: Please return the jewelry to _____its_____ former location.

1. Dana and Jonathan need to return many of _____ duplicate wedding gifts.

2. Jasmine wants another chance to correct _____ research paper.

3. They prefer to return all the phone calls _____.

4. The boy _____ is responsible for the trouble he has caused.

5. Ann and Ron put the new puppy in _____ cage for the night.

6. Javier insisted that the mistake was not _____.

7. Emma knew that _____ needed to end the relationship.

8. The mahogany chest was restored to _____ original beauty.

9. I gave _____ a pat on the back.

10. I try to give the children whatever _____ need.

Indefinite Pronouns

Because indefinite pronouns are nonspecific, writers often make agreement errors when using them. When an indefinite pronoun is the antecedent, you must first decide if it is singular or plural and then match the pronoun form accordingly. You should ignore any prepositional phrases following indefinite pronouns that are always singular or always plural. Look at these sentences:

Incorrect: *Neither* ~~(of the boys)~~ passed *their* test.

Correct: *Neither* ~~(of the boys)~~ passed *his* test.

The singular *his* refers to the singular indefinite pronoun *neither. Boys* is not the antecedent because it is part of the prepositional phrase *of the boys.* Using the plural *their* with the singular antecedent *neither* creates an agreement error.

Consider this sentence, making sure to ignore the prepositional phrase following the singular indefinite pronoun *each:*

Each of the buildings has (*its/their*) own entrance.

Buildings cannot be the antecedent because it is part of the prepositional phrase *of the buildings.* The antecedent is the pronoun *each,* which is always singular and must take the singular *its.*

Each of the buildings has *its* own entrance.

The plural indefinite pronouns cause few problems. They sound plural and are rarely misused.

Several of the employees brought *their* children with *them* to work.

The antecedent *several* is a plural pronoun and so takes the plural pronouns *their* and *them.*

With the third group of indefinite pronouns, those that can be singular or plural, usage is more complex. Finding the antecedent for this third group contradicts the rules just discussed. Because these indefinite pronouns can be singular or plural, you must look at the rest of the sentence for a clue to determine number. This clue usually comes in the prepositional phrase that follows the indefinite pronoun.

Some of the brownies had nuts in *them.*

Some refers to the plural noun *brownies,* so use the plural pronoun *them.*

Some of the cake had nuts in *it.*

Some refers to the singular noun *cake,* so use the singular pronoun *it.*

Practice Set 13–13

Directions: Write the correct pronoun in the blank. Underline its antecedent.

Example: <u>Neither</u> of the horses was in _____*its*_____ stall.

1. Each of the mothers meets _____ children at the bus stop.

2. Many of the flowers are still in _____ original plastic containers.

3. One of the boys left _____ backpack in my car.

4. Either of the women can present _____ case to the board of directors.

5. None of the furniture is in _____ proper place.

6. None of the chairs are in _____ correct locations.

7. All of the lizards have spots on _____ tails.

8. Most of the farmland is valued for _____ fertile soil.

9. Both of the drinks had ice in _____ .

10. Some of the dancers left _____ costumes in the dressing room.

Sexist Language

Writers should avoid using sexist language, but sometimes this effort can cause pronoun agreement errors. Masculine pronouns (*he, him, his, himself*) were once referred to as gender-neutral pronouns, that is, pronouns that could replace nouns that are masculine or feminine, such as *student, doctor,* or *athlete.* Today, however, most writers choose expressions that do not discriminate.

Sexist: *Every* student should bring *his* textbook to class.

To avoid sexist writing, use plural forms when possible.

Nonsexist: *Students* should bring *their* textbooks to class.

Another option is to rephrase the sentence to avoid using a pronoun.

Nonsexist: Every student should bring *the required textbook* to class.

Some writers use the inclusive forms of *he or she, him or her, his or her,* and *himself or herself* to refer to nouns that can be masculine or feminine.

Every student should bring *his or her* textbook to class.

This practice is easy to apply to single sentences, but when you are writing a long passage, the dual forms become repetitive. Therefore, choosing other methods of revision is preferable.

Practice Set 13–14

Directions: Rewrite the following sentences, eliminating sexist language.

Example: A doctor usually has many loans to repay after he finishes medical school.

Doctors usually have many loans to repay after they finish medical school.

OR

A doctor usually has many loans to repay after finishing medical school.

1. A police officer often risks his life to protect people in his community.

2. Everyone is responsible for submitting his own tax return to the government.

3. An attorney must be honest, detail-oriented, and flexible in his dealings with clients.

4. A good nurse gives her patients comfort as well as medication.

5. Nobody appreciates what he has until he loses it.

Compound Antecedents

Compound antecedents are usually plural and, thus, take plural pronouns.

The *child and the babysitter* have returned from *their* trip to the zoo.

There are some exceptions to this rule.

1. If the compound is a unit, refer to it by a singular pronoun.

   My *sister and closest friend is* on *her* way to see me.

2. If the compound nouns are preceded by the words *each* or *every*, use a singular pronoun.

   Each cat and dog receives its annual license tag from the city.

3. If the compounds are joined by the correlative conjunctions *either/or, neither/ nor, not only/but also* or the coordinating conjunctions *or* or *nor,* the pronoun selected refers to the antecedent closer to it.

   Neither the manager nor the *salesclerks* have received *their* Christmas bonus.

   Not only the elephant but also the *gorilla* is becoming extinct in *its* natural habitat.

QUICK TIP

This rule can be especially confusing when both subjects are singular but one is masculine and the other feminine. The sentence below follows the rule:

> Neither Mark nor his girlfriend likes her apartment.

However, this sentence would refer to the girlfriend's apartment, not an apartment that they share. If this is not the intent, you must recast the sentence, eliminating the need for a pronoun:

> Neither Mark nor his girlfriend likes the apartment they share.

Collective Nouns

Collective nouns are usually considered singular and take the singular pronouns *it* and *its*.

The championship basketball *team* lost *its* final game of the regional play-offs.

If a collective noun antecedent is plural because each member of the group is acting individually, refer to it with a plural pronoun.

The *class are* busily reviewing *their* old tests for the final exam.

Because these sentences are quite awkward, though, you should try to rephrase them.

The class *members are* busily reviewing *their* old tests for the final exam.

Practice Set 13–15

Directions: Write the correct pronoun form in the blanks.

> **Example:** Either the grocery store or the pharmacy will delay _____*its*_____ opening.

1. Each girl scout and troop leader must bring _____ sleeping bag to the campout.

2. The cast of the play presented long-stemmed roses to _____ director.

3. Ross and Kendra are studying for _____ comprehensive nursing exams.

4. The leftover spaghetti and meatballs is still in _____ container in the refrigerator.

5. Neither the paper nor the pencils can be found in _____ usual spot.

6. The two families are trying _____ best to get along with each other.

7. Not only the boss but also the employees hated _____ new salary schedule.

8. Every car and truck has _____ license plate in full view.

9. The jury gave _____ decision to the judge.

10. The president and CEO of the company were rewarded for _____ community service.

Practice Set 13-16

Directions: Rewrite the following sentences, using all plural subjects, verbs, and pronouns.

Example: His project is due after he submits his outline.

Their projects are due after they submit their outlines.

1. My brother is arriving at our condo at noon.

2. His life was a mystery.

3. Lunch comes with a drink and dessert.

4. A noisy alarm annoys me in the morning.

5. Everybody wants his or her life to be perfect.

Directions: Rewrite the following sentences, using all singular subjects, verbs, and pronouns.

Example: The medications have passed their expiration date.

The medication has passed its expiration date.

1. Their nephews are adorable.

2. The cadets salute during their initiation.

3. Those questions on the exam have no clear answers.

4. All children need their parents' supervision.

5. The chefs themselves serve the meals.

TEST YOURSELF

Directions: Circle the correct verbs and pronouns in parentheses.

Example: Not one answer in the answer keys (is/are) correct.

Each of the performers (wears/wear) (her/their) own gown to the recital.

1. Your excuse for your three tardies (is/are) unacceptable.

2. There (was/were) thousands of people who would have loved to be in your place.

3. Twelve miles (seems/seem) like a long way to travel to see a movie.

4. Either your attitude or your place of employment (changes/change) today.

5. Everyone in this class (expects/expect) to complete (his or her/their) homework.

6. Neither of the sisters (wants/want) (her/their) boyfriend to propose.

7. Mumps in young children (is/are) highly contagious.

8. A number of cubs in the litter (has/have) opened (its/their) eyes.

9. Her salary, as well as her bonuses, (makes/make) her rich.

10. (Is/Are) there anyone who can add two plus two correctly?

11. All of the files (appears/appear) to be in (its/their) proper folders.

12. *The Red Shoes* (is/are) a movie about ballet.

13. Every registered man and woman (has/have) the right to have (his or her/their) vote counted.

14. The number of questions (has/have) increased this year.

15. The worst part of those meetings (was/were) the speeches.

16. Arriving on time for the games (shows/show) your interest.

17. The professor, in addition to the deans, (tells/tell) the students to wait (his or her/their) turn.

18. (Has/Have) the mechanics included the estimates on (his/their) invoices?

19. One of the men (has/have) taken (his /their) daughter to lunch.

20. Neither the lasagna nor the meatballs (is/are) served in (its/their) own containers.

WRITE NOW

Directions: Using all singular subjects and verbs, write a 5–6 sentence paragraph on one of the following topics:

1. Finding a job

2. Raising a child

3. Surfing the Internet

Then rewrite the same paragraph, making all of your subjects and verbs plural.

GrammarSpeak ⟼＞

As a result of widespread usage, some people use the third-person plural pronouns (*they, them, their, theirs, themselves*) to refer to some singular indefinite pronouns (*everyone, everybody, someone, somebody, each, one*). This problem occurs most often when speakers use *their* with a singular antecedent. This usage, acceptable in informal speech, is still considered improper in all written English and formal speech.

Informal speech:	*Everyone* has the right to *their* own opinions.
All writing and formal speech:	*Everyone* has the right to *his or her* own opinions.
	OR
	People have the right to *their* own opinions.

You might hear sentences similar to those below in everyday speech. Correct them and practice saying the corrections aloud several times. Hearing yourself say them will help you break old habits and make you more aware of the correct forms.

Instead of:	**Say:**
Everybody should proofread their paper carefully.	Everybody should proofread his or her paper carefully.
	OR
	Writers should proofread their papers carefully.
Somebody left their backpack on the bus.	Somebody left his or her backpack on the bus.
	OR
	Somebody left a backpack on the bus.
Each person performs according to their own abilities.	Each person performs according to his or her own abilities.
	OR
	People perform according to their own abilities.
Everybody marches to their own drummer.	Everybody marches to his or her own drummer.
	OR
	Everybody marches to a different drummer.
One of the band members forgot their music.	One of the band members forgot his or her music.
	OR
	One of the band members forgot the music.

WORD WATCHERS

Some words and phrases seem interchangeable, but they really are not because of the rules of grammar.

bad/badly

Bad is an adjective; *badly* is an adverb. Use *badly* to modify verbs: He sings badly.

Use *bad* to modify nouns: He is a bad singer.

Use *bad* as a subject complement: He smells bad. Do not use *bad* as an adverb (as in *He sings bad*), and do not use *badly* as a subject complement (as in *I feel badly*).

different from/different than

Different from is nearly always the correct choice. *From* is a preposition. It is followed by a noun: Baseball is different from softball.

Than is a subordinating conjunction, so it introduces a clause: Movies are different now than they used to be. It is incorrect to use *different than* before a noun (as in *Baseball is different than softball*).

is when/is where/is because

These constructions are always incorrect. *Is* is a linking verb, so it must be followed by a subject complement—a noun, pronoun, or an adjective. *When, where,* and *because* introduce adverb clauses. Recast sentences to eliminate *is when, is where,* or *is because*. (*We leave on Saturday*, not *Saturday is when we leave*.)

like/as

Like is a preposition. It is followed by a noun: She looks like her mother.

As is a subordinating conjunction. It introduces a clause: I behaved as I should have.

real/really and **sure/surely**

Real and *sure* are adjectives. Use them before nouns: This is a real diamond. My bet is a sure thing.

Really and *surely* are adverbs. Use them to modify adjectives: I am really (not *real*) pleased with my new truck. He is surely sorry about forgetting her birthday.

try to/try and/ sure to/sure and

The *to* in *try to* and *sure to* is part of an infinitive: Try to behave yourself. Be sure to call me. It is incorrect to substitute *and* for *to* (as in *Try and behave yourself* or *Be sure and call me*).

good/well

Good is an adjective, so it modifies a noun: He is a good typist.

Well is an adverb, so it modifies a verb, adjective, or adverb: He types well. It is incorrect to say, "He types good." Both can fill the subject complement position because *well* can also be an adjective meaning *healthy*. *He feels good* means he feels happy. *He feels well* means he feels healthy.

Word Watchers Practice Set

Directions: Circle the correct word in parentheses.

Example: He was (really/real) disruptive during the meeting.

1. These directions are (different from/different than) the ones on page 26.
2. Gracie plays golf as (good/well) as a pro.
3. You were late yesterday, so try (and/to) arrive on time tomorrow.
4. I really feel (bad/badly) about losing that check.
5. Love me (like/as) I love you.
6. I banged my head so (bad/badly) that I have had a headache for a week.
7. If they continue to foul the other team, they will (sure/surely) lose the game.
8. I will not go out with him because he always acts (like/as) a fool in public.
9. Zack doesn't dance very (good/well), but he is always happy to try.
10. Be sure (and/to) close the door on your way out.

Modifier Usage

Modifiers are adjectives and adverbs—including single words, phrases, or clauses—that describe another word or group of words. Modifier placement can affect the meaning of a sentence.

LIMITING MODIFIERS

Place limiting modifiers—words like just, almost, even, hardly, only, merely, nearly, simply, scarcely, and exactly—next to the words they limit.

Look at the following sentence:

Jack said that he believed me.

Now add the modifier *only*. Notice how its placement affects the meaning.

Only Jack said that he believed me.

(No one but *Jack* said it.)

Jack *only* said that he believed me.

(Jack didn't mean it. He only *said* it.)

Jack said that *only* he believed me.

(Jack said that Miguel and Mary didn't believe me. Only *he* believed me.)

Jack said that he believed *only* me.

(Jack didn't believe Miguel or Mary. He believed only *me*.)

Careless writers frequently misplace single-word modifiers that modify amounts:

Improper placement: This car *just* costs $5,000.

What word does *just* modify? Placing just before the verb *costs* is wrong because it's not the verb that is being modified. The *amount* is being modified. This car costs $5,000, not $10,000.

Revision: This car costs *just* $5,000.

Improper placement: I *only* ran three miles today.

What word does *only* modify? I ran three miles, not five miles.

Revision: I ran *only* three miles today.

Practice Set 14–1

Directions: Move misplaced modifiers in front of the words that they limit. More than one placement may be correct.

Example: We only sold four units today.

1. They couldn't even stop fighting for five minutes.
2. She nearly paid $10,000 for that used car.
3. The scouts almost sold all of the cookies in one day.
4. Marcello plays three instruments, but Francesca just plays the flute.
5. The new owners nearly laid off everyone in the company.
6. Tonight's play only has two acts and an intermission.
7. Finn hardly takes any of the advice I give him.
8. He scarcely completed half of the essay before he turned it in.
9. The committee exactly adjourned at noon.
10. She has not even given one excuse for the delay in the project.

MODIFIER PLACEMENT

Place single-word modifiers, modifying phrases, and modifying clauses in positions that clearly indicate what they modify, usually next to or very near the word they modify.

Improper placement can cause some funny misreadings.

Improper placement: She destroyed the photographs of men that she had dated *at her new husband's request.*

Did she date the men at her new husband's request? No, she destroyed the photographs at her new husband's request. Revise the sentence by putting the adverb phrase next to what it modifies.

Revision: *At her new husband's request*, she destroyed the photographs of men that she had dated.

Improper placement: The Christmas lights were lovely to Janna, *hanging from the tree.*

Was Janna hanging from the tree? No, the Christmas lights were hanging from the tree. Revise the sentence by putting the adjective phrase next to what it modifies.

Revision: To Janna, the Christmas lights *hanging from the tree* were lovely.

Improper placement: We all admired the room for the baby *that Matt had painted.*

Did Matt paint the baby? No, he painted the room.

Revision: We all admired the room *that Matt had painted* for the baby.

Practice Set 14–2

Directions: Revise the following sentences, putting modifiers in the proper place. Indicate proper placement by underlining the misplaced modifiers and drawing an arrow to their proper location.

Example: She could see the people in the next apartment with her binoculars.

1. Mikela was thrilled when Foster gave her the gift-wrapped box with a shy smile.

2. He lowered his voice so that my brother wouldn't hear him intentionally.

3. We tasted the dish that he had prepared for the judges with saffron and curry.

4. I downloaded an app that shows me where I parked my car on my smart phone.

5. We served spaghetti squash to all of the guests topped with parmesan cheese.

6. The snow turned to ice as it covered the road that had melted in the sun.

7. She left the note telling of her whereabouts for her roommate pinned to the bulletin board.

8. I gently placed the kitten in my son's arms that had been meowing all night.

9. Marnie gave the bicycle to her neighbor's child that her kids had outgrown.

10. There is a sweater on the counter with two holes in the sleeve.

SQUINTING MODIFIERS

Do not place a modifier in an unclear or confusing position. These types of modifiers are called **squinting modifiers**. Squinting modifiers appear between two words and can modify either one. Consider this sentence:

Squinting modifier: Dining out frequently is expensive.

Does the sentence mean that it is frequently expensive to dine out, or does it mean that it is expensive to dine out frequently? Since either meaning applies, the modifier is not well placed.

Revision: Dining out is frequently expensive.

OR

It is expensive to dine out frequently.

Practice Set 14–3

Directions: Revise the following sentences in two ways, eliminating squinting modifiers. Indicate proper placement by underlining the misplaced modifiers and drawing an arrow to their proper location.

Example: Lucy said on Sunday we will go on a picnic.

On Sunday, Lucy said we will go on a picnic.

OR

Lucy said we will go on a picnic on Sunday.

1. Answering his questions clearly will get you off the hook.

2. Marching in place quickly makes me tired.

3. He said yesterday he was offered a new position with the company.

4. A letter to the editor I wrote once was printed in the local newspaper.

5. Angelica believed eventually life would get easier.

6. The fans thought throughout the game the pitching could have been stronger.

7. Repainting the house often makes it look more appealing.

8. I told my roommate when class was over I would give her a ride home.

9. What you wish for often will come true.

10. Turning suddenly made me dizzy.

AWKWARD SPLITS

If possible, avoid putting modifiers in positions that awkwardly separate important sentence parts.

Place subjects as close as possible to verbs.

                               S   **V**

Awkward separation: *Trey*, before he met his wife, *was* in the navy.

Revision: Before he met his wife, *Trey was* in the navy.

OR

Trey was in the navy before he met his wife.

Place verbs as close as possible to direct objects.

                               V   **DO**

Awkward separation: He *asked*, before I could stop him, an embarrassing *question*.

Revision: Before I could stop him, he *asked* an embarrassing *question*.

OR

He *asked* an embarrassing *question* before I could stop him.

Keep the verb phrases together.
Avoid unnecessarily splitting auxiliary verbs from main verbs.

aux. verb   modifier   aux. verb   main verb

Awkward split: Lacey *has* for an hour *been* *proofreading* her paper.

Revision: Lacey *has been proofreading* her paper for an hour.

Keeping infinitives together.

Try to avoid splitting the *to* from the verb form of an infinitive.

Infinitive modifier   infinitive

Awkward split: He wanted *to* carefully *address* her concerns.

Revision: He wanted *to address* her concerns carefully.

Practice Set 14–4

Directions: Revise the following sentences for proper modifier placement by underlining phrases that need to be moved and drawing an arrow to where they should go.

Example: They sang, after the speeches, a patriotic song.

1. She tried to slowly carry the vase to the table.

2. The dancer, after she regained her composure, continued with the performance.

3. He collected from everyone in the room money for the birthday present.

4. I am going to, if I can find the courage, tell her what I think.

5. The teacher was angry because the student had, during class, answered her cell phone.

6. Lily saw, before she could turn her head the other way, the terrible accident ahead.

7. I sold, when gas prices skyrocketed, my gas-guzzling car.

8. He wanted to privately explain why he had decided to quit his job.

9. Quinn, whenever Mike comes around, pretends she doesn't see him.

10. She often cooks, when she has the time, dinner for the entire crew.

AVOIDING DANGLING MODIFIERS

Dangling modifiers are phrases or clauses that have nothing to modify in a sentence. Consider this sentence:

Dangling modifier: *Hearing no further business,* the meeting ended.

Obviously, the meeting could not hear anything, and there is no word in the sentence for the opening phrase to modify; therefore, it is dangling. However, someone has to end the meeting, so add that person to the sentence.

Revision: Hearing no further business, the president ended the meeting.

Dangling modifier: *Cleaning the kitchen*, a giant cockroach scampered across the counter.

Since a cockroach can't clean a kitchen, the modifier is dangling. Similar to the previous sentence, we know that someone has to clean the kitchen, so again, add the person to the sentence.

Revision: Cleaning the kitchen, I saw a giant cockroach scamper across the counter.

OR

While I was cleaning the kitchen, a giant cockroach scampered across the counter.

Dangling modifier: *After brushing my teeth*, my tongue began to tingle.

Since my tongue can't brush my teeth, this modifier is dangling.

Revision: After brushing my teeth, I felt my tongue begin to tingle.

OR

After I brushed my teeth, my tongue began to tingle.

Dangling modifier: *While driving home*, the puppy slept in the back seat.

Since the puppy can't drive, this modifier is dangling.

Revision: While I was driving home, the puppy slept in the back seat.

QUICK TIP

Changing word order will repair misplaced modifiers, but it will not repair dangling modifiers.

Misplaced modifier: My favorite vacation photograph is the one of my grandmother as she sat atop a camel *wearing her red tennis shoes*.

Correct Revision: My favorite vacation photograph is the one of my grandmother wearing her red tennis shoes as she sat atop a camel.

The modifier *wearing her red tennis shoes* now appears next to *grandmother*, the word it modifies, so changing word order is effective.

Dangling modifier: *While sitting atop a camel*, my grandmother's red tennis shoes looked great.

Changing the word order in this sentence does not repair the dangling modifier. In order to correct a dangling modifier, you must add something to the sentence (most often a subject).

Incorrect revision: My grandmother's red tennis shoes looked great *while sitting atop a camel*.

This revision says that the tennis shoes were sitting atop a camel.

Correct Revision: While sitting atop a camel, my grandmother looked great in her red tennis shoes.

Practice Set 14–5

Directions: Revise the following sentences to correct dangling modifiers.

Example: Driving through Tampa, the orange blossoms smelled heavenly.

When I was driving through Tampa, the orange blossoms smelled heavenly.

1. Flying above the city, the people below looked like ants.

2. Cell phones should always be turned off when attending an important meeting.

3. While trying to study for my exam, the children playing in the street kept distracting me.

4. Quietly whispering a little prayer, the soldier's tanks crossed the desert.

5. In order to succeed, much planning is required.

6. Practicing my drum solo, the phone just wouldn't stop ringing.

7. To balance the books properly, all checks must be subtracted from cash on hand.

8. The shampoo bottle fell on the floor while singing in the shower.

9. Rushing to class, the bell let me know I was going to be late.

10. Sliding down the chimney, the soot covered Santa from head to toe.

Practice Set 14–6

Directions: Revise these sentences containing misplaced, squinting, or dangling modifiers. Write "correct" next to any that need no revision.

Example: While sleeping, the noisy television didn't bother Marta.

The noisy television didn't bother Marta while she was sleeping.

1. The orders he shouted quickly made the soldiers snap to attention.

2. I painted, with no one's help, three rooms in two hours.

3. This recipe only calls for four cups of flour.

4. While watching the season finale of my favorite television show, a telemarketer called.

5. Uncovering the truth, the case was closed by the detective.

6. It is important to thoroughly proofread your work.

7. The scientist was awarded his Nobel Prize wearing a golf shirt and khakis.

8. Mitch, when he wants to, can be charming.

9. Closing the car door, my skirt accidentally ripped.

10. The girl whom I see on the bus occasionally waits for me after class.

11. The streets in my neighborhood, whenever it rains, flood.

12. I only paid fifty dollars for that lamp.

13. Not paying attention, the soap splashed into my eyes.

14. Madison asked me to, when I could, call her to arrange a meeting.

15. Angry with his parents, the bedroom was a good place to cool off.

16. Being a fan of the rock group, the concert tickets seemed inexpensive.

17. Act II of the play just has two scenes.

18. The pianist played the song for the class using his sheet music.

19. Hungry for his supper, the dog rattled his bowl.

20. While driving down Main Street, the stoplights were out of order.

▼ TEST YOURSELF

Directions: Rewrite the following paragraph, correcting any misplaced or dangling modifiers.

Today started in the worst way. First, I set my alarm clock for 6:00 PM instead of 6:00 AM. Waking up at 7:30 AM, my day was already off to a bad start. Before taking a shower, my boss had to be called to report that I would be late for work. I was ready to finally leave when I discovered that my key ring was missing. My car keys had to be found before leaving the house. They neither were in my briefcase nor in my pants pocket. Looking under the couch, there they were. Quickly, I wrapped a Pop-Tart in aluminum foil from the toaster and ran out the door. My bad luck got worse. My car would not start. Being dead, I thought that I would have to buy a new battery, but my kind neighbor was able to use cables to jump-start my car. When at last arriving to work, everyone cheered.

WRITE NOW

Directions: Write an 8–10 sentence paragraph describing a product that you are trying to sell. Be sure to include at least one descriptive modifier in each sentence to help boost sales.

GrammarSpeak ⟶

The following exercise contains sentences with misplaced modifiers that people use in everyday speech. Practice saying the correct sentences aloud.

Instead of:	Say:
We should even raise taxes on the middle class.	We should raise taxes on even the middle class.
This car nearly costs $10,000.	This car costs nearly $10,000.
They were only counting the first two numbers.	They were counting only the first two numbers.
The choir was just singing the first verse.	The choir was singing just the first verse.
They simply were overwhelmed.	They were simply overwhelmed.

WORD WATCHERS

Weak words and clichés are so overused that they have become meaningless. Avoid these expressions in your writing:

nice	dead as a doornail	thing
fun	bored to death	happily ever after
interesting	quiet as a mouse	it is what it is

Word Watchers Practice Set

Directions: Rewrite the following sentences, replacing the boldfaced clichés or weak words with meaningful language.

Example: I couldn't persuade him to change his mind, so **it is what it is.**

Correction: I couldn't persuade him to change his mind, so we will have to accept his decision.

1. I let her go ahead of me in line because **what goes around comes around**.
2. I put all of my **stuff** in the locker and then left for class.
3. I think I did well on the test, **but time will tell.**
4. She doesn't have enough money to buy that house, but if she keeps saving, **someday her ship will come in.**
5. I finally agreed to let my children watch television on school nights **because if you can't beat them, join them.**
6. She thinks raising her credit card limit will solve her problems, but **there is no such thing as a free lunch.**
7. The party was **fun,** but Ruben looked **bored to death.**
8. He shouldn't worry about losing his job because **every cloud has a silver lining.**
9. When you are trying to lose weight, it is important to **take it one step at a time.**
10. Many people who have tried to find partners on the Internet have learned that **beauty is only skin deep.**

Sentence Coherence: Logic, Parallelism, and Shifts

SENTENCE COHERENCE

Coherent sentences make sense and result when writers use the appropriate parts of speech in the various sentence parts, such as subjects and complements.

Parts of the Sentence

Subjects

Subjects are usually nouns, pronouns, or forms of nouns like gerunds or noun clauses.

> The *dogs* barked loudly. (subject–noun)
>
> *Loud barking* annoys me. (subject–gerund)
>
> *That the dogs barked loudly* was the main complaint. (subject–noun clause)

Complements

Complements are nouns, pronouns, forms of nouns, or adjectives.

> The house was really a *mansion*. (subject complement–noun)
>
> A mansion was *what we really wanted*. (subject complement–noun clause)
>
> The structure of the mansion was *unstable*. (subject complement–adjective)
>
> Her comment about the mansion made me *angry*. (object complement–adjective)

Adverbs, Adverb Phrases, and Adverb Clauses

Adverbs, adverb phrases, and adverb clauses modify verbs, adjectives, or other adverbs. They cannot be the subject or subject complement of a sentence.

> ┌─────── adverb phrase ───────┐
> │ prep. gerund obj. of a prep. │
> *By   studying   hard*, I know that I will pass the exam.

In this sentence, *studying hard* is a gerund used as the object of the preposition *by*. The entire introductory adverb phrase *by studying hard* modifies the verb *will pass*.

Mixed Constructions

Faulty sentences use incorrect parts of speech for particular sentence parts.

Do not use a prepositional phrase as the subject.

adv. phrase   v
Incorrect: *By following the map will get you there quickly.*

In this example, a prepositional phrase incorrectly serves as the subject of the sentence, creating a **mixed construction**. There are several ways to correct this sentence.

1. Drop the preposition *by*, leaving a gerund phrase as the subject.

   ┌─── S ───┐   V
   Following the map will help you get there quickly.

2. Add a noun or pronoun as the subject.

   adv. phrase   S   v
   By following a map, you will get there quickly.

3. Recast the sentence.

   S   adj. clause   v
   Those who follow the map will get there quickly.

Do not use an object of a preposition as the subject.

prep.   op   v
Incorrect: *In Jane Austen's Emma tries to find her girlfriend a husband.*

In this sentence, *Emma* is the object of the preposition *in*, so *Emma* cannot serve as the subject.

You can correct this sentence by adding a subject.

prep.   op   s   v
Correct: *In Jane Austen's Emma, Emma tries to find her girlfriend a husband.*

Do not use an adverb clause as the subject.

adv. clause   pred.
Incorrect: *Just because she has a cold does not mean that she will miss class.*

In this example, an adverb clause incorrectly serves as the subject. You can correct this sentence in several ways:

1. Change the adverb clause to a gerund phrase.

   gerund phrase   pred.
   Her having a cold does not mean that she will miss class.

2. Add a pronoun subject.

   adv. clause   S   pred.
   Just because she has a cold, she will not necessarily miss class.

3. Recast the sentence.

   She has a cold, but she will not miss class.

Practice Set 15–1

Directions: Rewrite the following sentences, correcting the mixed constructions.

Example: Whenever I follow my instincts gets me in trouble.

Following my instincts gets me in trouble.

OR

Whenever I follow my instincts, I get in trouble.

1. Since his car wouldn't start meant he missed the interview.

2. By wearing jeans always makes me feel more comfortable.

3. Just because she got her driver's license doesn't make her a safe driver.

4. In Shakespeare's *Hamlet* does not know whether "to be or not to be".

5. After singing karaoke with my friend made me feel more confident.

6. By writing the information in my notes will make studying easier.

7. Because his car wouldn't start meant he had a bad battery.

8. In Leo Tolstoy's Anna Karenina leaves her husband for another man.

9. Even though we know the rules doesn't mean we obey them.

10. During her recital made me feel proud of her accomplishment.

More on Mixed Construction

Do not use an adverb clause after a linking verb.

Using *is where*, *is when*, or *is because* creates a structure problem.

Subject complements follow linking verbs. Subject complements are always nouns, pronouns, or adjectives, never adverbs. A mixed construction occurs when an adverb clause directly follows linking verbs such as *is/are* or *was/were*, especially in definitions or explanations.

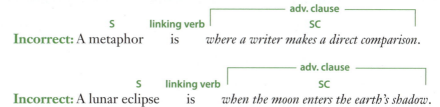

Incorrect: A metaphor is *where a writer makes a direct comparison.*

Incorrect: A lunar eclipse is *when the moon enters the earth's shadow.*

Avoid sentences using is when or is where.

You can correct these sentences by recasting them, eliminating the adverb clause after *is*.

Correct: A metaphor is a direct comparison that a writer makes.

Sometimes, you can keep the adverb clause by changing the verb from a linking verb to an action verb.

Correct: A lunar eclipse occurs when the moon enters the earth's shadow.

Avoid the construction the reason is because.

	S	linking verb	┌─── adv. clause ───┐ SC

Incorrect: The reason for our being late   is   *because we missed the bus.*

This sentence has an adverb clause after the linking verb *is*. In addition, the words *reason/because* and *reason/why* are similar in meaning and should not be used together. You can correct this sentence by doing the following:

1. Change the adverb clause to a noun clause:

    The reason for our being late is that we missed the bus.

2. Recast the sentence to avoid wordiness:

    We are late because we missed the bus.

Illogical Connections

Sentences are faulty when the subjects and predicates do not make sense together. In other words, they make an **illogical connection**.

                      S   pred.

Incorrect: The *decision* to take a cruise *would be fun for everyone.*

This sentence is not logical. It's not the *decision* that would be fun; *taking the cruise* is the fun part. Correct the sentence by using a subject and predicate that make sense.

Correct: Taking a cruise would be fun for everyone.

Practice Set 15–2

Directions: Rewrite the following sentences, correcting predicate errors.

    Example: The reason that the floor was so expensive was because the tiles were made in Italy.

    The floor was so expensive because the tiles were made in Italy.

1. Depleting fossil fuels is where we use too much coal and oil.

2. The purpose of the microwave was invented to cut cooking time.

3. The reason we recycle is because we want to reuse and preserve natural resources.

4. The length of the song was too hard to sing.

5. Through studying a culture's philosophy is a good way to understand its art.

6. When you attend class regularly will help improve your grades.

7. By wanting to save money is a good reason to open a savings account.

8. Aerobics is when a person exercises to improve his or her heart rate.

9. The veteran we are honoring is a great example of leadership.

10. By listening to quiet music is a great way to relax.

Illogical Comparisons

Sentences are faulty when they make **illogical comparisons**.

Do not leave out the word *other* in comparisons.

Comparisons are faulty when writers leave out necessary words in the comparison form. Sometimes the word *other* is needed to make a comparison logical. Examine this sentence:

Confusing: Jupiter is larger than any planet orbiting the sun.

Obviously, the writer means that Jupiter is the largest of the planets that orbit the sun. The sentence, however, says that Jupiter is *larger* than any of those planets. Since Jupiter *is* one of those planets, the sentence suggests that Jupiter is larger than itself. You can correct this problem by adding the word *other:*

Correct: Jupiter is larger than any *other* planet orbiting the sun.

Do not create two meanings with *than* or *as.*

Comparisons using the words *than* or *as* must be complete to avoid confusion. The following sentence has two possible meanings:

Confusing: Gwen treated Bob better than his friend.

Did Gwen treat Bob better than she treated his friend, or did Gwen treat Bob better than his friend treated Bob? You must add additional information to clarify the meaning.

Correct: Gwen treated Bob better than she treated his friend.

OR

Gwen treated Bob better than his friend did.

Do not leave out *as* when it is part of the comparison form.

Examine this sentence:

Confusing: The play is as long if not longer than the movie.

The comparison forms in this sentence should be *as long as* and *longer than*. All parts of both forms must be included.

Correct: The play is as long as, if not longer than, the movie.

Practice Set 15–3

Directions: Rewrite the following sentences, making the comparisons clear and complete.

Example: I paid Brett back before you.

I paid Brett back before I paid you back.

OR

I paid Brett back before you did.

1. The center on the basketball team is as tall if not taller than the guard.

2. The trip to Cancun was more fun than any vacation I have ever taken.

3. Jensen screamed louder at the cat than Matt.

4. Alaska is larger than any state in the union.

5. My neighbor's boxer is as vicious if not more vicious than my pit bull.

6. Were you as scared or more scared than I was last night?

7. Eric took more time with his project than any student in his class.

8. At last night's basketball game, she cheered more for her brother than her boyfriend.

9. Iowa produces more corn than any state in the United States.

10. The movie was as funny if not funnier than the book.

PARALLELISM

Parallelism uses the same form of words, phrases, or clauses for items that appear together, which helps make writing consistent and logical. Parallelism creates balanced sentences. Compare the following two sentences:

Incorrect: I have always enjoyed *reading about composers, to listen to symphonies,* and *then I go to concerts.*

Correct: I have always enjoyed *reading about composers, listening to symphonies, and going to concerts.*

In the first sentence, three groups of words appear together, but they are not parallel. *Reading, to listen,* and *I go* are three different grammatical forms: a gerund, an infinitive, and a clause. The second example uses three gerunds, *reading, listening,* and *going,* each followed by a prepositional phrase. These items are parallel in structure.

Parallelism with Coordination

Words, phrases, and clauses joined by coordinating conjunctions (*and, but, or, for, nor, so, yet*) should be parallel.

Parallel words: I try to avoid any activity that involves *diving* or *climbing*.

Parallel phrases: The squirrel ran *through the flower beds, around the benches*, and *over the statues*.

Parallel clauses: You should study for the test with someone *who has taken good notes, who has taped the lectures*, or *who has maintained a high grade point average*.

Pairs of words, phrases, and clauses used with correlative conjunctions (*either/or, neither/nor, both/and, not only/but also*) should be parallel.

Parallel words: She told the guests to bring not only *vegetables* but also *desserts* to the party.

Parallel phrases: My watch is either *in the car* or *on my dresser*.

Parallel clauses: Sydney always revealed not only *what she thought* but also *what all her friends thought*.

QUICK TIP

Remember to use both sides of the correlative conjunction. If you use *not only*, you must also use *but also*.

Incorrect: *Not only* milk *but* cheese is a good source of calcium.

Correct: *Not only* milk *but also* cheese is a good source of calcium.

Completeness

Parallel constructions should be complete. Be careful not to leave out words that are necessary to complete the meaning. Examine the following sentence:

Incorrect: The soprano *never has* and *never will* sing rock music.

The two helping verbs, *has* and *will*, signal a change in verb tense, one present perfect and one future, so they cannot "share" the main verb *sing*. *Has* requires the past participle form *sung*.

Correct: The soprano has never sung and will never sing rock music.

Incomplete parallelism also occurs with prepositions. Specific prepositions follow certain verbs in English, creating particular meanings. These expressions are **idioms**, word combinations peculiar to the language. For example, *waited **on**, waited **for***, and *waited **with*** all have distinct meanings. Examine the following sentence:

Incorrect: He capitalized and invested in the booming stock market.

The verbs *capitalized* and *invested* cannot "share" the preposition *in* because the idiom is *capitalize on*, not *capitalize in*. The sentence should say:

Correct: He capitalized *on* and invested *in* the booming stock market.

Directions: Rewrite the following sentences, correcting any faulty parallelism.

Example: I like to exercise in the morning, before lunch, and when it is evening.

I like to exercise in the morning, before lunch, and in the evening.

Example: He appealed and relied on the committee for his support.

He appealed to and relied on the committee for his support.

1. Are you here to apply for a job, buy something, or do you want to enroll in a cooking class?

2. My favorite ways to relax are to take a drive in the country, working out at the spa, and then watch an old movie.

3. Being late for work, forgetting to wear your identification badge, and too many coffee breaks will get you fired.

4. You should pursue either a career in nursing or become a teacher.

5. The teacher has always tried to be fair in his grading practices, suggest a number of ways to improve, and having very organized lessons.

CONSISTENCY

Consistency avoids confusion and makes writing flow smoothly. **Awkward shifts** occur when writers change **point of view, voice, verb tense**, or **expression** within a sentence.

Consistent Point of View

Maintain a consistent point of view throughout a sentence.

Changing pronouns, sometimes called **shifting point of view**, causes writing to become unclear and awkward.

- **First-person point of view** uses the pronouns *I* and *we*. Use first-person point of view for informal writing in letters, personal stories, or autobiographical essays.

- **Second-person point of view** uses the pronoun *you*. Use second-person point of view for instruction and commands.

- **Third-person point of view** uses the pronouns *he*, *she*, *it*, and *they*. Many writers reserve the third person for formal writing in essays and other research projects.

A problem occurs when writers unintentionally change person in the middle of writing. Examine the following sentence:

Shift in point of view: *Contestants* have a good chance of winning if *you* start practicing a year in advance.

Contestants is the third person. In the next part of the sentence, however, the second-person pronoun *you* refers to this same third-person word—*contestants*. The sentence contains a shift in person. To correct this problem, make the pronouns consistent:

Third-person point of view: *Contestants* have a good chance of winning if *they* start practicing a year in advance.

Second-person point of view: *You* have a good chance of winning if *you* start practicing a year in advance.

Practice Set 15–5

Directions: Rewrite the following sentences, correcting any shifts in person.

Example: Before a student gives a speech, you should rehearse before a mirror.

Before you give a speech, you should rehearse before a mirror.

OR

Before students give speeches, they should rehearse before a mirror.

1. Workers must file for compensation early if you expect to get paid this year.

2. She has always considered one's appearance her best asset.

3. I always leave early on Friday afternoons even when I know you shouldn't.

4. A person never really knows when you will be called on to give one's opinion.

5. Parents should always bear in mind your child's feelings about separation.

Consistent Voice

Maintain a consistent voice within a sentence.

In a sentence written in the active voice, the subject does the acting:

S V
I hit the ball.

In a sentence written in the passive voice, the action *happens* to the subject:

S V
The *ball was hit* by me.

Keeping the voice consistent is important. Examine the following sentence:

active voice
Voice shift: He *made* plans with some friends to go to the beach, and then he

passive voice
was asked by his boss to report to work.

The first part of the sentence is written in the active voice. The subject, *he*, does the action, *made plans*. The second part of the sentence shifts to the passive voice. The subject doesn't act; something happens to him. The subject *he* was asked by his boss.

active voice

Correct: He *made* plans with some friends to go to the beach, and then his boss

active voice

asked him to report to work.

Practice Set 15–6

Directions: Rewrite the following sentences, making the voice consistent in each one.

Example: After their vows were exchanged at the wedding, the bride and groom started to giggle.

After the bride and groom exchanged their vows at the wedding, they started to giggle.

1. After I finished ironing the last blouse, I was given two more wrinkled shirts by my sister.

2. Whenever I see the doctor, I am always told that I am in good health.

3. The technician tested our TV set and was instructed by my father to make the necessary repairs.

4. She poured the batter into the cake pan, and the pan was then placed into the oven.

5. When the escaped convict was caught by the police, they put him in handcuffs.

Consistent and Clear Verb Tenses

Maintain consistent and clear verb tenses within a sentence. Writers sometimes change tenses to show the natural progression of time.

present tense   future tense

After I   *go*   to the bank, I   *will go*   to the store.

In this sentence, the tense changes logically from present to future. A problem occurs when writers start a sentence in one tense and illogically shift to another:

present tense   past tense

Tense shift: He   *walks*   outside and   *left*   the door open.

In the following sentences, the tenses are consistent:

present tense   present tense

Correct: He   *walks*   outside and   *leaves*   the door open.

past tense   past tense

Correct: He   *walked*   outside and   *left*   the door open.

Practice Set 15–7

Directions: Rewrite the following sentences, correcting any illogical shifts in verb tense.

Example: I offered him a chair and sit beside him.

I offer him a chair and sit beside him.

OR

I offered him a chair and sat beside him.

1. One night last summer, we walked on the golf course and watch the meteor shower.

2. When I suddenly came upon a hummingbird, it flies away.

3. In March, Gary decides to give her a ring and married her in April.

4. The child was happy with her grade, but her mother is not pleased.

5. She picked flowers from her garden and gives them to her lonely neighbor.

Consistency in Discourse

A **shift in discourse** is a change in style from direct quotations to indirect quotations.

A direct quotation repeats someone's exact words.

Mary asked, "Will you go with me to the aquarium?"

An indirect quotation gives the same information without using someone's exact words:

Mary asked if I would go with her to the aquarium.

Both of these methods of expression are correct. Mixing them, however, is very confusing and awkward, especially in the same sentence. Often, sentences using mixed expression sound as if they contain a question in the middle of a statement.

Mixed expression: Mary asked would I like to go with her to the aquarium.

Practice Set 15–8

Directions: Rewrite the following sentences, correcting any shifts in expression.

Example: I wondered if she should go or should she stay.

I wondered if she should go or stay.

OR

I wondered, "Should she go, or should she stay?"

1. When the movie ended, we had to decide did we want to get something to eat or go directly home.

2. Truman asked if I had his cell phone and could he borrow my car.

3. Meteorologists are trying to determine if the hurricane returned to the Gulf and will it destroy our beaches.

4. A student in any technical program should always check their course requirements.

5. I am contemplating becoming a nuclear medicine technician, or should I become a nurse.

6. After the game, we tried to decide did we want to go to a movie.

7. John asked if I had the answers to the questions and could he borrow them.

8. The entomologists don't know whether the strange insect can protect itself or will it become extinct.

9. Please let me know if you can come over and will you bring your CDs.

10. The teacher told the class not to talk when she left the room and would the students please stay in their seats.

Practice Set 15–9

Directions: Rewrite the following sentences, correcting errors in sentence continuity, parallelism, and shifts.

Example: When one has a cold, you should drink plenty of fluids.

When you have a cold, you should drink plenty of fluids.

Example: By eating oatmeal will lower your cholesterol.

Eating oatmeal will lower your cholesterol.

1. *Jeopardy* has been on television longer than any game show.

2. The host gives the answers and the questions are asked by the contestants.

3. Just because you are really smart doesn't mean you ask the right questions.

4. After the host reads the answer is when the players must ring in to pose the appropriate question.

5. Many of the answers come from pop culture, literature, history, and where world capitals are located.

6. Some answer boxes ask do you want to double your money.

7. By betting all of your money makes the question a true "daily double."

8. It is not always the contestant who gives the most correct responses that won the most money.

9. It all depends on the contestant's recall and how you play the game.

10. When we play at home, my father gives me more correct responses than my mother.

TEST YOURSELF

Directions: Rewrite the following sentences, correcting errors in sentence continuity, parallelism, and shifts.

1. The quarterback is more likely to be injured than any player on the team.

2. He picked up the phone, and then the number was dialed with care.

3. Although you need a haircut doesn't mean you will look funny in the photograph.

4. A grand slam is when a batter hits a homerun when the bases are loaded.

5. You forgot to give me my allowance is why I don't have any money.

6. My hair stylist asked did I want my hair highlighted.

7. MacKenzie is either lying or Chloe has her facts wrong.

8. She won't buy anything from that store if it won't give you a discount.

9. I told Max the answer before Tom.

10. The height of the grass was hard to mow.

WRITE NOW

Directions: Write an 8–10 sentence paragraph on how to behave upon meeting a potential employer for the first time. Show parallelism at least once, use consistent tense and person throughout each sentence, and make logical connections. Do not use passive voice.

GrammarSpeak ├────────▶

The following sentences contain errors in sentence coherence that we often hear in everyday speech. Practice saying the correct forms aloud.

Instead of:	Say:
The reason we are hungry is because we haven't eaten lunch yet.	We are hungry because we haven't eaten lunch yet.
Where are my keys at?	Where are my keys?
I am taller than him.	I am taller than he.
A plan was made by us.	We made a plan.
John asked would I go with him.	John asked me to go with him.

WORD WATCHERS

Be sure that your writing does not include inappropriate or offensive language.

sexist language	Most words can be written as gender-neutral:
	waiter/waitress = server
	mankind = humankind
	fireman = firefighter
	mailman = postal worker or letter carrier
	steward/stewardess = flight attendant
obscenities and vulgar language	It is never appropriate to use language that can be offensive to your readers. Offensive words that have become part of your everyday vocabulary may not be suitable for an essay. If you are unsure, leave them out.
name calling	Do not use derogatory terms to refer to people. These include obviously offensive terms that you would not use in polite company, but they also include words that categorize or stereotype. Be careful about using impolite terms like *jerk* or *cripple*.

Word Watchers Practice Set

Directions: In the following sentences, replace sexist language with gender-neutral terms.

1. The waiter forgot to bring the ketchup but remembered the napkins.
2. Each voter should bring his registration card.
3. I really admire firemen because they often risk their lives to help others.
4. The discovery of penicillin has been important for all of mankind.
5. Airline stewardesses do more than just serve drinks to passengers.
6. All businessmen should take courses in management so they will know how to deal with people.
7. All department chairmen should report to the dean before Tuesday.
8. We will invite all of the doctors and their wives to the conference.
9. Because I love animals, I wear only clothes sewn with manmade fabrics.
10. I really appreciate the workmanship of the craftsmen who made this table.

Parts of Speech: For Further Study

On your journey through *Grammar to Go* thus far, you have learned the foundations of English grammar: the parts of speech, how words function in a sentence, phrases and clauses, and sentence structure. It seems like a lot, yet these essentials are just the beginning. This final chapter will add to your knowledge, taking you a little beyond the basics, helping you to increase your understanding of how the language works.

You have mastered grammar essentials, but there is more to learn if you want to fine tune your writing skills. This chapter will help you take the next steps.

BEYOND THE BASICS: VERBS

Verbs express action or condition. As the main word or words in the predicate, verbs are necessary to make a complete sentence. The forms of verbs change, depending on time, mood, voice, person, and number.

Principal Parts

Verbs have three principal parts that create all of the tenses.

Basic Form

The **basic form** is the one that you find in the dictionary. It is really the infinitive form (*to* plus the verb) without the *to*, so that *to dance* simply becomes the basic form *dance*.

We *dance* at the club on Friday night.

Past Tense Form

The second principal part of a verb, in this case *danced*, is the simple **past tense**, with no helping verbs.

We *danced* at the club last week.

Past Participle Form

The **past participle** combines with helping verbs to create certain tenses. For most regular English verbs, the past tense and the past participial forms are the same.

We *have danced* at the club every Friday for the past two months.

Two other secondary forms do not usually appear in typical verb lists. The first is the **-s form**, which is used for third person singular. The second is the **-ing form**, or **present participle**.

Regular and Irregular Verbs

Verbs may be regular or irregular in form.

Regular verbs form the past and past participle by adding *-d* or *-ed* to the basic form.

Basic	Past Tense	Past Participle
learn	learned	learned
mow	mowed	mowed
bake	baked	baked

Irregular verbs do not follow the regular *-d* or *-ed* pattern in the past tense. They form their past and past participle by changing some or all of their forms (*become/became/become; eat/ate/eaten*) or by not changing at all (*put/put/put*).

The following chart shows some common irregular verbs.

Basic	Past Tense	Past Participle
arise	arose	arisen
be	was/were	been
become	became	become
begin	began	begun
bleed	bled	bled
blow	blew	blown
break	broke	broken
bring	brought	brought
build	built	built
burst	burst	burst
buy	bought	bought
catch	caught	caught
choose	chose	chosen
come	came	come
dig	dug	dug
draw	drew	drawn
drink	drank	drunk
drive	drove	driven
eat	ate	eaten

feel	felt	felt
fight	fought	fought
find	found	found
fly	flew	flown
forget	forgot	forgotten
freeze	froze	frozen
get	got	gotten
give	gave	given
go	went	gone
have	had	had
hide	hid	hidden
hit	hit	hit
hurt	hurt	hurt
know	knew	known
lay	laid	laid
lead	led	led
lie	lay	lain
lose	lost	lost
make	made	made
pay	paid	paid
quit	quit	quit
read	read	read
ride	rode	ridden
ring	rang	rung
run	ran	run
see	saw	seen
set	set	set
shine	shone	shone
shrink	shrank	shrunk
sing	sang	sung
sink	sank	sunk
sit	sat	sat
slide	slid	slid
speak	spoke	spoken

spring	sprang	sprung
stink	stank	stunk
swim	swam	swum
swing	swung	swung
take	took	taken
teach	taught	taught
throw	threw	thrown
wear	wore	worn
write	wrote	written

Types of Verbs

Verbs are either action, linking, or helping.

Action Verbs

Action verbs show some type of action or activity.

> I *think* before I *speak*.

> The batter *popped* the ball into center field.

> Samuel *waited* for the rain to stop before he *left* the building.

Action verbs are transitive or intransitive. **Transitive verbs** take direct objects, which receive the action of the verb.

>   S   TV   DO
> She called the repairman after the storm.

>   S   TV   DO
> The pilot started the engine.

Intransitive verbs do not take direct objects; the action is complete without a word in the predicate to receive the action.

>   S   IV
> Forgetting to bring his sweatshirt, Marcus shivered in the freezing wind.

>   S   IV
> Under the shade of an umbrella, we read by the pool.

Linking Verbs

Linking verbs connect the subject to a subject complement, which is a noun, pronoun, or predicate adjective. You may remember that the subject complement renames or describes the subject. Linking verbs include the following:

1. All forms of *be* (*am, is, are, was, were, be, being, been*)

2. Verbs of the five senses (*feel, smell, taste, look,* and *sound*)

3. Other verbs like *appear, seem, become, grow*

S | linking verb | SC (noun)

Joseph Farmington　　*was*　　captain of the team for ten months.

Here the linking verb connects *captain* to *Joseph Farmington*, renaming the subject.

S | linking verb | SC (adj.)

After the long interview, the applicant　　appeared　　tired.

In this sentence, the linking verb *appeared* connects *tired* to the subject, *applicant*. There is no direct object that receives any action, but the subject complement *tired* describes the subject.

However, some verbs can be linking or action, depending on the sentence.

S | action verb | DO

He　　*tasted*　　the flavored coffee.

In this sentence, the subject is actually doing the action of tasting.

S | linking verb | SC (adj.)

The coffee　　*tasted*　　bitter.

Here the verb does not show action. It states a condition. It links the adjective *bitter* to the subject *coffee*.

Practice Set 16–1

Directions: In the sentences below, underline the verb twice and the simple subject once. In the first blank, identify the verb as transitive, intransitive, or linking. In the second blank, write the direct object or subject complement if there is one.

Example: He is a very good reader. 　　　　linking　　reader

1. A boy from India solved the difficult problem. 　　　　_____　　_____

2. Many graduates tossed their caps in the air. 　　　　_____　　_____

3. Austin applauded at the end of the long song. 　　　　_____　　_____

4. The sky grew dark with the approaching storm clouds. 　　_____　　_____

5. I sounded the whistle at the beginning of the race. 　　_____　　_____

6. The horn sounded loud in the quiet evening. 　　　　_____　　_____

7. Working later than usual, he finished at midnight. 　　_____　　_____

8. Simon planted the trees by the new fence. 　　　　_____　　_____

9. Time is money. 　　　　_____　　_____

10. Lightning struck the tall steeple of the old church. 　　_____　　_____

Helping Verbs

Helping verbs are also called **auxiliary verbs**. They combine with *-ing* verb forms and past participle verb forms to make verb phrases. The following verbs can be helping verbs or main verbs:

am, is, are, was, were, be, being, been, does, do, did, has, have, had

Helping verbs also include **modals**—*can, could, may, might, must, shall, should, will, would*. Modals never appear alone as main verbs.

verb phrase   verb phrase

I <u>have visited</u> the dentist many times, but I <u>must go</u> again soon.

Verb Tense

Verbs have **tenses** that show the time of the action or condition. The English language has three basic tenses.

Present Tense

The **present tense**, which uses the first principal part of the verb, indicates a current condition, present action, repeated action, or habitual action.

> You *are* hungry.

> He *sings* for his supper.

> I *walk* every day.

Past Tense

The **past tense**, which uses the second principal part of the verb, indicates that something has already occurred and is now finished.

> You *were* hungry.

> He *sang* for his supper.

> I *walked* every day last week.

Future Tense

The **future tense** indicates that something will happen. The future tense uses the first principal part of the verb plus the helping verb *will*.

> You *will be* hungry.

> He *will sing* for his supper.

> I *will walk* every day next week.

In addition to the three basic tenses, English uses three **perfect tenses** to show the relationship of time within a sentence.

Present Perfect Tense

The **present perfect tense** indicates an action that has started in the past and is either still going on or has recently been completed. To form the present perfect tense, use the helping verb *has* or *have*, plus the past participle of the main verb.

> Over the years, I *have found* many rare shells along the beach.

> He *has made* four calls to the cable company since yesterday.

> They *have supported* our organization since it began and continue to do so.

Past Perfect Tense

The **past perfect tense** indicates that one action in the past was completed before another past action. You would use the past perfect to indicate which action occurred first. To form the past perfect tense, use the auxiliary verb *had* plus the past participle of the main verb.

> Hannah used crutches because she *had broken* her ankle in a skiing accident.

> Neal *had* already *eaten* dinner by the time his mother arrived with the pizza.

Future Perfect Tense

The **future perfect tense** indicates an action that will be completed before a certain time in the future. To form the future perfect tense, use the auxiliary form *will have* plus the past participle of the main verb.

> We *will have worked* a total of sixty hours by the time the project is finished.

> By tomorrow, the sled dogs *will have crossed* the finish line.

Progressive Tenses

The basic tenses and the perfect tenses have corresponding **progressive tenses** to indicate action that is continuing in the past, present, or future. Form the progressive tenses by combining the appropriate tense of the verb *be* with a present participle.

The present progressive tense indicates that something is happening right now:

> **Present progressive:** I *am staying* for the second act.

The past progressive indicates something that was happening at some point in the past:

> **Past progressive:** You *were working* at the same store ten years ago.

The future progressive indicates something that will be happening at some point in the future:

> **Future progressive:** He *will be standing* for the entire ceremony.

The present perfect progressive indicates something that has been started in the past and continues to happen:

> **Present perfect progressive:** They *have been signing* autographs for hours.

The past perfect progressive indicates a continuous action that has been completed at some point in the past:

> **Past perfect progressive:** Everyone *had been studying* very hard.

The future perfect progressive indicates a continuous action that will be completed at some point in the future:

> **Future perfect progressive:** By noon today, we *will have been rehearsing* for three days.

Practice Set 16–2

Directions: In the following sentences, underline the verbs or verb phrases twice and indicate the tense of each in the lines provided.

Example: You <u>will have spent</u> your money

before the end of the trip.   future perfect

1. She had already sung her solo.   _____

2. The sun shone brightly on the porch.   _____

3. James will have arrived in Rome by morning.   _____

4. Eric threw his hat in the ring.   _____

5. Alicia and Taylor have given us no choice.   _____

6. I will wear something green for St. Patrick's Day.   _____

7. Willis has never swum in the ocean.   _____

8. The water had frozen in the pipes during the night.   _____

9. Phil chooses to create his own costumes.   _____

10. Have you quit your job?   _____

Mood

Verbs occur in three moods: indicative, imperative, and subjunctive.

Indicative Mood

The **indicative mood** expresses statements of facts or questions.

The U.S. government includes the legislative, executive, and judicial branches.

What is the longest river in the world?

Imperative Mood

The **imperative mood** expresses direct requests or commands. The subject of the sentence is always an understood *you*.

Feed the dog and take out the garbage.

Subjunctive Mood

The **subjunctive mood** expresses wishes, conditions contrary to fact, requests, and commands.

Wish: I wish I *were* sitting in the bleachers.

Condition contrary to fact: If he *were* a good swimmer, he could finish the race.

Request or command: She demanded that they *be* present. She requested that he *remain* quiet.

QUICK TIP

There are no -s endings in the subjunctive mood. Notice that *to be* in the subjunctive mood is always *were*, regardless of the subject:

> I wish *I were*, I wish *you were*, I wish *he were*, I wish *they were*
>
> If *I were*, if *you were*, if *he were*, if *they were*

Practice Set 16–3

Directions: Cross out any errors in mood, and write the correct word or phrase above each error.

> **were**
> **Example:** If I ~~was~~ the leader, we would not cross the rapids on a raft.

1. I wish Gavin Langwell was my trainer.

2. The store requested that he brings his copy of the guarantee.

3. If he was my brother, I would advise him not to go.

4. Sandy insisted that her friend is added to the eligibility list.

5. Serena wishes she was taller.

Voice

Verbs may be in active or passive voice.

Active voice indicates that the subject of the sentence is doing the action.

> The mice ate the cheese.
>
> The children tease the dog.
>
> Mr. Wilson has painted his house several times.

Passive voice indicates that the subject receives the action of the verb.

> The cheese was eaten by the mice.
>
> The dog is teased by the children.
>
> The house has been painted several times by Mr. Wilson.

Overusing the passive voice creates wordy and weak writing, so use it sparingly. However, on occasion you can use the passive voice for variety or to emphasize the receiver of the action rather than the actor.

> **Passive voice:**   The frightened deer was hit by the car. (This sentence emphasizes the deer.)
>
> **Active voice:**   The car hit the frightened deer. (This sentence emphasizes the car.)

QUICK TIP

The preposition *by* frequently indicates the passive relationship between the actor and the receiver of the action.

As the captain descended the stairs, he was welcomed *by* a large crowd.

The general was supported *by* his troops.

Practice Set 16–4

Directions: Rewrite the following sentences, changing passive voice to active voice.

Example: I was asked by the doctor to come in early for my appointment.

The doctor asked me to come in early for my appointment.

1. A part of our fence was destroyed by the strong winds.

2. The most expensive cars are often built by foreign companies.

3. The materials were bought by my uncle, and the shed was built by my cousin.

4. The letter was not written by me.

5. A good argument was made by the defense team.

Special Challenges

Some verb pairs create special usage problems. The verbs *lay/lie*, *set/sit*, and *raise/rise* present special challenges because they are so frequently misused in speech that many writers choose the wrong form. Understanding the difference between transitive and intransitive verbs clears up the confusion.

Form	Transitive (takes a direct object) *to lay*: to put or to place something	Intransitive (does not take a direct object) *to lie*: to recline
Present	lay(s) I lay the book on the desk every day.	lie(s) I lie in bed every day.
Past	laid I laid the book on the desk yesterday.	lay I lay in bed yesterday.
Present participle	laying I am laying the book on the desk now.	lying I am lying in bed now.
Past participle	laid I have laid the book on the desk.	lain I have lain in bed for an hour.

Form	Transitive (takes a direct object) *to set*: to put something in a specified place or position	Intransitive (does not take a direct object) *to sit*: to rest or recline
Present	set(s) He sets the mail on the table every day.	sit(s) He sits in a chair every day.
Past	set He set the mail on the table yesterday.	sat He sat in a chair yesterday.
Present participle	setting He is setting the mail on the table now.	sitting He is sitting in the chair now.
Past participle	set He has set the mail on the table.	sat He has sat in the chair for an hour.

Form	Transitive (takes a direct object) *to raise*: to lift something up	Intransitive (does not take a direct object) *to rise*: to go up
Present	raise(s) They raise the flag.	rise(s) They rise from their seats.
Past	raised They raised the flag.	rose They rose from their seats.
Present participle	raising They are raising the flag.	rising They are rising from their seats.
Past participle	raised They have raised the flag.	risen They have risen from their seats.

Practice Set 16–5

Directions: Circle the correct verb form in parentheses.

   Example: I (lay/laid) on the sofa and watched television.

1. He is (laying/lying) on the floor.

2. The pizza dough has (raised/risen) in the bowl.

3. The child (set/sat) by her mother's bedside for hours.

4. The potatoes have (laid/lain) in the fields since last week.

5. (Raise/Rise) your hand if you have a question.

6. He (laid/lay) unconscious in the hospital for two weeks.

7. I (set/sat) the notebook on the chair when I arrived.

8. Smoke (raised/rose) from all of the chimneys in the village.

9. Dylan has (laid/lain) the baby in the crib.

10. Let's (lay/lie) out by the pool for the afternoon.

BEYOND THE BASICS: NOUNS

Nouns name persons, places, things, or ideas. They act as subjects, subject complements, and objects in a sentence.

obj. prep.   S   IO   DO   obj. prep.

After the *recital*, the *director* gave *Marcie* a *lecture* about *rudeness*.

In this example, nouns function as many structural parts of the sentence.

Nouns also can be classified by purpose. The general categories of nouns include common and proper, abstract and concrete, count and noncount, and collective.

Common and Proper Nouns

Common nouns usually name a general class (*woman*, *clerk*, *mountain*, *river*, *house*, *ship*, *feelings*, *autumn*). They do not start with capital letters unless they are the first words of sentences. **Proper nouns** name specific people, places, or things (*Mr. Meyers*, *Mississippi*, *Saturday*, *December*, *Cheerios*, *Middle Ages*). They do start with capital letters.

Abstract and Concrete Nouns

Abstract nouns refer to concepts and ideas that you cannot experience immediately through the senses (*strength*, *fairness*, *beauty*, *diligence*, *truth*). Abstract nouns are singular.

Samson's strength was impressive.

Concrete nouns refer to persons, places, or things that you can see, feel, hear, smell, or taste (*books*, *chair*, *cake*, *flowers*, *smoke*, *highway*). Concrete nouns can be singular or plural.

The cake was too sweet.

The chairs need reupholstering.

Count and Noncount Nouns

Categorizing nouns as **count** and **noncount** determines whether or not to use the articles, *a*, *an*, and *the*.

As the name implies, **count nouns** refer to persons, places, and things that someone can count (*apples*, *children*, *cars*, *neighbors*, *laws*).

Use the article *a* or *an* before singular count nouns that are not specific.

He drove *a truck* in the parade. (You don't know which truck, so say *a truck*.)

Use the article *the* when you know more specifically which truck.

We told him to drive *the truck* in the parade. (Here you have a specific truck in mind, so use *the* truck.)

Noncount nouns name something that is not countable. They are sometimes called mass nouns because they do not consist of individual parts that you can separate and count easily (*dirt, music, flour, labor, pride, housework, sugar, cotton*).

Do not use *a* or *an* before noncount nouns. You would not say the following:

Incorrect: I put *a sugar* in the cake that I was making.

Noncount nouns often follow words like *some* or *any* that limit or qualify the noun. Look at the following examples:

I put *some sugar* in the cake that I was making.

Is there *any pride* in laziness?

Multiple Categories

Nouns can belong to more than one category. For example, nouns like *flour* or *furniture* are concrete, but they also are noncount. *Jealousy* is a noncount noun, but it is also an abstract noun because it cannot be experienced through the senses. Categorizing nouns helps in determining capitalization, subject-verb agreement, and article usage.

Practice Set 16–6

Directions: Indicate a category that fits the nouns in bold print. You will notice that most nouns can fit more than one category, but choose just one that fits. Compare your answers to your classmates' answers to see how many categories each noun fits. In the example, *courage* is categorized as an abstract noun, but it is also a noncount noun and a common noun.

abstract

Sometimes we find **courage** in the strangest places. We can certainly see **bravery** in soldiers when their **unit** is engaged in **battle**, but we can also find courage in far less dangerous **situations**. It takes courage to admit a **wrongdoing**, and even more to apologize for it, especially for those in the public eye. For example, **Robert McNamara**, Secretary of Defense under Presidents Kennedy and Johnson, apologized for **errors** in **judgment** made during the **war** in Vietnam. In addition, a **spokesperson** for the professional hockey **team** the Toronto Maple Leafs apologized to fans for seven disappointing **seasons** in a **row**. Owning up to our mistakes can hurt our **pride**, but most of us feel better when we try to make **amends**.

Singular and Plural Nouns

You can change most nouns from singular to plural by adding **-s** *or* **-es.**

Singular	Plural
watch	watches
apple	apples
witness	witnesses

When a singular noun ends in **y** *preceded by a consonant, change the* **y** *to* **i** *and add* **-es** *to form the plural.*

Singular	Plural
spy	spies
fly	flies
reply	replies

Some singular nouns ending in **f** *or* **fe** *form the plural by adding* **-s.**

Singular	Plural
belief	beliefs
chief	chiefs
safe	safes

Others change the **f** *or* **fe** *to* **v** *and add* **-es.**

Singular	Plural
knife	knives
wolf	wolves
thief	thieves

Singular nouns ending in **o** *preceded by a consonant form the plural by adding* **-es.**

Singular	Plural
hero	heroes
potato	potatoes
tomato	tomatoes

Singular nouns ending in **o** *preceded by a vowel form the plural by adding* **-s.**

Singular	Plural
radio	radios
cameo	cameos
folio	folios

Some singular nouns follow rules carried over from Middle English spelling. Note the following irregular plural forms.

Singular	Plural
ox	oxen
deer	deer
woman	women
goose	geese
mouse	mice
child	children
tooth	teeth

When nouns are compound, as in **mother-in-law** *or* **maid of honor**, *add* **-s** *to the most important word, which usually comes first.*

Singular	Plural
mother-in-law	mothers-in-law
attorney general	attorneys general
maid of honor	maids of honor

When a singular noun ends in **y** *preceded by a vowel, form the plural by adding* **-s** *to the word.*

Singular	Plural
attorney	attorneys
foray	forays
boy	boys

QUICK TIP

Making the word *woman* plural is especially confusing because in the plural form the first syllable changes pronunciation, but the second syllable changes spelling. Think about the words *man* and *men*. Then just add *wo-* to them.

Singular	man	**Plural**	men
Singular	wo–man	**Plural**	wo–men

Practice Set 16–7

Directions: Change the following singular forms into plurals.

Example: woman   women

1. sister-in-law   _____

2. sash   _____

3. fresco   _____

4. fox   _____

5. democracy   _____

6. rodeo   _____

7. donkey   _____

8. wife   _____

9. window   _____

10. sheep   _____

BEYOND THE BASICS: PRONOUNS

Pronouns take the place of nouns. There are many types of pronouns.

Personal Pronouns

Personal pronouns substitute for the nouns naming people, places, things, or ideas. These pronouns include the following: *I, we, you, he, she, it, they, me, us, him, her, them*

Intensive and Reflexive Pronouns

Intensive and **reflexive pronouns** end in *-self* or *-selves*. These pronouns include the following:

myself, ourselves, yourself, yourselves, himself, herself, itself, themselves

Intensive pronouns emphasize the nouns they follow by referring to them immediately.

The doctor *himself* was surprised at the patient's quick recovery.

Reflexive pronouns point to the subject of the sentence.

The snake sunned *itself* on the rock.

Intensive and reflexive pronouns are never the subject of the sentence.

                         I

Marc and ~~myself~~ got lost on the way home.

Demonstrative Pronouns

Demonstrative pronouns point to, point out, or show something. *This, that, these,* and *those* are the common demonstrative pronouns.

This is my new hat.

You must not repeat *that*.

INDEFINITE PRONOUNS

Indefinite pronouns are not specific and do not refer to particular nouns.

Anybody can sing.

I told *some* of the children to choose a game.

Here is a list of the most common indefinite pronouns:

Always Singular	Always Plural	Singular or Plural
one, each, another	both	some
either, neither	few	none
everyone, everybody,	several	any
everything	many	all
someone, somebody,		more
something		most
anyone, anybody,		
anything		
no one, nobody,		
nothing		

Interrogative Pronouns

Interrogative pronouns ask questions. Common interrogative pronouns are *who, whom, which, what, and whose.*

Who are you?

What do you want?

Relative Pronouns

Relative pronouns introduce dependent adjective and noun clauses. Relative pronouns include *which, whichever, that, who, whoever, whom, whomever, whose, what,* and *whatever*.

Adjective clause: The climber *who crossed the Himalayas* experienced frostbite.

Noun clause: The sponsors offered a reward to *whoever found the missing documents*.

Practice Set 16–8

Directions: Underline the pronouns in the following sentences.

Example: Is there <u>anyone</u> <u>who</u> doesn't love a Greek hero?

1. Hercules thought of himself as the strongest man in the world.

2. Hercules himself defeated the Amazons.

3. Who was Hercules' father?

4. Hercules' father was Zeus, who was the king of the gods.

5. Everyone knows about Hercules' Twelve Labors.

6. He had to complete twelve punishing tasks, which took him one year.

7. In one of them, he had to capture the three-headed dog that guarded the gate of the underworld.

8. Hercules did whatever King Eurystheus told him to do.

9. The labors themselves seemed impossible.

10. Hercules completed all of them, however.

BEYOND THE BASICS: ADJECTIVES AND ADVERBS

Adjectives

Adjectives are words that modify nouns or pronouns. They answer the questions *which one*, *what kind*, or *how many*.

shiny ring   *blue* sky   *unlikely* hero

Many words can function as both adjectives and pronouns or as both adjectives and nouns. Examine a sentence carefully to determine the word's use.

Demonstrative adjective:	*This* day will live in history.
Demonstrative pronoun:	*This* is a day that will live in history.
Indefinite adjective:	*Neither* car has air conditioning.
Indefinite pronoun:	*Neither* of the cars has air conditioning.
Proper adjective:	She speaks the *French* language fluently.
Proper noun:	She speaks *French* fluently.

Adverbs

Adverbs are words that modify verbs, adjectives, or other adverbs. They answer the questions *where*, *when*, *how*, *why*, and *to what degree*.

Michael shops *carefully*.   (how?)

Michael shops *daily*.   (when?)

Michael shops *here*.   (where?)

Many adverbs end in *-ly* (*frequently, really, quickly*), but not all words ending in *-ly* are adverbs. For example, *lovely, likely,* and *lonely* are adjectives.

The words *not, very, quite,* and *too* are commonly used adverbs.

Often, you can move adverbs around without significantly changing the meaning of the sentence.

Slowly she answered the question.

She *slowly* answered the question.

She answered the question *slowly*.

Degrees of Comparison

Adjectives and adverbs show degrees of comparison.

Positive Degree

Words in the **positive degree** make no comparison. They simply modify.

The *bright* light from the helicopter shone onto the sidewalk.

The fisherman dove *rapidly* into the water to save the child.

Comparative Degree

Words in the **comparative degree** compare two things.

The light from the helicopter was *brighter* than the light from the searchlight.

The fisherman swam *more rapidly* than the lifeguard.

Superlative Degree

Words in the **superlative degree** compare more than two things.

The light from the helicopter was the *brightest* of all the lights at the scene of the accident.

Of the three swimmers who were trying to save the child, the fisherman swam the *most rapidly*.

Adjectives and adverbs form the comparative and superlative degrees in three ways.

For most one- and two-syllable adjectives and some short adverbs, add *-er* for comparatives and *-est* for superlatives. For two-syllable adjectives ending in a consonant followed by a y, change the *y* to *i*, and add *-er* or *-est*.

Base Form	Comparative	Superlative
long	longer	longest
near	nearer	nearest
fast	faster	fastest
easy	easier	easiest
dirty	dirtier	dirtiest

For adjectives of three or more syllables and for most adverbs ending in *-ly*, add *more* and *most* or *less* and *least* to make the comparative or superlative forms.

Base Form	Comparative	Superlative
persuasive	more persuasive	most persuasive
important	more important	most important
beautiful	more beautiful	most beautiful
diligent	less diligent	least diligent
slowly	less slowly	least slowly
quickly	less quickly	least quickly

Some adjectives and adverbs have irregular comparative and superlative forms.

Base Form	Comparative	Superlative
good	better	best
well	better	best
bad	worse	worst
badly	worse	worst
much	more	most
many	more	most

James is a *bad* driver.

Jeremy is a *worse* driver than James.

Joseph is the *worst* driver of the three.

- Do not use *more* or *most* and the *-er* or *-est* endings in the same comparison.

    Incorrect: Atlantis was *more richer* in art than historians once believed.

    Correct: Atlantis was *richer* in art than historians once believed.

- Make sure that all comparisons are complete and logical. If you use a comparitive form, you must identify what you are comparing something to.

    Incorrect: The gold in the antique necklace seems shinier. (shinier than what?)

    Complete: The gold in the antique necklace seems shinier than the gold in my necklace.

    Incorrect: My solo got a higher rating than Margo. (A solo can't get a higher rating than a person—Margo.)

    Complete: My solo got a higher rating than Margo's solo.

- Do not use the superlative form when comparing two things.

    Incorrect: Between the two of us, who is the strongest?

    Correct: Between the two of us, who is stronger?

- Do not confuse adjective and adverb forms in comparison.

  Incorrect: Your car runs smoother than mine.

  Correct: Your car runs more smoothly than mine.

QUICK TIP

Good and *well* are frequently misused. *Good* is always an adjective. *Well* is an adjective when it means healthy and an adverb when it tells how something is done.

> **Incorrect:**   I did *good* on my test.
>
> **Correct:**   I did *well* on my test.
>
> **Correct:**   I don't feel very *well* after eating that hotdog.

Bad and *badly* are also frequently misused. *Bad* is an adjective, so it should follow a linking verb.

> **Incorrect:**   I feel *badly* about your loss.
>
> **Correct:**   I feel *bad* about your loss.

Practice Set 16–9

Directions: Rewrite the following sentences, correcting any errors in comparison.

Example: This is the more exciting of the three novels.

This is the most exciting of the three novels.

1. Dru was the better runner on her track team.

2. The light from the comet was the most clear in the night sky.

3. I like lobster better.

4. Victoria is the smartest of the twins.

5. Nathan ran quicker than Noah.

6. Of Los Angeles and New York, I like New York best.

7. She was the worst of the two spellers.

8. Among Josie, Angelina, and Sally, Josie is the taller.

9. A bassoon's tone is deeper than an oboe.

10. My new computer responds slower than my old one.

BEYOND THE BASICS: PREPOSITIONS

Prepositions connect nouns or pronouns to something else in the sentence by forming groups of words called prepositional phrases.

Prepositions are usually just one word, but sometimes a group of words can act as a preposition.

A noun or pronoun connected to a sentence by a preposition is called the *object of the preposition*. Prepositional phrases always modify something in the sentence.

Idiomatic Expressions Using Prepositions

Prepositions are often part of idiomatic expressions—groups of words having a special meaning when used together. For example, we say *interested in* but not *interested for*. Idiomatic expressions can pose particular problems for second language speakers, so it's important to consult a dictionary if you are unsure. Here are some other common words that combine with specific prepositions:

These words go with	these prepositions	These words go with	these prepositions
Acquainted	with	Disappointed	about, by, with
Agree	with, to, on	Fond	of
Angry	with, about	Grateful	to, for
Approve	of	Involved	in, with
Consist	of	Object	to
Correspond	with	Part	from, with
Depend	on	Responsible	for
Differ	about, from, with	Wait	at, for, on

Practice Set 16–10

Directions: Use the blanks below to fill in a correct preposition for the sentence.

Example: He is responsible ____for____ paying the bill.

1. We will wait _____ everyone to arrive before we begin.

2. He is angry _____ the new regulations.

3. Can we agree _____ a time limit for these presentations?

4. Max is heavily involved _____ the plans for the meeting.

5. The test will consist _____ an essay and some matching questions.

QUICK TIP

Many people believe that ending a sentence with a preposition is always incorrect; however, in modern usage, it is usually acceptable to do so if there is no other way to express the idea. For example, we say, "What are you looking at?" Saying "At what did you look?" sounds awkward.

BEYOND THE BASICS: CONJUNCTIONS

Conjunctions connect parts of sentences, often showing the relationship of particular words, phrases, and clauses to the rest of the sentence. Conjunctions may be coordinating, subordinating, or correlative.

Coordinating Conjunctions

Coordinating conjunctions connect words, phrases, or clauses of equal rank. *And, but, or, nor, for, so,* and *yet* are the coordinating conjunctions.

                              adj.   adj.
Joining two words: Alex was industrious *and* smart.

                                         prep. phrase
Joining two phrases: The lost contact lens must be in the drain *or*
prep. phrase
in the vacuum cleaner.

                        independent clause   independent clause
Joining two clauses: I can come to the dinner party, *but* I cannot stay late.

Subordinating Conjunctions

Subordinating conjunctions introduce dependent clauses, called subordinate clauses, and connect them to the independent clauses of sentences. The following is a list of the most common subordinating conjunctions:

after	even if	though
although	even though	unless
as	if	until
as if	since	when
as though	so that	whenever
because	than	where
before	that	while

   SC
When the mega-mall opened, the smaller shopping center closed.

                      SC
The pioneers traveled *where* no one had explored.

SC
If I want to finish the project, I will have to work during the weekend.

Correlative Conjunctions

Correlative conjunctions appear in pairs and join elements that are parallel in structure. Correlative conjunctions include the following: *both/and, either/or, neither/nor, not only/but also, whether/or.*

Neither Madison *nor* Holly took enough money to the garage sale. (correlative conjunctions connecting the nouns *Madison* and *Holly*)

She *not only* wrote to the governor *but also* circulated a petition among her neighbors. (correlative conjunctions connecting the verbs *wrote* and *circulated*)

Whether skiing *or* snowboarding, you should always check your equipment. (correlative conjunctions connecting the gerunds *skiing* and *snowboarding*)

Practice Set 16–11

Directions: Underline any conjunctions in the sentences below and label them as coordinating, subordinating, or correlative.

                subordinating   coordinating
Example: <u>Before</u>   I left home, I packed my bags   <u>and</u>   paid my bills.

1. Not only department stores but also specialty shops are coming to the new International Plaza.

2. Missy always walked to work because she wanted to get some exercise.

3. The back seat of my car was soaked, for I had left my windows open.

4. While the cat is away, the mice will play.

5. She did not eat any breakfast, so she ate a hearty lunch.

QUICK TIP

Prepositions, conjunctions, adverbs, and infinitives sometimes look alike.

Preposition:	*After* the game, we saw a movie.
Subordinating conjunction:	*After* we left the game, we saw a movie.
Preposition:	He bought a gift *for* her birthday.
Coordinating conjunction:	He bought a gift, *for* his wife's birthday was Saturday.
Preposition:	The mouse crawled *inside* the box.
Adverb:	The mouse crawled *inside*.
Preposition:	I went *to* the shop.
Infinitive:	I like *to* shop.

Practice Set 16–12

Directions: In the sentences below, label the words in boldface as prepositions, conjunctions, infinitives, or adverbs.

                         prep.   conjunction
Example: Everyone **but** Brandon stayed to work, **but** we still didn't meet our deadline.

1. He traveled **to** China **to do** research for his dissertation.

2. The rain came **down** heavily as we walked **down** the street.

3. I placed the document **before** the unsuspecting guests **before** they could say a word.

4. **Until** I gave her an alarm clock, she always slept **until** noon.

5. **To stay** physically fit, you must go **to** the gym.

Conjunctive Adverbs

Conjunctive adverbs join independent clauses. Below is a list of some common conjunctive adverbs.

consequently	however	similarly
finally	moreover	then
furthermore	nevertheless	therefore
hence	next	thus

Using different methods to join clauses adds variety to your writing. The three sentences below say the same thing but in different ways:

Coordinating conjunction: We will work together, *and* we will accomplish the task.

Subordinating conjunction: *When* we work together, we will accomplish the task.

Conjunctive adverb: We will work together; *consequently*, we will accomplish the task.

QUICK TIP

Both conjunctive adverbs and coordinating conjunctions join closely related independent clauses; however, it is important to note how punctuation differs with their use. A comma separates independent clauses joined by a coordinating conjunction. Remember to place the comma before the conjunction, not after it.

I need a new car, but I don't have the money to buy one.

A semicolon separates independent clauses joined by a conjunctive adverb. Place a comma after the conjunctive adverb.

I need a new car; however, I don't have the money to buy one.

Using a comma to separate independent clauses joined by a conjunctive adverb creates a comma splice, a type of run-on sentence.

Incorrect: I need a new car, however, I don't have the money to buy one.

INTERJECTIONS

Interjections are words that show surprise or strong feeling and are not grammatically connected to the sentence. Commas follow mild interjections; exclamation points follow strong interjections.

Oh, I understand what you are saying.

Wow! I am finally finished with this chapter.

Interjections are rarely appropriate in formal writing. Some interjections, however, can be offensive to readers and are never appropriate even in informal writing.

Practice Set 16–13

Directions: Write the part of speech above each word in boldface.

What country **boasts** the world's **largest** bird's nest? Beijing, China, revealed its

National Stadium to the world during the 2008 Olympics. This architectural **marvel**

made of intersecting **metal supports** weighs 42,000 tons and seats **nearly** 90,000

fans. **The** most visible features **are** the crisscrossed beams **and** the bowl-shaped

roof. **These** give the building the appearance **of** a large nest made **from** randomly

placed twigs **although** there is nothing random **about** the **construction**. It took

Swiss and **Chinese** architects years to finalize the plans for it. Amazingly, there are

no **external** supports holding up the 11,000-ton roof. Construction **teams** took **five**

years to build **it**. **Oh**, what an impressive sight! Today, **National Stadium stands** as

an engineering masterpiece and **one** of China's most popular **tourist** attractions.

TEST YOURSELF

Directions: This story contains examples of many of the grammar and punctuation issues you have learned about in this text. Find the errors and correct them as shown. We have done the first one for you, correcting a run-on sentence.

H

Harry Houdini was born on March 24, 1874. ~~h~~is real name was Eric Weiss. Houdini

worked in a factory after his family moved to the united states. First to Appleton,

Wisconsin; then to New York City when he was 13. He could of chosen to remain in the factory but he showed alot of interest in the trapeze, magic, and he liked performing escape acts. Always giving him standing ovations, Harry thrilled audiences by escaping, handcuffs', jails, and straightjackets. In one of his performances in a small theater he spotted a young dancer who he soon began to court and eventually marry Bess Rahmer had a tremendous affect on his life. Him and his wife performed together for the rest of his career. Houdinis big break came when his manager Martin Beck booked him in a vaudeville theater. He soon played to great crowds. Earning him the title, "Worlds Most Famous Escape Artist".

By 1912, one of his greatest acts were the Chinese Water Torture Cell. He was lowered upside-down into a locked glass cabinet filled with water. He held his breath for three minutes every member of the audience was holding their breath to. Many people think that Houdini died in the water chamber but their is more to the story. During a backstage meeting a college student J. Gordon Whitehead punched Houdini in the stomach three times. Although Houdini had gave he and his friends permission to punch him. These punches took Houdini by surprise. He died a few days later. Of a ruptured appendix. His legacy among magicians is unparalleled. Each of them remember his famous motto, "my chief task has been to conquer fear."

WRITE NOW

Directions: Write your own sentences using the parts of speech indicated below. Use the dictionary to help you.

1. Use *down* as a preposition.
2. Use *down* as an adverb.
3. Use *well* as a noun.
4. Use *well* as an adverb.
5. Use *like* as a preposition.
6. Use *like* as a verb.
7. Use *morning* as an adjective.
8. Use *morning* as a noun.
9. Use *brown* as a verb.
10. Use *brown* as an adjective.

Selected Answers to Chapter Exercises

CHAPTER 1

Test Yourself

      n   **v**   **adj n prep adj n**
1. Marco Polo planned a trip to the East.

   pn   **v**   **adj**   **n**   **prep**   **n**   **n** **conj** **v** **prep** **n**
2. He started his journey from Venice, Italy, and ended in China.

   interj **pn** **v** **adj** **adj**   **n**
3. Wow! That was an incredible journey!

    n   **v**   **adj**   **adj**   **adj**   **n** **prep** **n**
4. Polo entered the Mongol diplomatic service in China.

   adj   **n**   **v** **pn**   **prep**   **n** **prep** **adj**   **n**
5. His travels led him through Asia for fifteen years.

   adj   **noun**   **adv**   **v**   **pn**
6. The Genoese eventually captured him.

   pn **v** **adj** **n** **prep** **adj**   **n**
7. He wrote a book about his adventures.

   adj   **n**   **v** **adj** **n** **conj**   **v**   **prep** **adj**   **adj**   **n**
8. Many people read his book and thought about this courageous explorer.

      pn   **v**   **adj**   **prep**   **n**
9. Everybody was excited about China.

   adj   **n**   **v**   **adj**   **n** **prep** **adj** **n**
10. His adventures revealed the riches of the East.

CHAPTER 2

Test Yourself

Bill Mazeroski was one of the greatest second basemen ever in Major League Baseball (S/LV/SC). He played for the Pittsburgh Pirates from 1956 to 1972 (S/V). This fine athlete entered the Baseball Hall of Fame in 2001 (S/V/DO). He holds the Major League record for double plays by a second baseman (S/V/DO). This accomplishment earned him the nickname "The Glove" (S/V/IO/DO). However, his bat made him even more famous (S/V/DO/OC). He was the last batter in the ninth inning of the 1960 World Series (S/LV/SC). His coach gave him the chance to hit the only home run ever to win a World Series in game seven (S/V/IO/DO). The Pirates won with a score of 10 to 9 (S/V). Bill Mazeroski taught sports fans an important lesson (S/V/IO/DO). A master outfielder can hit the most dramatic home run in the history of baseball (S/V/DO).

Word Watchers Practice Set

1. affect
2. among
3. capital
4. except
5. chose
6. capitol
7. accept
8. effect
9. choose
10. between

CHAPTER 3

Test Yourself

1. the, oldest–adj.–modify *city*
   really–adv.–modifies *mean*
   the, oldest, European–adj.–modify *settlements*

2. Numerous, ancient, Native American–adj–modify *settlements*
   much–adv–modifies *earlier*
   earlier–adv–modifies *were established*
   the, great–adj–modify *cities*
   now–adv–modifies *call*
   our, "oldest"–adj–modify *ones*

3. the, northeastern–adj–modify *part*
   now–adv–modifies *is*
   a, popular–adj–modify *destination*
   many–adj–modifies *tourists*

4. the, 16th–adj–modify *century*
   the, Spanish–adj–modify *government*
   desperately–adv–modifies *wanted*
   a, secure–adj–modify *base*
   their, New World–adj–modify *settlements*
   the–adj–modifies *English*
   the–adj–modifies *French*
   also–adv–modifies *were*
   anxious–adj–modifies *who*
   the–adj–modifies *region*

5. a, famous–adj–modify *conquistador*
   somewhat–adv–modifies *famous*
   the, contested–adj–modify *land*
   the–adj–modifies *capital*
   Spanish–adj–modifies *Florida*
   two–adj–modifies *centuries*

6. a, bloody–adj–modify *century*
   the, native–adj–modify *population*
   some, English–adj–modify *privateers*
   the, industrious–adj–modify *Spanish*
   a, secure–adj–modify *fort*

7. The, sturdy–adj–modify *fort*
   still, today–adv–modify *stands*
   the, oldest, masonry–adj–modify *fort*
   the, continental–adj–modify *United States*
   certainly–adv–modifies *is*
   the, popular, tourist–adj–modify *attraction*
   most–adv–modifies *popular*
   the, old–adj–modify *city*

8. a, wealthy, oil–adj–modify *tycoon*
   the, ancient–adj–modify *city*
   a, popular, tourist–adj–modify *resort*
   very–adv–modifies *wealthy*
   wealthy–adj–modifies *people*
   the, nineteenth, twentieth–adj–modify *centuries*
   late–adv–modifies *19th*
   early–adv–modifies *20th*

9. several–adj–modifies *hotels*
   there–adv–modifies *built*
   the, magnificent–adj–modify *Ponce de Leon*
   a, luxurious–adj–modify *retreat*
   rich, famous–adj–modify *people*
   extremely–adv–modifies *rich, famous*

10. the, lovely–adj–modify *hotel*
    a, private, four-year–adj–modify *college*

Word Watchers Practice Set

1. continuous
2. further
3. site
4. complemented
5. immigrated

6. farther
7. continual
8. cited
9. compliment
10. emigrated

CHAPTER 4

Test Yourself

1. appositive phrase
2. prepositional phrase
3. prepositional phrase
4. verb phrase
5. appositive phrase

6. prepositional phrase
7. verb phrase
8. verb phrase
9. prepositional phrase
10. prepositional phrase

Word Watchers Practice Set

1. lose
2. led
3. number
4. passed
5. fewer

6. loose
7. fewer
8. lead
9. past
10. lead

CHAPTER 5

Test Yourself

His early training (G)

hearing his first jazz recordings (G)

to be a jazz trumpeter (I)

founding (P)

blending traditional Latin sounds with jazz, rock, and classical music (P)

to explore new musical territory (I)

Aided by jazz great Dizzy Gillespie (P)

Nominated twelve times for Grammies (P)

awarded three (P)

to excite music lovers throughout the world (I)

Cuban-born (P)

fascinated by his countryman's amazing life (P)

to tell Sandoval's story to the world (I)

to do so (I)

honoring Sandoval for his many achievements (P)

Word Watchers Practice Set

1. stationary
2. too
3. than
4. principal
5. whether

6. principles
7. too
8. principal
9. stationery
10. principles

CHAPTER 6

Test Yourself

1. Were lighthouses the first land-based guidance systems for ships?

2. (You) Read about the first true lighthouse, built in Alexandria, Egypt, under Ptolemy's rule, in approximately 280 BCE.

3. How did Ptolemy make his invention work without electricity?

4. There was a coal fire behind the lens inside the tower.

5. Do lighthouses still use fire as the main source of light?

6. In the United States, there are lighthouses guiding ships to shore.

7. Where are they found?

8. You can see them along most coastal states, especially Maine.

9. (You) Find images of famous lighthouses online.

10. Would you include a visit to a lighthouse on your next trip to New England?

Word Watchers Practice Set

(answers may vary)

1. They have been dating for a long time.
2. She is just a few weeks pregnant.
3. I would love to meet the drummer in that band.
4. I hope that the baby will go to sleep so that I will be able to watch the basketball game.
5. We packed just the important items, such as food, water, warm clothing, and blankets.
6. He tried to interest her in the brushes he was selling, but she didn't care about them.
7. Today, it is important to keep abreast of world events.

8. Markie, who hadn't eaten since breakfast that morning, told his mother that he was very hungry.
9. That strange looking bird is unique.
10. She was very casual in her attitude.

CHAPTER 7

Test Yourself

1. what you are doing – noun
2. When Cassius Clay changed his name to Mohammed Ali – adverb
3. which are common in Colorado – adjective
   that shimmer in the sunlight – adjective
4. because they care about their community – adverb
5. which took place on April 17, 1961 – adjective
6. whoever sold the most cookies – noun
7. how he will complete his research paper on time – noun
8. Where you work – noun
   that you must wear – adjective
9. where the parade began – adjective
10. as soon as the lecture is over – adverb

Word Watchers Practice Set

1. green
2. Moved or motioned
3. met
4. linked
5. if possible
6. consensus
7. announced
8. concluded
9. always
10. stopped

CHAPTER 8

Test Yourself

1. simple
2. complex
3. complex
4. compound
5. compound-complex
6. simple
7. compound-complex
8. complex
9. compound
10. simple

Word Watchers Practice Set

1. congradulated (congratulated)
2. writting (writing)

3. alot (a lot)
4. inconvience (inconvenience)
5. athelete (athlete)

CHAPTER 9

Test Yourself

(Answers my vary.)

One of the most intriguing figures of the Civil War was Major General George Mc-Clellan. A graduate of West Point, McClellan suffered from an inflated ego and an inability to take action, so much so that some even accused him of cowardice. When McClellan took command of the Army of the Potomac, the recruits were a ragtag bunch of farmers, who were inexperienced in the ways of war. He was an outstanding leader, organizing the troops and turning them into confident soldiers; however, he frequently showed a lack of respect for Lincoln, his commander-in-chief. He was nicknamed "The Young Napoleon," not only for his leadership skills, but also for his conceited and arrogant behavior.

McClellan's abilities did not extend to the battlefield, however. Often incorrectly convinced that his troops were vastly outnumbered and unwilling to put them in harm's way, he angered Lincoln by his refusal to engage the Army of the Potomac in battle or to push forward when they were close to victory. Lincoln's frustration showed in a famous letter he had once written to McClellan. The letter, addressed to "My Dear McClellan," said, "If you are not using the army, I should like to borrow it for a short while." It was signed, "Yours respectfully, Abraham Lincoln." Lincoln finally relieved McClellan of his command in 1862. Nevertheless, Lincoln had to tangle with him again when McClellan became the Democratic Party's candidate for president in the 1864 election.

Word Watchers Practice Set

1. judgement (judgment)
2. definately (definitely)
3. lisence (license)
4. occassion (occasion)
5. develope (develop) and seperate (separate)

CHAPTER 10

Test Yourself

1. Correct
2. Her nephew is a rude, obnoxious child.
3. People who have to, should leave the show at intermission.
4. Bill Gates, for example, supports many charitable causes.
5. I didn't read the book, nor did I see the movie.
6. Correct
7. All my cat does is eat, sleep, and make a mess.
8. The governor took office on January 10, 2010, in Raleigh, North Carolina.
9. Although he is my twin brother, we do not look at all alike.
10. "I am leaving now," the nurse said quietly to the patient.
11. The driver, his cell phone ringing loudly, was easily distracted.
12. Speaking in a very low voice, the politician admitted that he had lied in his campaign ads.
13. Correct
14. I need your raincoat, not your umbrella.
15. My father, who owns a dry cleaning business, was able to get the spot out of my dress.
16. New York, my favorite city, is very crowded in the spring.
17. Correct
18. Meredith, you are going to Los Angeles on business, aren't you?
19. Correct
20. You know, of course, that she is not coming to the seminar.
21. In fact, their credit card balance was far too high.
22. Correct
23. Correct
24. The basketball center for our college team is 7 feet, 3 inches tall.
25. In the middle of a huge project at work, the manager resigned.

Word Watchers Practice Set

1. regardless
2. have/have
3. themselves
4. supposed
5. anywhere
6. have
7. nowhere
8. himself
9. used
10. themselves

CHAPTER 11

Test Yourself

The March 1975 issue of Ms. Magazine published an article written by African-American novelist Alice Walker. Entitled "In Search of Zora Neale Hurston," this article awakened interest in the work of an artist who had died in poverty and obscurity, and it led to a Hurston revival. Born in January 1891 in Alabama, Hurston moved to Eatonville, Florida, at a young age, and it's Eatonville that lies at the heart of her work. Her short stories and novels are filled with childhood memories, characters, and vivid descriptions of life in Eatonville, chartered as an all black town in 1887. Hurston left Eatonville at thirteen, but she returned home for visits throughout her life. She began college at Howard University and finally graduated with a degree in anthropology from Barnard College in 1927. Hurston's interest in anthropology was evident in her work as she documented African-American folklore and created fiction filled with authentic dialect. Even before entering Barnard, Hurston had become active in the literary movement known as the Harlem Renaissance. Her well-known book Their Eyes Were Watching God was published in 1937.

For several decades, however, Hurston's work was ignored and underappreciated due to her conservative political views. She spent her last ten years working as a freelance writer, newspaper columnist, librarian, substitute teacher, and occasionally, a maid. After a stroke, Hurston died in a charity nursing home in 1960. Her public obscurity ended in 1973 when Alice Walker bought her a tombstone, calling her "A Genius of the South." Today Hurston's work is studied in English classes throughout the United States, and her life is celebrated at the Zora Neale Hurston National Museum of Fine Arts and the annual Zora Neale Hurston Festival of the Arts and Humanities in Eatonville.

Word Watchers Practice Set

1. It's
2. which
3. who's
4. there
5. you're
6. who
7. their
8. its
9. whose
10. they're

CHAPTER 12

Test Yourself

1. that
2. us
3. she
4. her
5. we
6. I
7. His
8. whoever
9. whom
10. who

Word Watchers Practice Set

(answers may vary)

1. casual
2. boys, guys, men
3. among
4. First
5. permitted, allowed
6. ignored, dismissed
7. man
8. all day and all night throughout the week
9. my mistake
10. unusual for him

CHAPTER 13

Test Yourself

1. is
2. were
3. seems
4. changes
5. expects, his or her
6. wants, her
7. is
8. have, their
9. makes
10. Is
11. appear, their
12. is
13. has, his or her
14. has
15. was
16. shows
17. tells, their
18. Have, their
19. has, his
20. are, their

Word Watchers Practice Set

1. different from
2. well
3. to
4. bad
5. as
6. badly
7. surely
8. like
9. well
10. to

CHAPTER 14

Test Yourself

(Answers will vary)

Today started in the worst way. First, I set my alarm clock for 6:00 PM instead of 6:00 AM. Because I woke up at 7:30 AM, my day was already off to a bad start. Before taking a shower, I had to call my boss to report that I would be late for work. I was finally ready to leave when I discovered that my key ring was missing. I had to find my car keys before I could leave the house. They were neither in my briefcase nor in my pants pocket. When I looked under the couch, there they were.

Quickly, I wrapped a toasted pop-tart in aluminum foil and ran out the door. My bad luck got worse. My car would not start. Since my battery was dead, I thought I would have to buy a new battery, but my kind neighbor was able to use cables to jump-start my car. When I arrived to work at last, everyone cheered.

Word Watchers Practice Set

(answers will vary)

1. I hope she will do the same for me one day
2. belongings
3. I won't know for sure until I see the results
4. she may have enough money
5. it was easier than fighting with them about it
6. she may find herself having even worse problems
7. enjoyable/bored
8. what appears to be a crisis sometimes turns out to have some benefits
9. set small goals first and then increase them as you gain confidence
10. attractive people don't always make the best partners.

CHAPTER 15

Test Yourself

1. The quarterback is more likely to be injured that any other player on the team.
2. He picked up the phone and then dialed the number with care.
3. Although you need a haircut, you won't necessarily look funny in the photograph.
   Your needing a haircut doesn't mean you will look funny in the photograph.
   The fact that you need a haircut doesn't mean you will look funny in the photograph.
4. A grand slam is hitting a home run when the bases are loaded.
   A grand slam occurs if a batter hits a home run when the bases are loaded.
   Hitting a home run when the bases are loaded is a grand slam.
5. Because you forgot to give me my allowance, I don't have any money.
   You forgot to give me my allowance, so I don't have any money.
6. My hair stylist asked if I wanted my hair highlighted.
   My hair stylist asked, "Do you want your hair highlighted?"
7. Either MacKenzie lied or Chloe has her facts wrong.
8. She won't buy anything from that store if it doesn't give her a discount.
   She won't buy anything from that store if it doesn't offer discounts.
9. I told Max the answer before I told Tom.
   I told Max the answer before Tom told him.
10. The height of the grass made it hard to mow.
    The grass was hard to mow because of its height.

Word Watchers Practice Set

1. The server forgot to bring the ketchup but remembered the napkins.
2. All voters should remember to bring their registration cards.
3. I really admire firefighters because they often risk their lives to help others every day.
4. The discovery of penicillin has been important for all humanity.
5. Flight attendants do more than just serve drinks to passengers.
6. All businesspeople should take courses in management so they will know how to deal with people.
7. All department heads should report to the dean before Tuesday.
8. We will invite all of the doctors and their spouses to the conference.
9. Because I love animals, I wear only clothes sewn with synthetic fabrics.
10. I really appreciate the talent of the artisans.

CHAPTER 16

Test Yourself

Harry Houdini was born Erich Weiss on March 24, 1874. "Harry" was not his real name; it was a nickname evolving from a variation of his first name. Harry Houdini worked in a factory after his family moved to the United States, first to Appleton, Wisconsin, and then to New York City when he was thirteen. He could have chosen to remain in the factory, but he showed a lot of interest in the trapeze and magic. He also liked performing escape acts. Always receiving standing ovations, Harry thrilled audiences by escaping handcuffs, jails, and straight-jackets. In one of his performances in a small theater, he spotted a young dancer whom he soon began to court and eventually marry. Bess Rahmer had a tremendous effect on his life. He and his wife performed together for the rest of his career. Houdini's big break came when his manager, Martin Beck, booked him in a vaudeville theater. He soon played to great crowds, earning him the title "World's Most Famous Escape Artist."

By 1912, one of his greatest acts was the Chinese Water Torture Cell. Held by his feet, he was lowered upside-down into a locked glass cabinet filled with water. As he held his breath for three minutes, all members of the audience were holding their breath, too. Many people think that Houdini died in the water chamber, but there is more to the story. During a back-stage meeting, a college student, J. Gordon Whitehead, punched Houdini in the stomach three times. Although Houdini had given his friends permission to punch him, these punches took Houdini by surprise. He died a few days later of a ruptured appendix. His legacy among magicians is unparalleled. Each of them remembers his famous motto, "My chief task has been to conquer fear."

Index